Rosie Jackson

Mothers Who Leave

*behind the myth of women
without their children*

 Pandora
An Imprint of HarperCollins*Publishers*

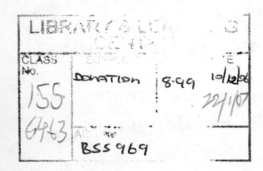
Pandora
An Imprint of HarperCollins*Publishers*
77–85 Fulham Palace Road,
Hammersmith, London W6 8JB
Published by Pandora 1994

10 9 8 7 6 5 4 3 2 1

© Rosie Jackson 1994

Rosie Jackson asserts the moral right to
be identified as the author of this work

A catalogue record for this book
is available from the British Library

ISBN 0 04 440899 4

Typeset by Harper Phototypesetters Limited,
Northampton, England
Printed in Great Britain by
Mackays of Chatham, Kent

for all women separated from their children
– for whatever reason.

Contents

PART FOUR
Inside Story – Making the Unconscious Conscious

Acknowledgements

This book has grown organically over the last few years and I am grateful to many people along the way who have made it possible. My ideas were still embryonic when the excellent BBC documentary about mothers who've left children, *How Could She?* was first transmitted on television in April 1990. It was this production by Sally George which encouraged me to take the project further, and I am grateful to Sylvia Paskin, whose collaboration on that programme introduced the subject to a wide audience in a sensitive way, and who generously passed on to me ideas and suggestions for this study.

My greatest debt is to all those women who were willing to share their histories with me. Their desire for anonymity makes it impossible to thank each one individually by name, but I am grateful to them all for the time spent recounting experiences that were often painful to re-examine. It was these women who kept reminding me of the importance of the personal and so stopped the book straying too far into abstractions. To all of them go my heartfelt thanks, also to the various selfless workers, past and present, of the British network MATCH (Mothers Apart from Their Children), who have provided vital support to many such women. Carol Findon and Kate Sayer were especially helpful to me in supplying information.

I am very grateful to Anna Christy for freely sharing memories of her mother, Elizabeth Fowles, also to John Fowles for his comments and permissions to reproduce material. Shirley Glubka kindly made it possible to reprint her article on surrogate mothering, whilst Maggie Mountford and Sarah Hopkins generously contributed previously unpublished poems.

From Susan O'Brien came a chance remark that first threw the switch of decision to do the book, Sarah Le Fanu gave helpful input at an early stage, Mary-Jayne Rust and Frances Howard Gordon offered insightful comments on a draft manuscript. Thanks too to Micky McCartney for patiently explaining the legal intricacies of The Children's Act and to Susan Mears, my agent, and Karen Holden, my editor at Pandora, both of whom have been extremely supportive.

Amongst many friends whose encouragement and inspiration during the gestation of the book have been invaluable, I would like to thank in particular Karen Cohen, Deirdre Burton, Diane Furlong, Nicole Ward-Jouve, Charles Harvey, Phoebe Clare and Lindsay Clarke. An extra special thank you goes to Jan Relf for her brilliant support and selfless sharing of contacts. I am also thankful to my son, for still being there, and for making it impossible for me not to learn some difficult lessons.

Finally, deep gratitude to John Hàrlow, whose genius in computing and practical matters, along with his inordinate love, patience and confidence, leaves me indebted beyond words.

Foreword

It seems part of our human nature, alas, that we should criticise and condemn one another. It is not only men who give women a hard time: women are very good at doing it to one another, in big and little ways – from stoning the adulteress to death or not talking to the neighbour at the bus stop because her kids don't get to bed on time. It seems that those who depart from 'normal' behaviour frighten us into bad behaviour, which can be both self congratulatory and cruel. And, though these days we train ourselves in empathy and have managed in this family-centred society of ours, over the last century, to tolerate a number of minority groupings – unmarried mothers, working mothers, divorced or single women, and wilfully childless wives – we have not yet come to terms with 'mothers who leave'. And it is to this phenomenon that Rosie Jackson's interesting and original book devotes itself, and to the unnecessary pain and guilt felt by women who are sensitive to society's opinion of them. 'Mothers who leave' have not only to struggle to forgive themselves for an uncommitted sin, but to face a society which remains unforgiving, no matter what.

Society makes no distinction between bearing children and rearing them: even less so than it used to. Wealthy women in England were once expected to hand over their babies to nannies; the nursery was set well apart from the rest of the house; public schools made men of healthy little boys, not their mothers. Now the pressure is the other way: 'why have a baby at all if you're just going to hand it over to child care?', 'take your baby into bed with you', and to send a child to boarding school is seen almost as parental cruelty. 'Women who leave' – in our contemporary society, in which everyone's assumed to be born pleasant and good, it's just that bad mothering makes them otherwise – have a worse and not a better time of it than they did, judging from the case histories related in this book. 'Mother love' must be single-minded, goes the current refrain, flawless and wholly reliable; 'mother love' must be capable of all sacrifice; 'mother love' is simply not open to least/worst solutions; say 'mother' and assume 'love'. Of course in real life it isn't so. The welfare of mothers and the welfare of their children overlap but don't necessarily coincide.

The price of charity, generosity, understanding, of building a kind and enduring society, is eternal vigilance against our worse, mean, backbiting, self-righteous, frightened selves. It takes a book like *Mothers Who Leave* to point out how far we have yet to go in pursuit of such tolerance. Mothers who fail, or refuse, or decline, or simply can't look after their children continue to earn our severest and most irrational censure. Men 'walk out', to a shrug and a sigh, but women who leave 'abandon' and get doors slammed in their faces.

If the woman, having succumbed to the almost universal urge to procreate, has done so in imprudent circumstances, or fails to discover in herself a maternal nature, if she can't arrive at the magic 'bonding' or fails to provide a stable home, or a permanent father, or is unable to sustain her own personality under the onslaught of that of her child, or that of its father; if she falls in love, or out of love, and decides her child, haplessly begotten, is better off without her, because if she stays it will be emotionally or practically impoverished, why then that's her out of court. An 'abandoning' mother, a pariah, and her own distress at what has happened not counted in her defence at all.

The marvel to me is that women have children at all: the marvel is that women so often stay, and don't leave. It is wonderfully to their credit when they do, not to their discredit when they don't. And to those in distress because they are apart from their children – for any one of the myriad reasons that Rosie Jackson suggests this happens – let me just say this: children don't stay little for ever, they grow up, gain their own volition, come back to you of their own wills, as like as not; no matter what's been said or done in the meantime, or who tried to turn who against whom, and a few years missing is nothing in a lifetime. And then the better your life, the better theirs. This is how it works out.

Fay Weldon, August 1993

Forgive me, I say,
for leaving you behind.
He stares into the distance.
A man by all accounts
yet still to me that child

who arrived back
finding a door I'd shut
only half an hour before
carrying all I could
in my two hands away.

Over ten years now
as we picnic in the car
and suddenly I've said it
for the very first time.

Forgive you? he echoes
and ruffles my hair –
a sign of affection
that I long to hurl back

at him, crying: No! No!
You don't understand!
No one ever understood!

In silence
we begin to eat –
our two small separate packs
seeming almost sufficiency.

Maggie Mountford 'Understanding . . .'

Introduction

The actions of, and reactions to, women who leave their children tell us a lot about motherhood, real and imagined.

Anne Karpf, the *Guardian* 3 April 1990

Could *you* walk out on your kids?

Honey

Goodbye, kids, Mother's leaving home.

Atlantic

A mother who leaves her children: the very notion conjures up myths of women tossing babies onto dunghills or ditching them on doorsteps in brown paper bags. We hear about her in sensationalised stories in the media, ranging from the hysterical hype of tabloids – 'Women Who Close the Door on their Children' – to the baffled curiosity of more serious broadsheets – 'How Could She?' the *Guardian*. Melodramatic headlines make her departure hard and definitive: 'When Mothers Walk Out' *Life Times*. An American family therapist recently described leaving your children as 'one of the last great crimes'.[1]

An absent mother equals a bad one, and probably a woman with loose morals to boot. Her actions are irresponsible, her departure damaging and difficult to justify. 'Walking out' is a reckless, cruel thing to do and has a sense of finality about it, as if any relationship between mother and child has come to an abrupt end. She has turned her back on her kids once and for all and, if she is now suffering for it – she is supposed to be an unhappy woman too – it is no more than her selfishness deserves.

If the myth of a mother leaving has always tended to invite a negative response, a new mixing of her motives with a crude version of feminism now fixes prejudice ever more firmly against her. She is merely out for a good time and her own ends, even more of a hard-hearted, pleasure-seeking bitch – 'What It's Like to Leave the Family Behind and Become a Weekend Mom' *Glamour.* Contemporary newspaper and magazine articles are still full of a shock-horror rhetoric and warnings against going down a similar route. 'Six Questions to Ask Before You Consider Divorce . . . You May Decide to Think Again' *Living.* 'Would You Ever Walk Out on *Your* Children?' *Woman's World.*

Yet the phenomenon of mothers leaving and living apart from their children is neither as rare – nor as scandalous – as the popular press would have us believe. It is an experience that has touched the lives of diverse women, women as serious as the writers George Sand and Charlotte Perkins Gilman last century and Doris Lessing this, as well as the wives of writers – novelists D. H. Lawrence and John Fowles both married women who had to leave their children to be with them. Women, too, as various as Ingrid Bergman, Shirley MacLaine, Diana Dors, Yoko Ono, Margaret Trudeau and Karen Silkwood. And, besides these more celebrated examples, there exist thousands of women who have left and do leave children, temporarily or permanently. The phenomenon is much wider, more far-reaching and more complex than we have been led to believe.

The reality is that structures and styles of parenting in the West are more fluid than they have ever been. There has been a widespread shift in patterns of child care from the late 1960s onwards, indicating a significant movement away from the nuclear family and from mothers having a monopoly on primary parenting. In the USA, between 1970 and 1978, the number of children under 18 living with divorced fathers rose by 136 per cent: by 1980, half a million divorced men were bringing up children whose mothers were no longer living in the family home. In the late 1980s and early 1990s nearly one quarter of all children in the United States were in single parent families, with the number expected to reach 50 per cent by the time of the next generation. [2]

In Britain, in the late 1980s, one family in eight had a single parent and an estimated 200,000 children lived with their fathers, whilst 20 per cent of children born in Britain in the 1980s were likely to have their parents divorce. Before the introduction of the Children's Act in

1991, between 10 and 15 per cent of fathers were granted custody after divorce. Recent figures for Britain show that in 1993 2.2 million children were being brought up in 1.3 million lone parent families, one in 10 headed by a father.[3] A significant 15 per cent of mothers are not living with their children.

Given that these are conservative estimates, they would suggest around 500,000 women now living without their children in the States and something in the region of 100 to 200,000 women in Britain. Not all these figures will reflect mothers who have 'left', but even where women have lost custody or live separately for whatever reason, the stigmas attached to living apart from their children can be much the same. *Mothering is for life.* To have broken that rule, whatever the circumstances, puts a woman in the category of the deviant and unnatural.

This book explores some of the contradictions facing such mothers. Why is it that a woman who leaves children is still as damned, or at least doomed, as she ever was, when a man who leaves can do so with relative impunity? (A survey of 'desertion' in the States in 1904 found that of 591 families in which a parent had left a family, only 17 were women.[4]

Is this underlying prejudice merely part of the current backlash against feminism, or is it something more profoundly rooted in the psyche? If, as the figures above suggest, the nuclear family is disintegrating all around us, why does this desire to hang on to its forms and structures seem to remain?

The following study moves towards answering these questions. Part One, 'Icons of Good Mothering', explores dominant ideas of mothering and asks what happens when they are broken, with specific attention to the *representation* of mothers who leave. For the way we see such women, the way we think about 'good' or 'bad' mothers, is not something innate – it comes from a particular code of thought as to what constitutes real mothering. This relates to the development of a specific ideology of motherhood, one that has evolved in the West over the last two centuries and is inseparable from social and economic shifts. Part Two, 'Out of the Doll's House', explores these changes in more detail, suggesting that it is precisely this historical transformation that has affected our way of seeing women who break the maternal ideal, and going on to discuss some of the external factors that have shaped the actual lives of mothers who have left.

What emerges is a close link between the rhetoric of mothering – the cultural construction of the Mother figure in novels, plays, films, popular media – and the demands of mainstream ideology. In other words, images of mothering do not merely *mirror*, so much as *reproduce* or manufacture, a specific set of values and rules about the role of women. The whole iconography of good and bad mothers is not simply a passive reflection of social reality, but an actively determining force, constantly renaming and reinforcing certain assumptions and definitions as to what properly constitutes maternity.

The images of abandoning and absconding mothers that have been given to us over the last 200 years are not necessarily mirrors of social actuality, but are fabrications, constructions that have *formed* our sense of that reality, formed, or deformed, our sense of ourselves. As I shall show, a specific language of mothering has evolved in the West since the Industrial Revolution – a language that is being constantly modified and renegotiated to try to accommodate social shifts – and it is within or against this language, as its dark underside, that there has also emerged an equally specific language and iconography surrounding and attached to a mother who leaves. I have devoted the initial section of this book to examining the cultural representation of mothers who leave because it is precisely this, the sexual politics of representation, that has largely determined how we think about such women and about female identity in general. [5]

Part One, then, is devoted to exploring ways of seeing and thinking about mothers and, more specifically, mothers who leave. It discusses some of the unconscious assumptions that still exist about mothers living without their children – prevailing ideas about the kind of women they are, the plots in which they are supposed to exist, the endings their lives are presumed to have – and I shall relate these to the stories about such mothers that have come down to us from a moralistic literary tradition. For it is nineteenth-century melodramas and fictions such as *East Lynne* and *Anna Karenin* that still shape our responses to absent mothers and whose ways of working therefore need to be understood in some detail.

I then go on to discuss how more recent twentieth-century texts – novels, Hollywood films, contemporary TV dramas – have perpetuated a similar tradition of hostility. In popular culture, from one of the best-selling novels of the 1930s, *Sorrell and Son*, through recent mass media programmes like American TV's series *Raising Miranda*, to current best-sellers such as Danielle Steel's *Daddy*, the absent mother is actively maligned, punished, trivialised or marginalised out of existence. No matter what the rationale for her leaving, there is still a block when it comes to a rational appraisal of her actions. In the late 1970s, for example, in both the novel and film of *Kramer versus Kramer*, we simply have the old bitch in new (designer) clothes: another woman who has walked out on a whim so she can put her own life and career first; a work that spells out too the lamentable impact of feminism – it makes a mother chuck aside her kid for her own pleasure.

In previous studies of the subject of mothers leaving, whether 'expert' or lay discussions, one constant has been to view it almost exclusively from the side of the child. Whatever the medium – popular press, Hollywood, law, social sciences or psychology – the customary perspective has been unremittingly the *child's*. Titles of magazine articles, research papers and books all make their emphasis clear: 'Where's Mummy Gone?' *Under Five*; 'When Mommy Leaves Home' *Family Circle*; 'When Mommy Moves Out' *New York*; 'Abandoned' *Options*; 'The effects of maternal deprivation', a World Health Organisation publication; 'Effects of psychological deprivation in infancy' in journals of paediatrics and psychiatry; *Mummy Doesn't Live Here Any More*. In all of these, the reader is being made to identify with the child (who is assumed to be abandoned) rather than with the mother (who is assumed to be abandoning). Thus there is an unconscious concentration of attention on the child's life rather than on the adult woman's: the *mother's* emotional and psychological reality, *her* inner needs, are left out of the picture.

This is partly to do with the enormous attention given to the child and the child's development in modern psychology. Starting with Rousseau's romanticisation of the innocent child and continuing, though in different form, through Freud's focus on infant development, the child has been the centre of modern psychological interest and sympathy. In cases of mothers and children being separated, the same preoccupation has revealed itself. Masses of research and tomes of child psychology exist studying the effect on the child of a mother's absence – for short and long periods of time, at different ages, in various contexts – but there has been very little of substance on the effect of this separation on the *mother*. Her emotional and psychological development have been eclipsed.

One of the main aims of this book is to redress that imbalance, by focusing unashamedly on the *woman's* position, and not on the child, children, husband or partner she leaves. I am as concerned with the effects on *her* inner and outer life as on that of her child or children. So although I do consider some of the implications for the child, especially in the final chapter of Part Two, 'Effects', my main priority throughout remains the mother herself – and how the emotional, social and legal repercussions of leaving affect *her*. This is a deliberate choice, but it should not be taken to mean that I underestimate the effect of separation on the ones left behind, nor that I mean to over-simplify the overall situation.

In order to give a sense of the reality of being apart from one's children and how this does affect the mother's life, for good or ill, Part Three of this book, 'The Mother's Point of View', is given over to personal accounts. The first of these are extracts from fiction and autobiographies, including writings by nineteenth-century feminist Charlotte Perkins Gilman, actress Ingrid Bergman, novelist Doris Lessing and the memoirs of Frieda Lawrence, wife of D. H. Lawrence. These are women who have given voice for the first time to some of the complexities of feeling involved in being separated (*apparently* willingly and by free choice) from their children. The rest of the stories in Part Three are taken from extensive interviews I made with contemporary women.

These women were contacted through a variety of sources. Some were from personal connections (once you start looking, there seem to be mothers who've left children round every corner); others contacted me following publicity in various newsletters, notably that of the self-help group MATCH (an acronym for Mothers Apart from Their Children; see the Key Addresses section for more information).

MATCH was set up in 1979, after Peg English, an American living in Britain, wrote to the *Guardian* to voice her distress at being separated from her children. The huge response to her letter generated the MATCH network, which now operates on a voluntary basis, linking women through individual area contacts and quarterly newsletters. MATCH offers basic information on legal aspects of separation, divorce, child welfare, access, rights and responsibilities, as well as general advice about personal support, aid and counselling. Like other self-help groups, it has proved invaluable in breaking down the sense of isolation with which women are often tormented. Many MATCH members have expressed the immense relief they have felt at discovering they were not the only one to be separated from their children, and to be able to share the mixed range of emotions – and response to social reactions – involved. In the States, Mothers Without Custody serves a similar function.

In total, I interviewed in person or received letters from more than five dozen women. From the vast range of stories I heard, I selected those which felt to me most interesting, representative or at odds with conventional stereotypes of mothers apart from children, though being a personal selection it will inevitably betray my own priorities. They are deliberately chosen from women with widely differing class, economic and educational backgrounds: amongst them are a truck driver's daughter and the daughter of a bishop, an unemployed single mother and a millionaire, a battered wife and the spouse of a well to do country doctor. Though their specific circumstances differed so enormously, each one felt compelled, or was forced, to leave her children – children of different ages, from infants to late teenagers. All, though, had children with whom some kind of link or bond was established before leaving.

All the contemporary accounts in Part Three are transcripts of personal interviews, except for Siobhan's, in Chapter 11, which was done through correspondence, and Shirley Glubka's, in Chapter 15, which was written and published in the States some years ago. In each case I made a direct transcript of the interview or letter, editing it down to a suitable length, and the women involved had the opportunity to read and correct the edited narrative. All accounts are reproduced with the women's permission. But it should be remembered that these chapters, 11 to 20, present women speaking in their own words and their oral material gives them a different feel and texture from the rest of the book. I have kept my introductory comments to these accounts to a minimum, but it should be obvious how the stories illuminate and overlap with themes raised elsewhere.

I have deliberately not tried to cover the experiences of women whose lives I feel ill-equipped to describe. Separation from children that comes about through fostering, racial difference, imprisonment or physical or mental handicap in mother or child have not been included. This is not because I think they are less important, but because they are highly specific areas and therefore need to be addressed on their own terms from within. I was reluctant to misrepresent them by talking about them in general or ill-informed terms from the outside.

Adoption is another such specialised area. Leaving illegitimate children at birth has always been a frequent social practice and one that has come to be condoned, not attracting the same negative stigma of relinquishing older children. The legendary 'Calamity Jane', Martha Jane Cannary Hickok, gave her baby daughter to surrogate parents and had only sporadic contact with her, never revealing her maternal identity.[6] Even the devout Christian author Dorothy Sayers, one of the first women to get an Oxford degree, had an illegitimate son in 1924, giving him away the following week to her cousin to mother and never sharing a home with him.[7] But whereas adoption at birth has come to be a more acceptable social practice, being separated from children at a later stage still has not.

It should be stressed that the personal accounts in Part Three are not clinical case studies, nor is this a book for those who want sociological surveys or catalogues of statistics and percentages. I made no use of formal questionnaires, but instead asked women to focus on those issues that they felt had been most important to them. Social scientists might ask for 'proof' that these personal stories are representative, or object to their 'truth' value. Obviously, naming one's own history is a complicated process, and memory inevitably distorts and refracts events in particular ways. But all the women were telling their experience as they saw it, and I make no apology for this presentation of *their* version of events. This movement away from a neutralised voice of scholarly generalisation is a conscious choice, a deliberate attempt to give a sense of what it is like – from the inside – for mothers who leave. For readers impatient with such a subjective approach, more abstract and impersonal studies are recommended in the Bibliography.

The stigma attached to mothers living apart from their children is still so great that nearly all the women involved – even the most liberated and successful in worldly terms – asked to remain

anonymous. Whether reluctant to attract more ne
or anxious to protect children and relatives from m
or hurt through publicity, they did not wish to disc
identities. The women's names, therefore, and those
children and, in some cases, places too, have been changed.
reasons I have not included my own story at length in Par   ce,
though each of the accounts mirrors and parallels some aspect of other
of my own experience and I have no wish to disguise the fact that my
involvement with this book is deeply personal.

When my first marriage disintegrated, in the early 1970s, my son
(our only child) remained living with his father in the family home.
My son was then aged three and a half. The reasons for this were
various and complex. I was only 19 when we married and was totally
unprepared for motherhood, its unremitting demands and the
isolation that – through the force of our circumstances – it entailed.
The pregnancy came in the middle of my undergraduate course at
Warwick University, and the next two years I remember only as utter
chaos and fatigue, torn between midnight essays on Lear and madness,
buckets of vile-smelling *Napisan*, rushing at lunch-time to the
excellent university crèche (free to students), baby-feeding and sitting
in Germaine Greer's seminars on Ibsen and European theatre trying
to hide my wedding ring. Puzzlingly, although my ex-husband co-
operated generously whilst I completed my degree, fully sharing in
domestic tasks and child care, it all became more problematic when
I wanted to proceed to post-graduate work, and tensions grew between
us.

Also, in retrospect highly unwisely, we moved away from our home
and friends in Leamington Spa to one of the most rundown outer
suburbs of Leeds, several miles from the city centre. Whilst my ex-
husband taught full-time in a state school, I was isolated in our
terraced house, with no money, no transport and 24-hour-a-day child
care to juggle alongside my research work. Neither of our families
lived close enough to help out and we had no money for paid child
care. A state nursery to which I applied refused even a part-time place,
on the grounds that it served only broken families.

Occasional sallies to York University, where I was registered to do
a Ph.D., only left me feeling guilty and anxious at having left my son
with female neighbours with whom there was no affinity other than

geographical closeness and who thought both my husband and I were weird radicals. I would rush out of tutorials with my supervisor to get an early train back to Leeds, sweating with panic at the thought of the neglect or abuse to which I feared my son might be subjected.

After two years of this desperate isolation, compounded by difficulties in the marriage – many, I admit, caused by my own depression with the overall situation – I went up the wall. A GP's prescription of Valium did not help. I could see no way out. Knowing we had to resolve things, my husband and I went together to a solicitor in Leeds to discuss how we could effect legal separation in the friendliest way possible, one that would damage neither our son nor ourselves. The solicitor laughed in our faces. 'Come back,' he said, 'when you've actually split up. There's always acrimony. You can't avoid it. There's always a fight.' After going round in circles exploring various possibilities that then proved impossible, we eventually opted for my moving to York and father and son staying in Leeds, where I would visit weekly, or have my son to stay at weekends.

Sadly, though, the solicitor's ominous words proved right. The civil behaviour we had both fully intended soon collapsed after our actual separation. Because I was the one who had done the actual physical moving, the scenario could be (and was) construed in terms hostile to me: I had '*left my child*'. So, although the plan had been mutually agreed, legally I was the one deemed to have 'deserted', and hence carried the major blame for the separation. Eventually we divorced and although we shared custody, my ex-husband had care and control.

There were heavy recriminations from relatives and, from the outside, it must indeed have looked like a wilful and self-regarding act, one in which I put my own needs before those of husband or child. I went to live alone in a room in a student house on a noisy ring-road in York, where I cut off from my confusion and grief – indeed from all real feelings – by engrossing myself in academic research. It was as if, once I had left, I *had* to succeed and excel intellectually – any existing drive in that direction compounded by a need to justify leaving – and for the next few years I became thoroughly addicted to intellectual work (an addiction from which, fortunately, I later extricated myself). Accusations and attacks that I was 'more concerned with my education than with being a proper wife or mother' stung with their bitter ring of truth – from my external actions, it must indeed have seemed that way, that my maternal instincts were pretty atrophied.

There were further difficult ramifications when, the following year, my ex-husband moved away to live with his own mother – at a distance that, without money or my own transport, was impossible for me to manage – and any assumptions I had held about frequent on-going contact with my son were rapidly disillusioned. From then on, our relationship was frustrated and bedevilled by physical distance and, at times, issues around access.

I do not want to misrepresent this. Some of these problems were partly caused by my own distress at the situation and by my not knowing how to handle it or the negative projections put on to me from various sources. And further physical moves on both sides didn't make things any easier: in 1976 I moved to Norwich to take up a lectureship in English literature at the University of East Anglia, whilst my ex-husband had gone to Birmingham to another teaching post there. He remarried and was to have two more children, but although I too have since married again, something (largely unconscious) steered me away from having any more children. It was as if I knew there were too many profound issues for me around this whole experience that had to be resolved first.

Even with the best will in the world, circumstances such as these create tensions and difficulties in relationships. The necessarily sporadic nature of meetings with my son have made that bonding vulnerable and it has taken effort and pain to sustain it. Over the years this has taken its inevitable emotional toll (often denied and unadmitted) on both sides. Now, happily, any animosities seem to have subsided and my relationship with my son, though still intermittent, is much stronger. Yet we both tend to acknowledge and identify our relationship as a good friendship rather than the mother-child bond that, in our different ways, we still fantasise is the norm.

Looking back, it is easy to see how the separation could be misconstrued and constructed in the way it was, but from the inside, it felt very different and confused. There was nothing calculated nor ambitious, nothing even particularly conscious about it. Leaving was simply a blind desperate measure, a muddled attempt to escape what felt like an impossible living situation and a profound despair. Acting from the midst of one of those emotional pits where the depression of the present clouds any thought of future reality, leaving was simply an unwitting move in the dark, with *absolutely no sense* of the long-term repercussions and consequences for either my son or myself. There was no projection forwards to the future at all, no awareness that the difficulties I was struggling to resolve by leaving might be exacerbated so intensely by the additional pain of living apart from my son throughout his childhood and adolescence that it would take much more struggle to resolve this too.

The irony is that one *does not* ever leave one's children behind: the umbilical cord is not so easily severed. Indeed, the paradox might be that children become more of a preoccupation absent than present and that for some mothers who are separated from their offspring, the wound is so great that there is virtually an *obsession* with the children they have lost or left behind – an awareness of that link that nothing else can appease.

It has taken two decades for me to come to terms fully with my own experience of 'leaving', with all its implications and aftermath. Only through the support of long-term psychotherapy, many women friends and some valuable new relationships have I finally managed to overcome, or at least find some equanimity in living with, the emotional and psychological effects of being separated from my son – and with some of the underlying causes for that event having happened at all.

Researching and writing this book has been an essential part of that process, for it has encouraged me to look at the situation from a perspective wider than my own individual one. As I have tried to understand the various implications of a mother leaving, on personal, social and political levels, I have come to realise that some of the anguish I have experienced was caused not by the physical separation alone, but by the ways in which that separation is regarded and constructed socially, by the isolation it imposes and the difficult emotions it brings in its wake.

In that strange, lateral way in which our deepest understanding so often proceeds, I gradually came to see that the phenomenon of mothers leaving children has its own peculiar meaning and history, yet it is a phenomenon that has been almost totally hidden from view. Not only is it (unsurprisingly) off the map of mainstream culture, but it is even largely invisible in women's and feminist writings. Either no other woman had gone through this experience (which I doubted) or the naming of it had, till now, been too exposing to risk.

Those suspicions were confirmed as I hunted for literature on the subject. I found very few women who dared to name the fact that – willingly or unwillingly – they had left their children: amongst these few were Charlotte Perkins Gilman, Doris Lessing (and then, very obliquely) and Ingrid Bergman. The equally scant number of books dealing with the theme hid behind scores of statistics and tables, or were from academics or liberals approaching the experience second-hand and therefore without a deep sense of its devastating emotional and social impact. None was informed by a feminism that might read the event in both personal and political terms.

Yet this kind of experience, like many others, is neither wholly personal nor wholly social: it exists at the interface between the two, where individual and cultural pressures meet and intersect. There is no one single cause, whether in the woman or in society, for a mother leaving, only a complex interaction of internal and external factors. And if we are to get at the various strands of meaning surrounding such experience, inner and outer cannot be separated from one another: one of the best lessons feminism has taught us is that the personal and social, individual and political are woven and meshed deeply together.

Thus, as I re-examined the reasons for my own separation from my son, I saw that their origins were both outer and inner. Some were obviously and immediately social and empirical – poverty, immaturity, an unplanned pregnancy in the middle of my undergraduate degree course, a weak early marriage, lack of emotional support from family, domestic isolation, inadequate child care provision – but others were more deeply rooted in my particular personal and familial history, reaching back through my own childhood to the mothering I received, and beyond that again, to my mother's mothering (these in turn deeply affected by social and economic factors too).

This made me begin to wonder whether it was possible to discern any particular set or structure of internal factors that might tip the balance between a woman going or staying. For compared with the limited numbers of mothers who do leave, there are millions of women, in circumstances not too dissimilar to those described in the personal stories in Part Three, who do *not* leave children, but manage to find other ways out of their dilemmas. What is it, I thought, that tips that balance? Obviously each case and set of circumstances will have its own unique aetiology, but even so, could it be that some emotional or psychological factor comes into play, so that it is possible to see women who abdicate the mothering position as having some unconscious element in common? Many women fantasise leaving husbands and families at some stage, but relatively few act it out: what is it that makes the difference?

These are some of the issues explored in Part Four of this book, 'Inside Story – Making the Unconscious Conscious'. Here I look at the unconscious forces moving around images and realities of the mother who has left, thereby understanding more deeply some of the prejudices against her, so that we can start to undo, or resist, the projections and think about our situations in more realistic and helpful ways. I examine too some of the unconscious factors that play in and around the mother-child bond and are handed on from mother to daughter, exploring those elements in a woman's unconscious life and history that may trigger her leaving, and how these might leave her feeling when she has left.

And I ask about the possibilities for the future and for her relationships – with her children, with others, and with herself – offering examples, too, of restitution and reparation, where mother-child bonds are repaired. Thus, in Chapter 23, the moving account by John Fowles' stepdaughter, Anna Christy, gives a marvellous testimony of her mother, Elizabeth Fowles, and reveals how, despite the pain of their separation in the early 1950s, their future contact more than healed the wound, indeed brought them to an unusually close intimacy.

Many of the final stories in Part Three will have been seen to feed into this more positive reading of mothers who leave. These come from women who, like myself, have been fortunate enough to find the means and support – whether through education, psychotherapy, careers, creativity, or new relationships – to rethink the meaning of their being apart from their children and to transform what may have been a painful experience into something more positive. I have deliberately included these accounts, with their affirmative and relatively happy endings, largely because there are so few images of unconventional mothering that have not back-fired. Our culture gives us such little sense of mothering *in absentia* that can work, affords such rare glimpses of women *not punished* for looking after themselves and their own creativity as well as their children, that I made a conscious choice to focus finally on some personal stories that are examples of hope.

But if I have erred on the side of narratives with relatively happy outcomes, this does not mean I am unaware of those equally real ones where rifts with children have not been allowed to heal. Many mothers have *not* had the means of reparation – to themselves or their children – and have been punished by their children's fathers and deprived of seeing them, some even pushed by all these circumstances into despair and suicide. Popular mythology wants us to believe that such tragic endings are the rightful and inevitable destinies for mothers who break the rules, but my own emphasis shows that this is not so. Even women who have transgressed some of our deepest cultural ideals *can* still have rich, fulfilling lives *and* improved relationships with their children.

However, I hope it will be obvious that nowhere am I advocating that women *should* leave children. This would be as ridiculous as claiming that anyone defending the right to choose of a woman who has terminated a pregnancy is actually saying abortion is desirable. Leaving children is less an option to recommend than a choice between equal impossibilities. So although feminist thought and theory profoundly inform my arguments and position, I should stress at the outset that I am not in any way making an equation between feminism and leaving one's children.

At the beginning of the second wave of feminism, in *The Female Eunuch*, Germaine Greer made a passionate plea for unclouded thinking on this issue of mothers leaving:

> Most women, because of the assumptions that they have
> formed about the importance of their role as bearers
> and socializers of children, would shrink at the notion
> of leaving husband and children, but this is precisely the
> case in which brutally clear rethinking must be
> undertaken. [8]

My own book is intended to contribute to such a process of clarification, but this is *not* the same thing as turning a mother who has left into a feminist heroine. Greer may have been right to play devil's advocate about women leaving the nuclear family – her argument continues –

> A wife who knows that if she leaves her husband she can
> only bring up the children in pauperdom, although she
> could support herself, must make a sensible decision,
> and reject out of hand the deep prejudice against the
> runaway wife.

but this is easier said than done, and overlooks many complexities, not least of them the difficulties of the *mother's* position and her *emotional* tie with her offspring. None of the women I met identified her action as a feminist gesture, nor saw it as a clear-headed or 'brutally' rational decision. Sequences of events were far messier, the result of unfortunate combinations of circumstances – pressures, drives, contingencies – that felt impossible to withstand.

So although it would be difficult to make sense of the phenomenon of mothers leaving without reference to a feminist reading of the situation – and my study relies throughout on feminist theory, history and analyses of culture and sexual politics – it needs to be remembered that these readings are retrospective. They may give meaning *after* the event, but they are not its primary motive.

One British women's press considering a proposal for this book asked for something more unequivocal – it wanted stories of women who *had consciously* chosen to leave, as if somehow mothers abdicating were part of a feminist agenda, a deliberate rebellion, proving that freedom and childbearing are incompatible. But to go along with any equation that converts leaving one's children into a feminist enterprise is dangerously misleading, and I will be arguing strongly against it. Such confusion both caricatures feminism (reducing it to that crass level of bra-burning and child abandonment that delights the backlash press) and hardens the real social prejudice against mothers who are separated from their children. It associates their actions with hard-headed political choice, as if their hearts have nothing to do with it.

Leaving children is *not* an item on the feminist agenda, and to my understanding never has been. The circumstances that compel the separation are always complex and far-reaching, and usually more by default than by choice or design. Contrary to popular assumptions, I found that *no mother leaves a child lightly, easily, entirely willingly, or in cold blood.* Many mothers are separated from children *involuntarily,* or through selfless decisions about what seems to be in the children's best interest. Because of this, some women, especially amongst the MATCH membership, object to the use of the very term *mothers who leave*, on the grounds that it implies too much active agency on the mother's part, links up with notions of abandonment and feeds into sensationalised assumptions about the event. I am aware of these misgivings and admit there are dangers in the phrase being misunderstood, but at the same time I feel it is important to face the issue head on and refuse to occlude it in something more euphemistic. The account by Charlotte in Chapter 18, 'Leaving by Default', throws more light on this, stressing the importance of our taking responsibility for all our actions and history, however negative or (apparently) victimised they may seem. I have therefore let the term stand.

For if, on the one hand, there is a danger of trying to turn the mother who leaves into a heartless feminist heroine, on the other there is a tendency to want to view her as perpetually miserable and in a penance of life-long abjection for her 'crime'. This was the response of a non-feminist press to my book proposal – they wanted something more sensational and salacious, where women were seen to be regretting and suffering being apart from their children. Some mothers I met *were* apparently locked into difficult and deprived circumstances, both economically and emotionally, and I do not want to underestimate the very real hardship and pain they endure. But there is no need to stay in this position. No matter how hostile the context, it is possible to come to terms with the separation and slide out of the doom-laden projections we are supposed to carry.

The only British publication on this subject to date is Helen Franks' *Mummy Doesn't Live Here Any More* (1990). This was a much needed contribution in that it was the first book to open up rational public debate and to argue for a more lenient approach towards mothers who do not fulfil the traditional role. But there are many gaps and shortcomings in Franks' approach, not least of which is that the overall picture she paints is this conventional, unremittingly negative one. Mothers not with their children are seen primarily as hapless social victims trapped in a political and personal wasteland. They are unable to get their lives together (or, presumably, write a book for themselves) and the very categories in which Franks places them – leaving children for affairs, ambition, lesbianism, literal imprisonment – imply deviance, failure or criminality. Most are seen to have suffered agonies and to be permanently guilty and unhappy.

There is no sense of the phenomenon being seen positively, no inclusion of women who have worked through the experience creatively or independently and come out strongly on the other side. Fay Weldon's review of Franks' book rightly picked up this forlorn impression, noting that the mothers all belonged in various 'categories of misfortune', and that when they spoke it was in 'voices which have the sad and melancholy flavour of hopeless lives, hopefully lived: voices of the oppressed, the under-educated, the misunderstood, waiting for rescue, gently keening.'[9] As the following chapters show, it is possible to extend the range of that female choir into something less passive, less victimised and much less pessimistic.

There are other flaws with Franks' work. There is no awareness of the significance and impact of *representations* of mothers who leave – yet it is precisely these that have determined the way we think about them and about ourselves, and which need to be challenged if the way they are seen is to be changed. Nor is there much sense of the *historical formation* of mothering as we know it: the valid arguments Franks does make for greater compassion and tolerance towards women who break the rules would be stronger if we knew exactly where the rules had come from and how relative (and relatively new) they are.

But, most importantly, mothers who leave are seen by Franks very much *from the outside*. She emphasises, with some relief, that she herself is *not* a mother who has left. Indeed, there is a strong polarising of 'us' (the normal, moral majority, like herself) and 'them' (the different, deviant – non-moral? – minority of absent mothers). The sad result of this polarisation is that it works against the very sympathy for which, on a conscious level, Franks argues. For the constant subtext is one that alienates from the women themselves, so that one is left feeling identified as a kind of strange subspecies. Franks conducted interviews with some MATCH mothers, and includes clips from these in her evidence, but they are all mediated through her kind explanatory commentary, and many of the women involved, along with other MATCH mothers, have expressed unease with Franks' methods and position, feeling themselves to have been misrepresented and patronised.

Nevertheless, *Mummy Doesn't Live Here Any More* was a welcome introduction and I am indebted to some of its findings, as I am to the other three publications, all American, that have dealt directly with the subject. The first sympathetic study, *Absentee Mothers* (1982) was by Patricia Paskowicz, an American who had herself left her children, and it includes brief extracts from first-hand accounts, though its overall bias is towards generalised sociology. Geoffrey Greif's and Mary Pabst's *Mothers Without Custody* (1988) is highly academic and statistical, useful from that point of view but with no attention to women's subjectivity. Harriet Edwards' *How Could You? Mothers Without Custody of Their Children* (1989) is a more accessible Californian publication and is partly a self-help manual aimed at women finding ways to support themselves. Edwards has an excellent bibliography, too, of both fiction and non-fiction dealing with mothers who leave, and this was an invaluable source of material for me.

My hope is that this book will suggest, to the thousands of women who have 'left' their children, a way of placing their actions within a framework that links the personal to the social and political and so takes away some of the guilt of separation. I also hope it might encourage, amongst those millions of mothers (and fathers) who have not left, more insight and compassion into the lives of those who have and so inspire more flexible attitudes towards parenting. That those who were once left – as children – by their mothers might, as adults, read this study and so come to understand the situation more fully and sympathetically, would be the best outcome of all.

PART ONE

Icons of Good Mothering –
And What Happens to
Women Who Break Them

The Abandoning Mother:
Popular Myths and Images

'Mother' and 'Father' as social roles are in transition in
lived culture, but images deal with such changes in
ideologically bound ways . . . As always, it is precisely
because of prevailing mother-constructs that we expect,
or indeed demand, that mothers be gentle and self-
sacrificing. Their deviation is then all the more
reprehensible.

E. Ann Kaplan *Motherhood and Representation*

Andrew Morton's recent biography of Princess Diana has been a major
coup, not only by rapidly becoming an international best-seller, but
also by persuading an audience of millions to sympathise exclusively
with Diana's point of view. This is no mean feat and the way he achieves
it is of particular interest to this study. The actual saga of her life opens
as follows:

> It is a memory indelibly engraved upon her soul. Diana
> Spencer sat quietly at the bottom of the cold stone stairs
> at her Norfolk home clutching the wrought-iron
> banisters while all around her there was a determined
> bustle. She could hear her father loading suitcases into
> the boot of a car, then Frances, her mother, crunching
> across the gravel forecourt, the clunk of the car door
> being shut and the sound of a car engine revving and
> then slowly fading as her mother drove through the gates
> of Park House and out of her life. Diana was six years
> old. [1]

It is hard to see how anyone could resist such rhetoric, for it pulls out
all the sentimental stops. The reader is drawn ineluctably on to the

side of a little girl whose mother, it seems, has suddenly and inexplicably vanished. No device could be better guaranteed to elicit that sympathy and support on which the rest of Morton's narrative relies – we are being plunged here into immediate identification with Diana *as abandoned child*.

This kind of structuring at the start of *Diana: Her True Story* is typical, indeed symptomatic, of the ways in which accounts of mothers who leave are told. As the audience, we are placed on the side of the child rather than the mother; there are strains of high melodrama and emotional tension; and the experience is taken to be a lasting and ineradicable trauma – 'a quarter of a century later', it is still this, according to Morton, which is Diana's central formative memory.

All the mythologising that surrounds a mother who leaves is implicit here, as if nothing more need to be done than hint at the archetype for her to be conjured up. The mother herself is a vague, inaccessible figure, sensed only in the distance, and wilfully closing the door (a door that is both literal and symbolic) on her children, as if all contact between them is over. She *drives out* of her daughter's life, the natural equation being that any mother who leaves is *assumed to have abandoned* her children. Yet if we read on through the later chapters of the biography, a very different impression surfaces.

In fact, Morton shows himself far more sensitive to the mother's position than this opening would ever lead us to expect, and although our glimpses of the mother are tantalisingly brief, Frances Shand Kydd does come across as a person with her own complex motivations and emotional pain. She is seen as having a 'vivacious personality', 'fiercely proud, combative and tough-minded', and making strong interventions on Diana's behalf at various points in subsequent years. We learn that her departure came about only after years of marital unhappiness and that she was deeply concerned for the children she was leaving behind when her marriage collapsed. In 1968, at the time of her divorce, she did everything in her power to obtain custody of her four children and to have them living with her after she had moved to London. [2] But even her own mother, the late Ruth Fermoy (lady-in-waiting to the Queen Mother) testified against her suitability as a parent (two months earlier, Frances had been cited as the third party in Shand Kydd's divorce). Accordingly, the judgement went in favour of the father – whose greater wealth and privilege, it seems, as well as conventional moral judgements, influenced the verdict. 'Lady Althorp sued for custody of the children, an action started with every hope of success as the mother usually wins – unless the father is a nobleman. His rank and title gave him prior claims.'[3]

In other words, in stark contrast to the ogre-like figure summoned up in Morton's melodramatic opening, Diana's actual mother was caring and involved. Far from being indifferent to her daughter's life, she has remained supportive and in contact over the years. Her relationship with her four children did *not* end with her departure but was sustained, even in the face of considerable difficulties and opposition. Yet despite these facts of history, it is still the myth of the abandoning mother that hangs over Morton's saga of Princess Diana and determines our emotional response to it. Structurally, from that opening paragraph onwards, all our sympathies are ensconced firmly on the side of the deserted child.

Popular representations and thinking about mothers who leave have invariably been characterised by this kind of mythologising process. As in the example from *Diana*, the language, structure and rhetoric of melodrama have alienated readers and viewers from the mother and aligned them with the child. It is the *mother* who has been assumed to be actively in the wrong, and so she has been easy to ostracise and revile.

Interestingly, among divorced parents it is mothers not with their children who are viewed most negatively.[4] Indeed, according to a recent survey in the United States, non-custodial mothers are one of two social groups most vulnerable to popular censure – the other one being homosexuals. By contrast, non-custodial *fathers* are not only accepted, but even approved of *more* than single people.[5]

Perhaps the most notorious case this century to demonstrate public condemnation of a mother who leaves is the celebrated one of Swedish actress Ingrid Bergman. In 1950, when Bergman moved from America in order to live and work with the Italian film director Roberto Rossellini, she left behind her, with her first husband, their one daughter Pia, to be brought up in the country and language with which the child was familiar. To judge from the outrage this evoked in the national and international press, one would assume Bergman had committed murder. The furore reached such a pitch that she was even censured from the very heart of male power, the floor of the United States House of Congress.

On 14 March 1950, Edwin C. Johnson launched an attack on Bergman in the Senate itself, reviling her as 'one of the most powerful women on earth today – I regret to say, a powerful influence for evil', and damning her 'assault upon the institution of marriage'. He went so far as to muse on the possibility that she might be suffering from 'the dreaded mental disease schizophrenia' or might she be the victim of 'some kind of hypnotic influence?' For surely 'her unnatural attitude toward her own little girl indicates a mental abnormality.' According to Senator Johnson, Pia now had 'no mother' and the villainous Bergman, an 'alien guilty of turpitude', was banished from the USA, forbidden to set foot on American soil ever again. [6]

It would be tempting to try to place Bergman's rejection in the context of the early 1950s, interpreting it simply as part of that decade's increasing 'feminine mystique', were it not for parallel instances in more recent times. Diana Dors' autobiography, *Dors by Diana* (1981) reveals immense hostility towards her from the popular press when – largely through force of history and financial circumstances – she had to leave her two young sons with their father Richard (Dickie) Dawson in Hollywood in the early 1960s. (A full-time residential nanny was employed and remained with the family until her death at the time of the children's late adolescence.) It was to sustain the expensive lifestyle to which relatives and intimates seemed to have become addicted that Diana was pressurised into resuming a hectic schedule of world-wide acting and cabaret work immediately after the birth of her first child, but her (exaggerated and one-sided) reputation for infidelity combined unfortunately with the scandal of leaving her children to draw on to her a nasty whiplash of scorn and abuse from the American press. She was portrayed as a heartless, terrible woman, who had run off with other men and abandoned a loyal husband and their innocent children. [7]

In 1977, Margaret Trudeau, married to Pierre Trudeau who was then Prime Minister of Canada, left her three young sons with their father when her marriage disintegrated. Although she had continued access and saw her children regularly – initially an average of five days every two weeks – her departure and pursuit of an 'independent career' was constructed by the media and popular opinion as sheer selfishness. A violent swing of public sympathy to the side of the 'abandoned' father and sons was reflected by a 17 per cent increase in the Prime Minister's popularity ratings and Margaret Trudeau herself was swamped with hate mail and threats of violence and attacks against her life. [8]

Because women who leave children go against the grain of the selfless, masochistic and self-sacrificing function that our culture expects of mothers, they invariably invite censure from the system they seem to offend. Karen Silkwood, the woman whose life was dramatised in the film *Silkwood* (which had Meryl Streep in the title role) suffered from damning assumptions made about her because she had left her children. Yet her circumstances had been impossible. Her husband drank heavily, was sexually unfaithful and left to her the full onus of child care. When his behaviour finally led to bankruptcy, Karen tried to divorce him, but he insisted on having custody of the children. Unable to accept this, Karen refused, only leaving – on the husband's terms – after another few years of their miserable marriage.

Despite the distance between Oklahoma and the children's home in Texas, she maintained regular contact and saw them as much as possible. Meantime, working at a plutonium plant for the Kerr-McGee Nuclear Corporation, she discovered its violations of legal requirements and exposed these to the Atomic Energy Commission. Within months she was contaminated by a number of 'leakages' and suffered threats against her that culminated in a fatal car 'accident'. Kerr-McGee were prosecuted, but in the trial they tried to rest a large part of their defence on the alleged unreliability of Karen Silkwood's evidence. This, they claimed, was obvious in her disturbed, if not immoral, character – she had left her family, 'walked out' on husband and children. What better proof of mental and emotional instability?

This aspect of the corporative conspiracy against Karen Silkwood was excluded from the film version of her story, yet in the opening sequences there are shots of her with the three children she has 'left'. Reading the film from this angle, it is not implausible to suggest that what is taken in from it, subliminally, is that a woman who breaks out of the 'normal' family unit can expect to be punished. For Silkwood not only challenged the power of the nuclear plant, she also challenged the power of the nuclear family. She left her children behind. And no matter how sympathetic Streep may make her character, the plot – killing off Karen Silkwood – ultimately enshrines an old moral message: a mother who leaves cannot be allowed to succeed or survive.

Thus, on an unconscious level, part of the film's implicit and unacknowledged meaning is that the mother's death is an inevitable, if not 'rightful' punishment for her deviance.[9]

Historically, in the modern period, mothers have often met with heavy retribution for leaving children. Across Europe in the sixteenth and seventeenth centuries, the penalties included public humiliation, whipping, being put in the stocks or house of correction, even – as with Bergman 300 years later – exile. One of the earliest cases recorded in Britain, from London in 1556, gives a graphic picture of the sentence such a mother could expect:

> for leavynge and forsaking of a childe in the streates [a woman] shulde be whipped at Bridewell and from thence sent unto the govrnors of Christes hospitall for a further reformacion . . . [then] sent unto the pillorye . . . wyth a paper on hir hed wherein was written in greate letters Whipped at Bridewell for leavynge and forsakinge hir childe in the streates, and from thense caryed into Southwerk and banished for hir offence out of the citie.[10]

No matter what the reasons for her actions, nor how far these were out of her own control, as in extreme poverty, it was the mother rather than society that was held to blame. Once her crime was discovered, she would be chastised and forced to take the child back.

With the enlightenment of the eighteenth and nineteenth centuries, punishment became less physically barbaric, but the values informing the treatment of the absconding mother remained much the same. If she was not prepared to take on the proper nurturing role, she must be bad or mad. In 1739, a woman's ambivalence or inability to care for her children was so far from the assumed norm that a British mother who said she could not love her children was certified as insane.

On this level, not much has changed. In 1980, a Baltimore lawyer dealing with a custody dispute claimed that: 'The courts are prejudiced against fathers. Unless the mother is a prostitute, a drug addict or a mental defective, she is automatically assumed to be the better qualified to have custody.'[11] Obversely, then, if a mother *does not* take on full child care, it is reasoned she must be in a morally suspect or mentally deficient category. Charlie Chaplin and Cary Grant both had mothers who did not live with them and were deemed disturbed or ill. [12]

The assumption is that if you have left your children, you just cannot be a good woman, let alone a good mother. In the early 1980s, John Lennon highlighted this when he talked about the media witch-hunts that pursued Yoko Ono. Before her involvement with Lennon, Yoko had been married to Tony Cox, with whom she had a daughter, Kyoko, who was five at the time of their separation. Despite a fierce battle, Kyoko was subsequently legally granted to Cox – apparently after he had virtually kidnapped her – yet it was Yoko who had to take the blame for having 'allowed' her daughter to go and whose questionable mothering then came under attack. In Lennon's words: 'Yoko got steamed into a guilt thing that if she was not attacking them with detectives and police and the FBI, then she was not a good mother looking for her baby.' [13]

Relinquishing your child is not only presumed to be bad mothering, but is also made synonymous with leaving them for ever, severing all ties and thus made equivalent to abandonment. This is the myth played on so effectively in the opening of *Diana*. A mother leaving means curtains down. Her actions are final and irrevocable.

Yet empirical evidence suggests these general assumptions and equations to be untrue. Studies show that the absent mother struggles, frequently against much hostility, to continue sustained contact. An American survey found 60 per cent of mothers maintaining at least once and mostly twice or more monthly visits with their children after separation. Less than one mother in 10 had no contact, a rate much lower than that of non-custodial fathers – studies in Britain and the States have found between 40 and 50 per cent of men having no contact with their children two years after divorce. [14]

Part of the popular prejudice against mothers who leave comes from the view of motherhood that is so deeply ingrained in our patriarchal and Christian tradition. In the collective Western mind the very way of seeing mothers, the construction of the Mother image, is shot through with assumptions and messages that have come down from a Christian iconography. With the 'Virgin' Mary as the focus of Christian and maternal love, mother as virgin is the very emblem of female purity and anything moving away from that ideal is impure, deviant and bad. So powerful is the cult of this (Virgin) mother in mainstream culture that women who do not approximate to it are turned into female anti-Christs, fallen and scarlet women, bad mothers who simply do not exist, mothers who – like Princess Diana's – are deemed to have walked (or driven) off the map.

Through the visual tradition of Christianity, the Madonna and Christ child has become our central icon of mother-child relationships. As the one picture of mother and child constantly in front of our eyes this reinforces our sense of their being a single indivisible unit, one from which the mother simply cannot move away. In this icon, mother and infant are viewed in a deeply romanticised way, with the baby suckling at the breast, the body of the Mother fetishised, or mother and child gazing at one another in an enclosed, mutually ecstatic reverie.

It is significant that, through this unquestioned tradition, the figures of mother and child are effectively bonded together into one physical unit. The mother-child dyad is held to be an engrossing, symbiotic bond into which nothing external can impinge and from which nothing can be taken away. Thus in the reified, if not deified, images of (rapturous) Madonna and child in our cultural heritage – Michelangelo's famous *Pietà* in St Peter's, Rome, Raphael's *The Madonna del Granduca*, Titian's *Madonna and Child* – there is an exclusive and single-minded focus on the mother-child bond. Mother is not seen or sensed in any way as a separate person, but only as part of this (deeply physical) unit with her child, bound to and with it in a cocoon that is isolated from the rest of the world and from history.

Although we know that the child will eventually move out and grow away from this mother-infant dyad, we know too that the mother will not. Only the child will separate out and become other, necessarily renouncing the mother in that process of individuation – as does Christ himself when he disowns the mother: 'Woman, what have I to do with thee?' But, by definition, Mother is the one who cannot separate or grow away. She is the wholeness *from which* the child's separation occurs, and it is upon her, the mother's (ever-present) body that the child's individuation relies. Thus in the visual arts, there is no image of a mother outside the mother-child icon (except mourning over dead children, where the enclosing unit and exclusive preoccupation remain).

In this dominant Western tradition, then, what artistic representation can there possibly be of a mother who leaves? If woman is defined as mother by being a mother to the child, how can she claim to be mother without the child? What representation can there be if she moves out of that mother-child dyad? Indeed, outside her relationship to her child, how can a mother exist at all? In the very leaving she is assumed to have ceased to be a mother – her functional, defining relationship to her child has supposedly come to an end.

If feminist aesthetics have analysed the construction of women as objects (of the male gaze) rather than subjects in their own right, nowhere is this more true than in cultural representations of the mother.[15] In all the visual arts, from classical painting to contemporary cinema, there is no view of the mother's world from within, no sense of *her* complex subjectivity. Mother is only an imagined ideal – the good all-nurturing provider, object of fantasy – and is always linked into, defined by, her *relationality* to her child. In this light, a mother who leaves becomes a kind of grammatical nonsense.

It is as if there is an internal grammar of motherhood, a correct (and imperative) way to be and behave, which involves women remaining attached to their children. To depart from this, to advertise separation, throws this deepest syntax askew. A mother who leaves jolts all the usual expectations about women into such disarray, it becomes hard to find images or words to describe her: as if an absent mother is a contradiction in terms, a grammatical impossibility.[16]

And just as in the visual arts a mother not aligned with the Madonna myth moves out of frame – like vampires, with whom they are often symbolically associated, they have no reflection in the glass of mainstream culture – so in literature mothers who leave are notable for their lack of representation. Such mothers are either not represented at all, remarkable only by their absence, or are tied into narrative lines aimed at defining them in highly negative ways, and bringing them to punitive, destructive ends.

The fate of one such story about a mother who leaves is a case in point. In 1989, the BBC screened *The Ginger Tree*, a popular drama about a woman separated from her child. Set in the early 1900s, it tells how Mary Mackenzie, a Scottish girl, travels to the Far East to be married to a British military attaché. On every level the marriage is a disappointment and Mary lives in a stupor of unfulfilment until her love affair with a Japanese count, Kentaro Kurihama. Discovering she is pregnant by him, Mary leaves her marriage and – under Kurihama's financial protection, effectively his concubine – has her son in Japan. The baby is only a few months old when Kurihama has it kidnapped and given to Japanese parents as their *yoshi*, or adopted son. Mary is dumbfounded by her son being stolen, but under Japanese law she has no right to reclaim him.

The TV dramatisation of Mary's loss and frustration as she mourns and tries to find her son are moving, especially to any mother who has been separated from young children. It is many years before she meets her son again, not in fact until the outbreak of the Second World War, at the moment of her enforced repatriation to Britain. Her son, now adult, is a Japanese fighter pilot, preparing for a suicide mission to save his country. Mary – this mother who is no mother – has to come to terms with having a child who is a stranger on every level, culturally as well as personally, and the complex feelings involved are conveyed with unusual sensitivity.

However, comparing the TV series with the novel on which it was based, there is one striking omission from the plot which says much about mainstream attitudes to mothers who leave. In the original, Oswald Wynd's *The Ginger Tree* (1977), prior to her affair with Count Kurihama, Mary (whose name so obviously links her with traditional icons of mothering) has a child, Jane, inside her marriage. When her husband discovers her infidelity, he not only compels her to leave, but prevents her from taking baby Jane with her – and forbids any further contact. Jane is sent back to England to be brought up by Mary's mother-in-law. This episode – and, even more so, the fact of its omission from the TV adaptation – is highly significant.

First, the episode itself shows that a woman leaving her marriage and child has to be punished in kind. Mary leaves husband and daughter only to be left by lover and son: a neat moral symmetry is deeply embodied in the plot, so that her punishment perfectly fits her crime. One baby pays for another. For stealing away her mothering from her first baby, her mothering of her second is stolen from her – and she suffers deeply for it. 'It is when I am weakened by tiredness that all I want is my baby back, at any price to me personally . . . I will never see Tomo grow, I will never see the changing face moving out of childhood towards the man. Already he is recognising someone else as his mother.'[17]

Secondly, its deliberate omission suggests that the BBC could not risk a drop in audience ratings by having a sympathetic portrayal of a woman who has left her child. In order for Mary (played by Samantha Bond) to remain a character of whom the viewer could approve, the controversial issue of a mother walking out had to be dropped. Even as late as 1989, though a woman's adultery may have become a morally acceptable theme, her leaving a child had not.

In the last decade, this resistance to a serious or sympathetic appraisal of mothers who leave has intensified in both Hollywood and the mass media. In the current backlash against feminism, motherhood has undergone yet another popular revival and regressive fantasies about the fulfilment to be found in maternity have once again taken centre stage. Films and TV soap operas have concentrated on making motherhood as seductive as possible, with young women (and men) craving for babies. In response to the real disintegration of the family and the threat of more fluid forms of mothering, popular culture has once more raised the family into a necessary refuge against social upheaval and has elevated mothering (or a sentimentalised version of it) into a noble role.

In this current climate, women taking unconventional roles or positions are mocked. Lesbianism has been turned into a theme for comedy shows, strong women have virtually disappeared from screen. Women who reject motherhood before the event are humiliated and seen as eccentric failures, whilst rejecting it afterwards is the ultimate irresponsibility. If feminism does surface, it is only to be derided as outdated and unfashionable, or turned into a joke. Hardly surprisingly, against this backdrop, mothers who leave are not only not taken seriously, but seem to have become part of the stock material of TV comedy.

Recent popular culture either briefly indulges – then reclaims – the mother who leaves home, as in *Shirley Valentine*, or (if she persists in her folly) ridicules her as negligent and delinquent. In the American TV series *Raising Miranda* a mother who leaves is shown up as self-indulgent and inadequate – the condemnation coming not only from men but, much more effectively, from the daughter who has taken over her mother's domestic role as the good wife.

The quest of the liberated wife who leaves home in
Raising Miranda is reduced to a pathetic joke. Mum ran
away after attending a 'self-improvement workshop',
snickers Miranda, the superior daughter, an adolescent
who becomes the dutiful surrogate mum to her macho
blue-collar father. Her abundant housekeeping skills
serve as a not-so-subtle rebuke of delinquent mum who,
Miranda tells us disparagingly, 'couldn't do a load of
laundry'. On *Blossom*, another deserted daughter is
similarly disgusted with her indulgent mother. 'She is
supposed to be in the kitchen, waiting for me after
school,' she decrees, not 'on the road, fulfilling her
needs.'[18]

In Britain's TV soap opera *Coronation Street*, when Deirdre Barlow
became involved with local politics and non-domestic activities her
marriage started to disintegrate: thus audience sympathy was quickly
manoeuvred away from the hard, termagant character of a woman
wanting to get out of the doll's house. In this desperately post-feminist
culture women who leave marriages or children have to be constructed
as 'bad' mothers who are meanly putting their own lives first, clumsy
parodies of 'macho feminists'.

Contemporary popular culture, far from being a reflection of what
is happening in society at large, is not giving any sensitive attention
at all to the complex ways in which mothering and parenting are
shifting their sites. Women's roles are simply being thrown back into
domestic models, mothers who leave – and all women taking different
'deviant' positions – being represented in a language and imagery
calculated to diminish and degrade. As with the story of *Diana*, no
matter what the reality, the characterisation of such mothers tends
towards the mythological – they are driven by a selfish ambition or
carelessness – and the rhetoric surrounding them is still one of
truancy and desertion.

It is as if, in the 1980s and nineties, dominant ideology has been
reacting to the threats of feminism's second wave in the 1960s and
1970s and, rather like King Canute, has been doing everything it
can to try to stop the tide. If feminism is feared for (supposedly)
wanting to destroy the family, or at least for destabilising the mother
figure, then popular culture and the mass media have been rushing

to salvage, resurrect and promote that besieged good mother as fast
as they can. Behind their comic shows and moral parables lies a deep
panic, evident in the desperation with which they try to foster in
women 'a renewed *desire* to occupy the mother position.'[19]

The most recent images of mothers who leave, then, in mainstream
culture, have been cleverly hostile or defensively humorous. Icons of
perfect mothers, of the blissful Madonna and child, have once more
been held up against them, like crucifixes or pieces of garlic meant
to protect against vampires.

But the iconography of Christian art and religion is not the only
source from which popular myths of good and bad mothers have been
able to draw. Just as powerful and influential as the sacred tradition
of the visual arts has been the secular heritage of modern culture –
particularly the vast amount of written material that has evolved in
the West from the Industrial Revolution onwards. It is in this body of
literature that we first find stories about mothers who've left, stories
that have fed into many popular myths and that have done as much
as anything to shape the tales we are told – and tell ourselves – about
such women.

For although it might be thought that hostile representations of
mothers who slip out of the conventional mothering role are nothing
new, it is in fact only in the modern period, particularly in the
eighteenth and nineteenth centuries, that moral narratives have
emerged telling us specifically how mothers should or should not
behave, and giving us dire warnings about what happens to the ones
who break the rules. Later on, I shall discuss how this cultural
development relates to the emergence of a new ideology of motherhood
in the post-Industrial period. But first, in the next three chapters, I
shall be exploring some of those long narratives that have come out
of Europe and America to form many of our moral judgements and
prejudices about mothers who leave. For it is here, in mainstream
Western culture of the last two hundred years – first in the novel, then
in cinema – that the most popular myths about such mothers have
their immediate roots.

Morals and Melodrama:
East Lynne Revisited

> The very hour of her departure she awoke to what she
> had done: the guilt, whose aspect had been shunned in
> the prospective, assumed at once its true, frightful
> colour, the blackness of darkness; and a lively remorse,
> a never dying anguish, took possession of her soul for
> ever. Oh, reader, believe me! Lady-wife-mother! should
> you ever be tempted to abandon your home, so will you
> awake!
>
> Ellen Price *East Lynne*

Much of the general reluctance to think lucidly or compassionately
about the lives of mothers who leave has come from fictions absorbed
from our literary tradition. Amongst the earliest references in the
modern period is Daniel Defoe's novel *Roxana* (1724), where a mother
who abandons her children is a dancer and prostitute. It is as if only
a woman of loose morals would do such a thing, forsaking her children
as willingly as her virtue, and this assumption of immorality in a
mother who leaves runs throughout mainstream literature.

In nineteenth-century fiction, mothers are forced to relinquish their
children because of the scandal of their illegitimacy. Dickens' *Bleak
House* has Lady Dedlock give up her daughter Esther – conceived out
of wedlock – and the mother is hounded to an early grave as a result
of her bittersweet passion. Elizabeth Gaskell frequently returns to
the theme of lost mothers, children separated from mothers or mothers
from children: 'All the earth,' she writes, 'though it were full of kind
hearts, is but a desolation and a desert place to a mother when her
only child is absent.' Novels by Thomas Hardy include sensitive
portraits of women unable to cope with the consequences of
illegitimate offspring, but again the mothers' ends are untimely deaths
or exile.

But no matter what the writer's sympathies towards the woman, the demands of the novel – and the social and sexual morality the genre enshrined – drove their narratives towards tragic endings, delivering mothers who leave children into fates worse than death if not death itself. Flaubert's *Madame Bovary* (1856–7) gives a punitive and highly sadistic death to the adulterous mother. Kate Chopin's *The Awakening* (1899) has a woman leaving her husband and children to pursue a romantic dream, but its heroine finds her freedom only symbolically, in the sea where she drowns. Laurence Housman's play of 1911, *Pains and Penalties*, depicts the life of Queen Caroline, wife of George IV, exiled and separated from her children and learning about the death of her daughter in a newspaper. She had to be seen to suffer for not being a good mother – the play was even refused a licence by the Lord Chamberlain. [1]

The implied warning of doom facing mothers who leave has been just as strong and eloquent in writings by women as by men. Indeed, of all novels to shape popular response towards the idea of leaving children, it is one by a woman – the highly acclaimed *East Lynne* (1861) – which spells out the direst consequences. Here, leaving is not only a heinous crime against marriage and family, but the most self-destructive act imaginable on the part of the mother.

East Lynne was the second novel of Ellen Price, more properly known under her married name as Mrs Henry Wood. She was born in 1814 and after a spinal disability in her early teens was partially invalided for life, with a forward curvature of the spine. In 1836, after a studious and well-educated childhood, Price married a rich banker, Henry Wood, with whom she lived in France and had one son. By Victorian middle-class standards, her life was exemplary, her very name a by-word of female rectitude. She certainly did not leave husband or child, and seems to have remained entirely faithful to her dull spouse, of whom even the son recorded that he 'had not a spark of imagination . . . It was an effort to him to read a novel.'[2]

Yet it was from the pen of this morally upright Victorian lady that there emerged one of the most extraordinary stories of an absconding mother, a novel that is a remarkable fantasy of female desire and its castration. In *East Lynne*, the woman is so full of (forbidden) personal and sexual longings that she has to do violent damage to them, resulting in peculiarly self-tormenting, masochistic behaviour.

Its heroine is the orphaned aristocrat Isabel Vane, who marries Archibald Carlyle – a brilliant lawyer whose hard-won wealth and inheritance enable him to purchase East Lynne, Isabel's former family estate. They have three children together, Isabel Lucy, William and Archibald, but in reality Isabel is a token mother. Carlyle's sister manages the household; nurses and servants care for the children. Hardly surprisingly, in this powerless situation Isabel – like Mrs Henry Wood herself – suffers various psychosomatic illnesses, and is sent abroad to recover. In France she meets Byronic villain Francis Levison, tries to flee her desire for him by returning home, but Carlyle coincidentally invites Levison to stay. The plot tightens around her. Tormented by what seems to be Carlyle's intimacy with a former girlfriend, Barbara Hare, Isabel is ready to fall prey to Levison's evil designs. In a moment of impetuous desperation, she leaves with him in a dramatic midnight flight from the marital home.

That is as much joy as she is allowed. From the second Isabel leaves, 'tearing at a furious pace' through the leafy splendour of East Lynne, she regrets her move. Not for an instant is her liberation seen as being worth the price. In the very next chapter we are transported to the Continent, a year on, only to discover Isabel drowning in guilt. She has had not a glimpse of gratification, not a second free from searing self-reproach.

> How fared it with Lady Isabel? Just as it must be expected to fare, and does fare, when a high-principled gentlewoman falls from her pedestal. Never had she experienced a moment's calm, or peace, or happiness, since the fatal night of quitting her home. She had taken a blind leap in a moment of wild passion; when . . . she had found herself plunged into an abyss of horror, from which there was never more any escape; never more, never more.

Thus, from the instant of Isabel's departure, the whole momentum of the narrative twists into this harrowing retribution against her. She is obsessed with her guilt as a failed mother and there is not one second when she is not tormented by the thought of the children she has left behind:

I do not know how to describe the vain yearning, the inward fever, the restless longing for what might not be. Longing for what? For her children. Let a mother, be she a duchess, or be she an apple-woman at a standing, be separated for a while from her little children: let *her* answer how she yearns for them. She may be away on a tour of pleasure . . . but as the weeks lengthen out, the desire to see them again becomes almost irrepressible . . . Oh! that she could see her children but for a day, an hour, that she might press one kiss upon their lips! Could she live without it?

The rest of *East Lynne*'s half-thousand harrowing pages is nothing but crack-down: not only through Isabel's 'adder stings' of conscience, but through a plot that stretches sensation and melodrama to their limits – 'her whole future existence . . . would be one dark course of gnawing retribution.'

The punishments Isabel meets are piled ludicrously high. Francis Levison abandons her – when she is already pregnant, so she is forced to give birth in deprived circumstances – and returns to his life as an infamous rake. Isabel decides the only way she can atone for her sins is life-long penance, and she is given ample opportunity for it. *En route* to a governess position, she is involved in a railway accident. Her new baby is killed outright and she herself sustains enormous injuries. She is crippled, her once lovely face disfigured to the point of non-recognition.

Indeed, the accident is so bad, witnesses assume her to be dead, which is the news that reaches East Lynne, so that from then on her children think of her only as a ghost. But in fact, Isabel survives – to endure the worst humiliation Mrs Wood's complex sado-masochism can devise. She returns to East Lynne to be governess to her own three children, a manoeuvre that compels her to add to her regrets the torment of seeing at first hand her faultless and devoted Carlyle now married to the envied Barbara. In the many agonising scenes that follow, the torture that is heaped on Isabel is thick and furious. It is not enough that she has to be in close contact with her children on a daily basis, with them believing her dead so that her unmotherly behaviour is perpetually confronting her; not enough to witness scenes of loving intimacy between Carlyle and the children's stepmother; not enough to have salt rubbed in the wound by hearing the kids talk about their darling lost mother and have Barbara forbidding her to spend her wages on presents for them; but, to cap it all, the caddish Levison turns out to be a murderer. She gave up Carlyle for *that*! Everything is exaggerated to maximise her pain. Her former beauty has been smashed, so she has to wear shapeless clothes, ugly hats and thick blue spectacles to conceal herself.

Isabel is effectively one of the living dead in her own home and the pain of her exclusion reaches its climax when her son William falls fatally ill. Even on his death-bed, she is not allowed to reveal her identity to him. She is the ghostly, unnameable mother, the woman whose awfulness cannot be revealed. With her 'heart sick unto death', watching with Carlyle as their son dies of consumption, Isabel endures the worst torment of all.

> Down on her knees, her face buried in the counterpane, a corner of it stuffed into her mouth that it might help to stifle her agony, knelt Lady Isabel. The moment's excitement was well nigh beyond her strength of endurance. Her own child; his child; they were alone around its death-bed, and she might not ask or receive from him a word of comfort, of consolation!
> . . . Lady Isabel fell sobbing on the bed. No; not even at that last hour when the world was closing on him dared she say, I am your mother.[3]

The trauma of her son's death finally does for her – though there is just enough time to squeeze in one more crucifying death-bed scene, her own, where Isabel makes confession to Carlyle and he (extremely reluctantly, and only when her death is assured) grants absolution.

George Meredith, Chapman and Hall's reader, thought the novel 'foul' and duly rejected it, but he mistook the palate of the Victorian female reader. *East Lynne* turned into one of the biggest publishing hits of the day and century. Of all those women's fictions in the 1860s known as sensation novels, this was the greatest and best-selling. By 1897, the 500-page saga had sold 400,000 copies and innumerable theatrical adaptations had been made.

Sensation novels were highly popular anyway, and flight from a repressive marriage was a recurrent theme, but what *East Lynne* did was to take the usual stock-in-trade – suspense, secrets, exaggerated feelings, shock, the (soap operaish) motifs of 'bigamy, adultery, illegitimacy, disguise, changed names, railway accidents, poison, fire, murder, concealed identity, false reports of deaths, doubling of characters or incidents'[4] – and refocus them in a new way that was highly pertinent to women locked in marriages and motherings they might hate but could not escape.

The message to these women readers is unmistakable:

> . . . Whatever trials may be the lot of your married life, though they may magnify themselves to your crushed spirit as beyond the endurance of woman to bear, *resolve* to bear them; fall down upon your knees and pray to be enabled to bear them: pray for patience; pray for strength to resist the demon that would urge you so to escape; bear unto death, rather than forfeit your fair name and your good conscience; for be assured that the alternative, if you rush on to it, will be found far worse than death![5]

But the strange power of *East Lynne* (and part of the reason for its immense and enduring popularity) is that it is not in any way a cold moral tract warning women to stay at home with husbands and children. It is far more intense. The agonising physical and emotional punishments inflicted on Isabel are so much in excess of the crime, so superfluous to the needs of the plot, it is as if they show the enormity of the desire her transgression embodies. The movement of the plot is so deeply vindictive and sadistic, so brutal towards Isabel's deviant impulses, it is as if only immense imaginative overkill can stop that excess of female desire in its tracks. Not only in the tormented and repressed psychosexual world of Mrs Henry Wood herself, but in the inner landscape of her female readers, there is a peculiar fantasising process going on, as if the passion and threat Isabel embodies are so great they can only be countered by this enormous frenzy of violence.[6]

In the mid-nineteenth century, when divorce was virtually impossible and the law defined both property and children as belonging to the man, few women had any means of support outside marriage. Fantasies of leaving *had* to be repressed: the consequences *were* – as *East Lynne* reveals in exaggerated form – just too appalling. The passion informing Ellen Price's writing and the extent of the suffering and punishment inflicted on the abdicating mother show just how urgent the message – and the need for repression – were. *East Lynne* was the effective *deterrent* women needed, echoing their own desperate containment of their equally desperate passion and desire.

Seen in this light, *East Lynne* is an extraordinarily sado-masochistic fantasy, and one that powerfully affected the collective female response to a mother escaping from husband and children. More than a century later, women are still filled with dire warnings about how awful the consequences would be if they were to leave. Once a mother, all that lies outside mothering has to be forbidden.

Shortly after *East Lynne* came another famous tale of a mother leaving, Tolstoy's *Anna Karenin* (1874–6). Less melodramatic than Wood's warning parable, Tolstoy's version reveals the social hypocrisies and tragic impossibilities facing a woman trying to free herself from a dead marriage. When Anna falls in love with Vronsky, her husband Karenin accuses her of being 'without honor, without heart, without religion . . . a lost woman! . . . in the depths of his soul he desired that she should be punished.' This is easy to do: when Anna leaves Russia for Europe with Vronsky and the illegitimate baby she has had by him, Karenin refuses to let her take their own son with them. Indeed, the eight-year-old Seriozha is told that his mother is dead. On a return trip, Anna is denied all access to the boy and rightly senses he will be brought up to despise her. 'This wounded Anna to the bottom of her soul.'

As the third party and the man, Vronsky gets off relatively lightly. It is Anna, the wife and mother who has left who suffers social persecution. Relatives and friends ostracise her, even Vronsky's sister-in-law refuses to be seen in her company, as if Anna has prostituted herself by leaving her family: 'We must call things by their right name. I cannot receive her.' The animosity is so strong that Anna becomes unable to bear it and looks for a way out of the guilt and pain. Tormented by Vronsky's growing alienation and 'feeling the impossibility of struggling', her final desperate gesture is to hurl herself under the wheels of a moving train. Her last thoughts are not of the man for whom she has sacrificed everything, but of the son she lost, amazed at how she relinquished him for a love that has proved finite.

Anna Karenin has none of the melodramatic pyrotechnics of *East Lynne*, and so is far more persuasively realistic. Yet for all Tolstoy's sympathetic portrait of Anna, once again his narrative is caught up in the demands of nineteenth-century novels for particular resolutions and these are deeply ingrained in our moral consciousness. We might be moved, or feel uneasy, at Anna's premature death, but at the same time there is a sense of aesthetic rightness and moral inevitability about her ending. And although this may be an authentic version of what was likely to have happened in such a case at the time, it is also important to recognise that it is not just an innocent mirroring, but a work that has formed our sense of reality – it is precisely these *imaginative reconstructions* of events that shape and fashion our expectations.

The subliminal and lasting effects of works like *East Lynne* or *Anna Karenin* are to convince us that for mothers who leave there is no hope. Either retribution will hit us from the outside – ostracism, hostility, misunderstanding – or we will internalise these judgements and devote our lives to guilt, penance and self-recrimination. Over the last century, despite legal shifts and social changes in the role of women, most representations still show us as shallow and selfish, our behaviour made acceptable only by life-long atonement. If a woman has been so heartless as to leave her children, the least she can do is suffer for it: her anguish is the penance for her crime.

It is telling that one of the few works of art to give a positive vindication of the rights of women – mothers or not – to leave oppressive marriages, Ibsen's *A Doll's House* (1879), is unable to take us past the point of a mother's actual departure. We are only shown the impossibility of her staying, as if even Ibsen's imagination fell short when it came to projecting a happy aftermath.

And as we shall find in those (male) twentieth-century fictions discussed in the following chapters, for all the historical shifts that have occurred, in mainstream culture the morals and myths of mothers who leave remain much the same as those of Victorian melodrama: catastrophe is bound to await us. There is still too much at stake to draw portraits of absconding mothers that are lighter, happier or less punitive.

Father as Mother:
Twentieth-century Heroics

> . . . if men are to begin to share in the 'work of love' we
> will have to change our ways of loving them. This means,
> among other things, that we cease praising and being
> grateful to the fathers of our children when they take
> some partial share in their care and nurture. (No woman
> is considered 'special' because she carries out her
> responsibilities as a parent; not to do so is considered
> a social crime.) . . . It means that we begin to expect of
> men, as we do of women, that they can behave like our
> equals without being applauded for it or singled out as
> 'exceptional'; and that we refuse them the traditional
> separation between 'love' and 'work.'
>
> Adrienne Rich *Of Woman Born*

In my own life, the earliest and therefore most formative image I can
recollect of a mother who leaves was in Warwick Deeping's *Sorrell and
Son*. Originally published in 1930, this was a highly popular novel in
England in the years leading up to and following the Second World
War. It ran to three reprints within a month and became a minor
classic, its appeal still evident in a recent television adaptation,
starring Richard Pasco as Sorrell and reaching millions. Although it
is better known to our parents' generation than our own, it is worth
discussing in some detail as symptomatic of the way mothers who leave
have been constructed in many literary works (before and after
feminism) this century.

Our family copy had been presented to my father as a Sunday school
prize, and sat proudly sandwiched in our small bookcase between a
Bible and a Pears encyclopaedia. I devoured it repeatedly during
childhood and early adolescence, unwittingly absorbing its intense
misogyny and only now, rereading it, have I come to realise the

appalling view of women I was taking in. Here, the terrible woman who has abandoned her child is nothing less than a vampire and whore: even incest might be within her range.

Sorrell and Son is set shortly after the First World War, and focuses on an exclusive father-son relationship. Captain Stephen Sorrell, recently demobbed, is a single parent to his only son Christopher, Kit, who is 11 when the novel begins. Sorrel is reduced to working as a porter in provincial hotels until his innate worth is recognised by a wealthy entrepreneur establishing a national chain of luxury hotels. In a magical rise of fortune, Sorrell ends up not only managing the best of them, The Pelican, but entering into partnership with their owner and running a lucrative antiques business on the side.

Sorrell's major investment, though, is his son. Somehow saving enough capital from his porter's salary, he funds Kit's private education and sends him to Trinity College, Cambridge to read medicine. The emotional climax of the story comes when Sorrell is dying from an inoperable stomach cancer. Kit, now an eminent surgeon, injects him with a lethal dose of morphine – a tear-jerking scene in which the son is his father's lover and murderer rolled into one.

There is no mention of Kit's mother for some time, and the reader assumes she must be dead, but it is gradually leaked that she 'walked out' on them, leaving Sorrell to parent alone – a role he assumes with all the single-mindedness of a military campaign. The absent mother, Dora, is re-introduced only when Sorrell's high moral integrity and close loving relationship with Kit have been firmly established and any sympathetic response to her is precluded. We are told that Dora's motives for leaving husband and child were twofold: money and sex. A greedy nymphomaniac! What better reason could Sorrell have for denying her access, or Deeping for cutting her out of the novel? Whenever she appears, Sorrell's panic breaks out once more, as if she is a man-eater, a vampire, wanting to devour all men, their son included.

> But the rampant sex of her! Those bold clear eyes, the
> nose broadening slightly at the nostrils, the luscious yet
> shrewd mouth! She was the very essence of sex . . . and
> it was this impression of her sex . . . that had disturbed

> him . . . that mixture of passion and shrewd, worldwise
> contriving . . . In his mental diary he wrote her down
> a vampire, a woman, who, having had all the
> satisfactions she desired from men and sex, was seeking
> other satisfactions. That red mouth of hers was ready
> to feed upon the young vitality of her son . . . now
> Christopher was to be the one creature to be desired,
> a young man to be debauched by the maternal passions
> of a woman who was growing old.

The plot is crudely manipulated to prevent any identification with
Dora, yet even so there is evidence that her actions in leaving were
those of a desperate and trapped woman. Piecing together the factual
jigsaw, we find that it was not till she was 40 – after 12 years of
marriage to Sorrell, of which even he admits only the first four were
happy – that she left. In other words, she had persisted for eight
miserable years in a bond with a man who by anybody's standards is
deeply repressed, repelled by the female sex, nostalgic for pre-war
Edwardian England, and blatantly misogynistic. Dora's departure was
hardly sudden or unjustified. The only wonder is that with her energy
and appetite for experience, she stayed so long.

What is most striking is how ruthlessly Sorrell (and Deeping) exclude
her and turn Kit against her. From the moment of her 'melodramatic
disappearance', Dora is refused all contact with her son, and is not
allowed to offer any emotional or financial support. She is not even
informed of his schooling or changes of address. Sorrell's 'whole
purpose had been to perfect a complete comradeship between himself
and his son . . .' and for this the mother has to be excluded: 'he was
desperately serious in his desire to keep her and Christopher apart.'

Through Sorrell, Deeping takes a self-righteous stance against the
mother who has left, even implying that once she has 'walked out', her
child never enters her head. As in many contemporary newspaper
articles, leaving is taken to mean ending all relationship with the
children. The cumulative effect of all this is deeply punitive. One of
the most extraordinary lines in this sadistic novel comes when Sorrell
ponders on Dora's reappearance. He wonders: *Did the mother ever
think of the boy? He hoped not'* (my italics). The notion of a woman
who has borne a child, raised him at home for 11 years and tolerated
eight years of a miserable and sexually unsatisfactory marriage for his

sake, finally leaving, aged 40, in a last bid to live, and being punished
by not being allowed to see her son again, the idea of this woman never
even wondering about him – *'Did the mother ever think of the boy?'* –
is quite astounding, and makes one gawp at Deeping's insensitivity.

But of course Dora has broken the rules of good mothering, and has
to pay a high price for her 'freedom'. She is not allowed to know where
her only son lives, she is not allowed to write him letters, she is not
allowed to send money or presents. Anything that would imply real
or responsible parenting, any on-going link, would give her a foot in
the door and is taboo. Dora is totally excluded from her son's life and
Kit is tainted with the same shallow portrait of her. When she finally
tracks him down to the austere masculine calm of his rooms at Trinity,
he gives her a cruel brush-off. 'So – this is the woman who let my
father down.' Her own 11 years of caring for him have been forgotten,
eclipsed by Sorrell's heroism in taking over the parent role (though
he employed female care-takers), and Kit's view of her is as warped
as his father has wanted:

> Had she expected him to rush at her and to cry –
> 'Mother'? Of course not! . . . For nine years she had
> been less than a shadow . . . His mother had deserted
> his father at a time of wounds and misfortune. She had
> gone away with another man. Nine years had passed,
> and Sorrell had been both mother and father to him . . .
> The man that was Christopher took sides, and his
> nascent manhood was on the side of his father . . . His
> father was a great man. He loved him.

Dora makes one desperate last-ditch attempt to explain the real story
to Kit, to point out there were two sides to the marriage failure, but
it falls on wilfully deaf ears –

> He would remember how she had walked about the
> room, weeping, pressing a handkerchief to her mouth,
> looking at him ever and again with a kind of passionate
> rage. 'You won't understand. I – always – wanted you.
> You are my boy . . . He's poisoned you against me. It was
> not my fault that I couldn't love him.'

– and Dora is at last wiped out of the novel.

Sorrell and Son is a vicious attack upon mothers who leave. The whole story is told from a male point of view, and Kit's last words to his mother, 'I belong to the pater,' reveal the real thrust of the novel – to give the triumph to men against women. Indeed, the male bond of 'Sorrell and *Son*' is inscribed in bold print at the top of every page: father and son close their defensive ranks against the powerful mother who might interrupt their all-male bonding. [1]

Sorrell and Son is a significant work, not only on a personal level, in that it so powerfully shaped my own views of female sexuality and mothers who leave (no wonder I later felt I had no right to fight for my son), but because it is so typical of the tales and images of 'abandoning' mothers that have fed the collective mind this century.

I mentioned previously the case of Diana Dors, whose two sons Mark and Gary remained in Hollywood with their father (and a full-time nanny) whilst Diana was earning money to support them throughout the 1960s. Yet it was their father, Richard Dawson, who was to be transformed by the media into a martyred and heroic figure. When Hollywood magazine headlines turned Diana into the wicked (sexual) mother, they simultaneously elevated Richard – who had eventually managed to get a TV series of his own called *Hogan's Heroes* – into the noble (wronged) father: 'The time Richard Dawson became a real-life hero.' [2]

Thus, if not having actually set the tone, the kind of patterning found in *Sorrell and Son* can nevertheless be taken as *representative* of the general picture that has become prevalent in recent years – a picture that shows bad mothers having left to do their own (immoral) thing and heroic fathers nobly remaining behind (by default) to pick up the pieces (with a little help from friends, nannies and relatives).

Most particularly, *Sorrell and Son* can be seen as anticipating two very popular modern fictions which have made full use of the theme of mothers who leave and fathers who stay: the novel and film of *Kramer versus Kramer* (1978 and 1979) and Danielle Steel's best-selling novel *Daddy* (1989; a television dramatisation was screened in Britain in 1993). I shall explore *Kramer versus Kramer* in much greater detail in the next chapter, but the striking thing about all these works is their identical focus on – and sympathy with – the father's rather than the mother's viewpoint. Structurally and emotionally, they all engineer the woman's exclusion and make the male point of view paramount. This fits in with that single-minded focus on the father that is necessary if he is to remain at all central.

What is most telling about the sexual politics of *Sorrell and Son*, *Kramer versus Kramer* and *Daddy* is that (like the Hollywood version of Diana Dors' story) they all elevate the father as single parent to the status of hero. In Steel's novel, although we are given an initial glimpse of the wife and mother, Sarah Watson, as a woman who is increasingly frustrated by her domestic role, from the moment she leaves – to pursue a career, starting with studying at Harvard (!) – it is as if she has waived all claim to our attention and she disappears from the text. From then on, the focus is exclusively on her husband, Oliver Wendell Watson, an advertising executive, and *his* struggle to survive. Moreover, despite their having three children – one daughter and two sons – it is Watson's relationship with his *male* offspring that is given priority, along with his relation with *his* own father in turn. The novel was promoted on precisely these male lines: 'Three generations. Three men', whilst the lives of the women – grandmother, mother and daughter – are utterly marginalised. Taken in isolation, this emphasis might seem accidental or innocent, but set against the context of other modern fictions about mothers who leave, it shows exactly the same sinister anti-female, anti-feminist prejudice.

In *Daddy*, as in *Kramer* and *Sorrell and Son* before it, it is the mothering father who becomes a martyr, the superman who is intended to arouse all our admiration and sympathy. This is one of the manipulated responses to shifting parent roles this century. Whereas mothers as parents, whether single or married, receive little real appreciation or cultural recognition, when the father takes on the parenting role, he is transformed into a hero. He is now the 'natural' good mother that the real one, turned bad, cannot be.

Even the reputedly radical playwright Bertolt Brecht could not avoid these kinds of stereotypes when it came to his portrayal of women. His play *The Caucasian Chalk Circle* (1949) re-works the theme of the mothers at King Solomon's court, contrasting a 'bad' mother who leaves with a 'good' one who picks up the pieces. Here, the first is a wicked empress/queen, more interested in hanging on to her jewels and furs than her only child, and the surrogate one is an innocent peasant girl. 'The Augsburg Chalk Circle', Brecht's short story on which his play was based, makes this polarity and prejudice even clearer. There is no complexity or inside view of the real mother's position and she is thoroughly trivialised and rebuked:

> the judge turned to Frau Zingli and wanted to know from her whether she had not simply lost her head at the time of the attack and abandoned the child. Frau Zingli . . . said in injured tones that she had not abandoned her child. Judge Dollinger . . . asked her with some interest whether she believed no mother could abandon her child. Yes, that was what she believed, she said firmly. Did she then believe, the judge asked further, that a mother who nevertheless did so ought to have her behind thrashed, regardless of how many skirts she wore over it? [3]

The child is then removed from its 'slut' of a mother.

Brecht was in America when he wrote this, and it is interesting to note how his stance reflects widespread reaction against feminism in the States in the late 1940s. Brecht's hostility to the abandoning rich queen/'bad' mother and idealisation of the poor peasant/'good' mother is of a piece with embattled debates then being conducted around women's independence and child care. As in Britain, too, women's newly won advances in employment rights during the Second World War met with a violent conservative reaction in the post-war years and traditional myths of motherhood were rolled back on to the scene.

Thus Brecht's reductive polarity of good and abandoning mothers corresponded perfectly to the moral rhetoric resituating women in their proper domestic roles. Just like Brecht's rich bad queen, in America and Britain in the 1940s and 1950s, women who placed their children in day care were dubbed selfish 'fur-coated mothers'. [4] Types of mothers found in fiction and fairy tales have fed only too well into the language of our modern (sexual) political economy.

Mothers 'On The Lam':
Hollywood Pictures

The father's absence from his child is seen here as
redeemed, the mother's absence . . . unredeemable.
                    Rebecca Bailin on *Kramer versus Kramer*

Hollywood cinema has made the most of the motif of women leaving
children. No less than six film versions of *East Lynne* appeared
between 1913 and 1931, tightening the novel's moralising aspects and
glossing over its questioning of the institution of marriage.[1] *Anna
Karenin* went through various film and TV adaptations; *East Lynne*
and *Sorrell and Son* have also ended up on the box.[2]

But if earlier melodrama and cinema depicted women seduced away
from mothering by sexual affairs, newer Hollywood dramas have
shown women seduced by economic independence. It is no longer her
desire for another man so much as her desire for liberation that now
draws the mother away – and brings the same bad end. This is
Hollywood's version of the backlash against feminism – too much
freedom and women will be unhappy and lose out on (the joys of)
motherhood.[3]

The most successful modern film to focus on the issue of a mother
leaving her child is *Kramer versus Kramer* (1979). I shall discuss this
in some detail to show how the Hollywood dream machine has dealt
with women's advances since the sexual revolution of the 1960s, for
Kramer is one of the first of the backlash movies, setting both tone
and theme for many to come. It still conveys the dominant view that
mothers who leave are 'mothers on the lam' – a slang phrase found,
as we shall see, in one of the male reviews of the film, and connoting
such women as irresponsible, absent without leave, on the run, playing
truant.

The novel of *Kramer versus Kramer* was published in New York in

1978, its male author, Avery Corman, claiming that its addressing of the experience of fatherhood made it the first 'post-women's liberation' fiction. It is effectively an update of *Sorrell and Son*: a story of a father and son left together when mother walks out, and with exactly the same emphasis. Once again the male perspective is unremitting and it is the father who becomes the heroic centre of the narrative.

All sympathies are manoeuvred away from Joanna Kramer, the mother who leaves. There is little insight into her plight before the separation, and none after it. She is registered only by her absence, the wife and mother who is not there, as if outside these roles she has none worth showing. Corman's novel is more than 'post-women's liberation': it is positively anti-feminist. Ted mocks his wife when she tells him her leaving will be applauded by feminists – 'What feminists? I don't see any feminists.' – and the political dimension of her act is never mentioned again.

Joanna Kramer's leaving is not allowed to be seen as a protest against the conditions of mothering in general. Instead, it is put down to her being a 'spoiled brat', an over-indulged and hard-hearted bitch who wants more time – to play tennis. This is the trivial and banal swamp into which Corman sinks feminism: a woman leaves her four-year-old son, not for meaningful or paid employment, not for a deeper adult relationship, not even for any imperative quest of self, but to be free to lob a few tennis balls round a court – a caricatured version of the feminist cause.

The novel's timing is critical here. *Kramer* came out in 1978, when the second wave of the women's movement had really been hitting America, and it shows how dominant culture was trying to deal with the challenge. It set the scene for the popular reaction – evident in subsequent films and TV programmes – which responded to feminism by becoming 'obsessed with fantasies of the mother abdicating her role as wife and mother to pursue her own ends, leaving to the father the domestic terrain that he found increasingly rewarding . . . The 1980s became increasingly the decade for fantasies of the Father as nurturer.'[4]

Ted Kramer is the white middle-class male struggling to accommodate the new state of affairs, and amidst the chaos of social upheaval and sexual mobility, he finds only one point of stability: his bonding with his son, Billy. Ted's defensive retreat into this bonding reproduces the unconscious drive of *Sorrell and Son*, and again it is no coincidence that Kramer's child too is *male*. Men – father and son – withdraw into a closed male bonding that women cannot hurt. Feminists can do what they like, but the heroic male couple will never be divorced.

The film version of *Kramer versus Kramer* is part of the same 'benign backlash' and it reinforces the novel's anti-feminist bias, closing ranks against the woman who threatens the dominant social order. 'How much courage does it take,' Hoffman's Ted asks ironically, 'to walk out on your kid?' Once again, we have neither an insightful nor sympathetic portrait of a woman who has left her child. The plot is hostile to the absent mother and the characterisation remains simplistic, human complexity reduced to Hollywood sentiment and melodrama.

All the initiating figures behind the film were men.[5] Stanley R. Jaffe at Columbia loved Corman's novel and was desperate to turn it into a film.[6] Jaffe, a 38-year-old father of two, identified with Ted Kramer, and said they were making the film 'for our children'. His publicised motives were unashamedly male-orientated: 'This movie is about love between parent and child, the kind I have not seen on the screen before: *an homage to motherhood using the father*' (my italics).

Choosing Robert Benton as the film's director and writer coincided very neatly with this orientation. In the 1950s, Benton had been art director of the porn magazine *Esquire*, and more recently had been a screenwriter for *Superman*. Even more revealingly, he was currently working on a screenplay called *Stab!* – a film for United Artists about a female Jack the Ripper – to which he returned after *Kramer*. In fact one does not have to dig too far beneath the surface of *Kramer* to detect these two deeper preoccupations of Benton's creeping around: *Superman*, with its myth of man as heroic superstar, and *Stab!*, with its fear of the free woman as a destructive, indeed fatal attraction.[7]

As models for *Kramer*, Benton studied old Hollywood classics like *The Awful Truth* (1937) and *Mildred Pierce* (1945). This genre of Hollywood melodrama invariably shows independent women coming to a sticky end, and any mother daring to break the traditional family mould is punished by losing her child. This silencing of powerful or 'unmotherly' women in Hollywood in the 1930s and 1940s repeats itself in the counter-reaction to feminism in the late 1970s and 1980s: *Kramer versus Kramer* is effectively a re-write of *Mildred Pierce* for modern times.

Jaffe claimed that 'The character Ted is really a kind of hero. It isn't easy for a man to accept the role of a working mother.' Once again, whereas women taking responsibility for children is natural, men doing what women do all the time is heroic. Selecting Dustin Hoffman to play Ted Kramer fitted in with this heroism perfectly, for his previous film roles had established specific meanings that would build up audience expectation and response.

From *The Graduate* onwards, the star figure of Hoffman assumed the position of the heroic anti-hero: martyred, misunderstood, but ultimately victorious. His repertoire included *Midnight Cowboy* (1969), *Little Big Man* (1970), *Straw Dogs* (1972), *Papillon* (1973), *Lenny* (1974), *All the President's Men* and *Marathon Man* (1976). With such a lineage, all Hoffman had to do to elicit sympathy was appear on screen, for he already carried the right symbolism: the downtrodden hero/victim, little big man, wronged innocent.

The choice of Meryl Streep for Joanna was equally deliberate and set the tone for her subsequent roles as women of ambiguous morality: as the sexual other woman in the film version of John Fowles' novel *The French Lieutenant's Woman* (1981), as the mother in *Sophie's Choice* (1982), who has to choose which child to relinquish and – once again – as a mother who leaves her children in *Silkwood* (1983). Streep tried to make Joanna more sympathetic than the one-dimensional character in Corman's novel, and she does dramatise poignantly some of the dilemmas involved in being apart from children, as well as make an assertive appearance in the court scenes, talking (in her own words) about seeking an identity 'outside of being somebody's daughter, or wife, or mother'. But the problem with Streep's characterisation is that it misleads the audience. It camouflages the film's essential anti-feminism, so that it is hard to see just how the core issues around gender and parenting are being fudged.

When Streep's Joanna leaves husband and son, Hoffman's Ted moves in to fill the gap. In the novel, Kramer (like most men in his position) employs another woman to take the role of surrogate mother (or they find a free one in neighbours, girlfriends, mothers or mothers-in-law). But in the film's greater heroics, Hoffman does not need to employ anyone. He can do what Joanna failed to do, and he sustains his full-time professional work alongside his single parenting. No matter about the inconsistency or simplicity of characterisation, with bad husband and father changing overnight to Supermom, juggling work and fatherhood with one hand tied behind his back, no matter that single mothers (who grossly outnumber single fathers) might wonder why single fathering suddenly receives such adulation: the point is that single male parenting has to be transformed into a star turn.[8]

At the very moment when feminism's second wave was exposing woman's role in the family as problematic, *Kramer* turns up a novel solution – *to uphold the myth of motherhood without the woman present.* As Jaffe said, the film is a paean to paternity, '*an homage to motherhood using the father*', an 'homage to fatherhood in the liberated seventies'.[9] But it is not really a new family structure at all. When Joanna leaves, the Kramer family is simply reorganised by a magical device: the new (super) man steps in to fill the gap. It may look progressive, but it is the opposite. The myth of the nuclear family is simply being upheld in revised terms, in which the man plays the parts of both father and mother. Women may abandon their duties, but men will not forget theirs. Feminist mothers may let the side down, but not fathers. Like some modern Greek hero, superman Hoffman battles on, carrying the banner of family continuity and responsibility.

Shifts in plot from novel to film point to other magical devices. In the novel, Joanna ends up renting out *Hertz* cars at LA airport, but in the film she is upgraded into a Smith graduate and highly successful sportswear designer whose lucrative salary exceeds Ted's. These are unrealistic changes: in 1977 the average US family income in households headed by women was $7,742, whereas the Streep character easily finds a re-entry job at $31,000 a year – a device which is not out to argue for women's power so much as boost audience sympathy for the abandoned Hoffman, whose own job prospects plummet when he is left holding the baby.

The court case on which the *Kramer versus Kramer* title rests is even more implausible. Having moved to California and allowed Ted custody, Joanna later returns to New York and contests the order, claiming her decision had been made 'under the mental anguish of an onerous marriage' that made her confuse leaving husband with leaving child. She says she has never stopped loving her son, and now has her own secure environment and income to give him a good home. On grounds of 'natural' mother right, she wins the case: her son is declared legally as well as biologically hers.

So far so good. But in term of sexual politics, Hollywood cannot go so far. A mother who leaves her child *and* gets him back? A woman who succeeds on male *as well as* female terms? No sooner has Joanna triumphed through a challenging and expensive law suit, than – inexplicably – she changes her mind. In the novel, she telephones Ted in a state of self-loathing verging on the hysterical: " 'I just can't make it . . . I – can't – get it together . . . The responsibilities . . . I guess I'm not a very together person . . . I won't fight you for him any more . . . You know, I guess I am a failure. I'm a failure, just like your lawyer said. You can have him, Ted. He's yours." . . . and Ted Kramer got to keep his son.'[10]

Streep makes the backing down more respectable, turning it into an act of generosity towards the good little big man, but in both cases the woman is shown as unable to claim job *and* child. Streep renounces Billy because she believes Hoffman is the worthier parent, and because if the film is to retain sympathy for the mother, it has to show her finally letting go: female heroism means self-denial. Thus *Kramer* recants the threat of castration that the independent woman represents.

The moral is that unless a woman is rich enough to pay for full-time surrogate care, she cannot have a career *and* mothering. This is an either-or scenario played into by some notorious cases of women leaving. The outrageously 'male' figure of George Sand left husband and children in rural France in 1831 to pursue a writing career in Paris.[11] Actress Shirley MacLaine, who left her daughter Sachi in Japan to be brought up by Sachi's father, said 'Spending twenty years with a husband and child would drive me into the ground. I would not be able to breathe.'[12] These reinforce the myth that a woman has to choose *between* children and career: the loss of children is the cost women are presumed to pay for success in masculine terms.

But in *Kramer*, except in terms of its unconscious attack on women, this scene is utterly illogical. The idea of a mother who has just survived the trauma of a difficult and costly legal battle to regain custody of the child she loves, going to pieces and meekly surrendering him back to the father, is highly unrealistic. Moreover, *Kramer*'s version of court proceedings, in being so benign towards the mother, is anachronistic. In the late 1970s, it was no longer the case that the argument of 'natural' mother right would automatically win custody for women. Indeed, with so much evidence stacked against Joanna – having 'deserted' the family home and having had extensive psychotherapy, which would be seen as evidence of instability – she would be unlikely to have won. 'Courts attack a woman's fitness as a mother on the basis of her poverty, her politics, her lesbianism, her heterosexual connections, her class, or her "mental health."' [13] Contemporary court cases in both America and Britain in that period often showed the father winning, reinforcing the fantasy on which *Kramer* is based: that the Father has now replaced, and is superior to the Mother. As if a parodic rewrite of the fight over the baby in Solomon's court, the child is once more awarded to the 'good' surrogate mother – but in the midst of the reaction against feminism, this just happens to be the father.

The film's trump card is that it is not the court that gives the child to the father, but the mother herself who relinquishes it. There is no one but her to blame for her loss. Not the Law, and certainly not the father – such a nice, inoffensive chap – no one could be less vindictive. If patriarchy (in the form of Law and marriage) are so clearly exonerated, then Joanna losing her child is only her fault. Any problems to do with mothering have to be put at her door, originating in her own muddled psyche. Once again, any political dimension has been neatly removed. A mother's departure and losing her child are shrunk to the level of personal neurosis: it is all *her* fault and *her* choice. [14]

The remarkable achievement of *Kramer* is that its coercion of audience response is such that even the most alert female viewer can be confused into thinking the outcome right, even positive. This is managed by sustained filmic identification with the (male) world of father and son rather than with the mother who has disappeared. From the instant of her departure, we do not see Joanna's point of view, we have no inside view of *her* development or expansion. We only see what she has left behind, constantly reminding us of the fact that *she is not there*, of her absence as crime.

As the family circle closes tightly round the gap the absent mother has made, response hardens against her. The audience is made to identify with a male world not only through a plot that plays on fears of loss of family security, but even more effectively through visual positioning. Camera shots are predominantly from a male point of view. Whilst we have extensive shots of Kramer and Billy – at the top of imposing tall skyscrapers – Joanna is glimpsed only fragmentarily, mostly creeping around on ground level. She is cut off from the audience, put behind dark windows and screens, an ominous and sinister figure who is linked with disaster and peers like a ghost on to the happiness from which she has exiled herself. Camera angles privilege Hoffman and attack Streep, particularly in the court scene, where the 'camera's gaze is used to create a sense of punishment'. The entire visual composition of the film works to prevent identification with the woman, thus ensuring male supremacy by making it seem natural and inevitable. [15]

The exclusively male world that emerges after Streep's departure takes on the quality of a closed, hermetically sealed universe where Hoffman becomes not only the boy's father, but his mother, playmate and partner. [16] Their relationship is deeply romanticised. As in *Sorrell and Son*, there is a strong element of male narcissism, one further legitimated here by a long American tradition celebrating male bonding – a bond from which women are excluded and in which the female is established as something to be feared. [17] Indeed, even some male critics have identified the subtext of *Kramer* as being misogynistic, if not sadistic towards the woman. [18]

By contrast, in a remarkably sexist review in *The Listener*, Gavin Miller revealed the malevolence that still tends to greet mothers who leave. After praising *Kramer* for being 'a very decent film', realistic(!) and full of 'great restraint, scrupulous choice and patient observation', Miller proceeds to slander the mother. Claiming that Joanna Kramer has some 'catching up' to do with the rest of the human race, he admits to not being able to feel any sympathy for these 'mothers on the lam'. It would seem that Jaffe and co. had clinched their 'post-women's lib' deal.

Far from being a healthy sign of fluid parenting, then, or a radical exposition of father rather than mother assuming child care, *Kramer* is the opposite. Within the context of backlash sexual politics, it is yet another symptom of male fantasy, a dream of a Utopian men's world undisturbed by demanding or emasculating women, part of what

Faludi has called a 'hypermasculine dreamland'. It reinforces the stress on *masculine power* found in the New Right movement throughout the 1980s, masking within the role of father as mother the dream of father as omnipotent. 'If the "pro-family" movement was "pro" anything, it was paternal power.'[19]

When Gary Bauer formulated the US government's position on family policy in the mid-1980s, he not only used terms echoing those in *Kramer*, but made a direct allusion to the film to justify conservative sexual politics. His 1986 report, 'The Family: Preserving America's Future', laid the blame for social breakdown on women – women who work, women who divorce, women who put their children into care, unmarried mothers, mothers who discard husbands, children and marriages 'like paper towels'. Paralleling the fantasies and fears found in *Kramer*, Bauer's main obsession too seemed to be the potentially damaging effect of all this on *male* offspring. In Faludi's words, 'Bauer concerns himself only with the fate of the sons (a one-gender fixation typical of New Right writings on the subject).'

Kramer is the one text that Bauer later cites as example – and proof – of that female selfishness that lies behind declining family standards:

> There are going to be serious consequences for free society if we continue down this path . . . Take *Kramer vs. Kramer*. There's that poignant letter the mother leaves behind addressed to her son, where she says, 'That's not all there is in life. Mommy has to do some other things.' I think that was a real symbol of the times. An excuse for women to run out on their responsibilities.[20]

Kramer is neither an isolated nor an innocent work merely reflecting social values, but a text that has helped *shape* them. Representative of Hollywood's response to the women's movement, it has served to intensify fear of feminism, largely by making this synonymous with erosion of the family. As Malloy writes: 'Apparently criticised by the film, the institution of the family is really protectively upheld even in its fracturing.'[21] Moreover, the film's clever displacement of women from the centre of attention and its reassertion of men as the focus of heroic interest and power was to be typical of the new counter-attack against feminism: from then on Hollywood lost no time in deflating and trivialising 'women's lib' even further.

In films from the 1980s and 1990s, the whole issue of broken families, of mothers leaving or staying, problems of single parenting and child care are reduced to the level of male heroism or comedy. The unremittingly male focus of *Parenthood* (1989) again makes the father the film's central point of interest, celebrating fathers for doing work that has never made mothers at all heroic and has certainly not drawn them into the centre of mainstream film. [22]

The very titles of *Three Men and a Baby* (1987) and its sequel *Three Men and a Little Lady* (1990) make their priorities clear. Like *Three Men in a Boat*, the primary interest is the bonding between three male friends and how they handle a baby that has been left at their apartment by its mother: the *woman's* life and character, or her inner world, are utterly marginal. Like *Kramer*, *Three Men and a Baby* turns men into heroes for doing what women do all the time. Its comedy comes from an assumption that the norm – mother bringing up baby – has been broken, and the plot never actually challenges that assumption.

> the movie does not propose that men take real responsibility for raising children. It derives all its humour from the reversal of what it deems the natural order: mother in charge of baby . . . [and it] keeps anxiously bolstering its male characters' masculinity. As if terrified that having a baby around the house might lower the testosterone level, the guys are forever lifting weights, sweating it out on the playing fields and jogging to the newsagent's for the latest issue of *Sports Illustrated* and *Popular Mechanics*. [23]

When the baby's glamorous young mother Sylvia finally confesses her need for help if she is to reconcile parenting and work, the three men rush to her aid, promising to share the responsibility and they will all live together happily ever after. It is a perfect fairy tale resolution: maiden in distress and three heroes to rescue her.

In *Baby Boom* (1987) there is a similar use of comedy to tone down any serious addressing of the real contemporary crisis in parenting, a similar glossing over complexities facing women. Diane Keaton as single parent (gaining a child through a magical inheritance rather than any stigma of illegitimacy) also runs into difficulties reconciling her career with good mothering. Babies and business do not mix. But here the solution is pure regression. Her dormant maternal instincts are just waiting to be tapped, so that she willingly relinquishes a lucrative business offer to stay at home with baby – and heterosexual romance with local vet in the offing. '*Underneath they're all lovable.*' Once again, *underneath, all real women are mothers.*

So although in one way, films like *Three Men and a Baby* are a welcome relief, with their non-punitive treatment of a mother who has left her child, and although it is good to have men depicted doing the day-to-day routine of child care, the basic thrust of such films contradicts these advances. Not only is there an utter lack of realism in the men's characterisation (outdoing even Ted Kramer's metamorphosis, they transform overnight from phallic worshippers to doting diaper-changing dads) but the fantasy finale shows that their parenting is less in aid of women than an added boost to their own narcissism and sexual attractiveness. The last shots of the three males with (female) baby in the park turns their fathering into an image of potency that makes them even more alluring to the bevy of admiring girls. These may be *new men*, but they are Hollywood's version of them – fathering and domesticity only make them *more* virile. Neither their jobs, identity nor sexuality have been put at risk by their taking over child care. Far from being punctured by parenting, their macho image has merely been enhanced.

The *Three Men* films are part of a spate of comedies about men raising children, either alone or for the first time sharing more fully in the process of child rearing. *Raising Arizona* (1987), *Parents* (1990) and the recent British BBC series *May to December* (1993) show men rediscovering the joys of parenting. Partly this is a negative response to feminism, a turning of the spotlight back on to new men rather than new women, but it is also indicative of the attempt to reinstate the family as prime source of value, implicit propaganda for the pro-family lobby.

E. Ann Kaplan sees the underlying trend of these parenting films as part of a political drive aimed at putting Mother back in her usual place, even if, as in *Kramer* and *Three Men*, it is in a less traditional living pattern. 'These films play out unconscious fantasies of abandonment (the bad mothers in these films who drop off their babies) . . . and end with the old values, in that the *mother* has to be re-inserted at the end, even if we are left with a slightly unconventional "family".'[24]

Lying behind all these films, then, are some familiar double standards. If a woman is a good mother, she gets no recognition; if she is a bad mother she gets punished for it. What is deemed bad mothering in a woman is accepted as normal in a man, so that when the father assumes the role of good mother, he is elevated into superman. In her perceptive and witty review of *Kramer* in the *Observer*, Sally Vincent stressed the impossible deadlock this produces for the mother who leaves:

> Only a man may take leave of absence from a family and find redemption. If a woman does it, all the love and longing she feels will be mouthed into stark silence and quickly transferred to the father, who will thereafter express his love and longing against a background of Purcell trumpet concerto and associated heroic sounds. Then so deep will be her female guilt, and so perfect his male innocence, there will be a wondrous conclusion to the effect that heads she loses and tails he wins.[25]

Mommy doesn't live here any more? No big deal. Daddy's a much better (super) mother anyway.

PART TWO

Out of the Doll's House –
The Politics of Leaving

Background: The
Institution of Mothering

Good mothering is an invention of modernization.
Edward Shorter *The Making of the Modern Family*

Although mainstream culture promotes an idea of the mother as an eternal, archetypal essence, maternity as we know it is actually a specific institution, indeed an invention of post-Industrial society. Far from being transcendental, as the iconography of Madonna and child would have us believe, mothering has been constructed and defined historically, its very forms shifting according to changing economic and political needs. The model of mother that dominates our own thinking is the one that evolved in response to the Industrial Revolution and its needs for women's roles to change.

Adrienne Rich's brilliant and impassioned study, *Of Woman Born: Motherhood as Experience and Institution* (1976) shows that it is only in the last century and a half that maternity has been elevated into such a 'sacred calling' and woman's role in the nuclear family turned into a 'natural' affair. Far from being a trans-historical ideal or an innate instinct, such full-time, exclusive motherhood is a relatively recent event, a specific doctrine evolved during the eighteenth and nineteenth centuries to support the sexual and political economy (patriarchal and capitalist) of the newly industrialised West.

Prior to the model of the nuclear unit that we take so much for granted, the existence of extended families and more communal forms of child care made the experience of mothering much less inflexible or confining. Medieval women, for example, could leave their children behind for long periods without reprisal.[1] But whereas women in a pre-capitalist economy were *producers* (many based in cottage industry in the home), the Industrial Revolution turned them into *consumers*. No longer an equally active part of the work force, they became secondary and passive, reliant on men to provide for them and their children.

This gradual but rapid economic shift led to a new defining of woman's place, indeed of woman herself. For the first time, production (outside the home) became the occupation of men, whilst reproduction (inside the home) was the main preoccupation of women. This was a novel sexual division of labour, identifying woman by her position *within* the family (private) and man outside it (public). *Woman's* primary social identity was now her role within the family – *as mother.* Cocooned at home with her children in an isolated unit, she was effectively imprisoned in a domestic cloister. Theories and ideologies of gender division and mothering quickly evolved to explain and defend this (artificial) scheme of things as natural.

A whole moral and sentimental discourse of mothering emerged, making motherhood a vocation as serious – and sacrosanct – as the Church. Rousseau's theories were particularly influential, putting a primary focus on the needs of the *child* and stressing the importance of the biological mother's care for its healthy development. Although his own five children were farmed out to a foundling hospital, Rousseau insisted that no *real* mother would give her child to a hired nurse but would breastfeed, otherwise the child's natural growth would be affected.[2] Yet wet-nursing and surrogate child care have been widespread practices throughout cultural history, and – as Germaine Greer points out in *The Female Eunuch* – do not seem to have resulted in races of psychopaths.[3]

The effect of Rousseau's pontifications was to invent the mother as we know her. From then on, mother was constructed as a being whose purpose was to be there for the child, the sole and best caretaker of its physical, emotional and moral well-being. Indeed, so much was invested in her presence that the future of the human race itself was held dependent on her fulfilling her role – a position currently revived in the New Right's pro-family lobby. Morality, feeling, responsibility for relationships, are all invested in the woman – intensifying the split between the public, intellectual domain as the man's and the private, emotional domain as the woman's sphere.

From Rousseau onwards, in America and Europe, writings about the mother promoted her role as a moral influence, redemptive of her own children in particular and – through them – the human race in general.

> Mothers have as powerful an influence over the welfare
> of future generations, as all other earthly causes
> combined . . . The world's redeeming influence, under
> the blessing of the Holy Spirit, must come from a
> mother's lips. She who was first in the transgression,
> must yet be the principal earthly instrument in the
> restoration. It is maternal influence, after all, which
> must be the great agent in the hands of God, in bringing
> back our guilty race to duty and happiness.[4]

Mothers were to be new embodiments of Christ's mother, the Virgin
Mary, 'the earthly type of perfect love',[5] and to emulate her purity,
self-surrender and sacrifice. In an effectively secular post-Industrial
culture, the family became the new religion in the West, with the home
a sacred place and mothers the ministers to other people's needs. Like
God's love, a mother's was supposed to be unconditional. Her own
longings, wants or needs did not come into the question.

The Bible was wheeled on to justify this new creed. If woman,
descended from Eve, was originally sinful she could redeem her sin
through childbearing – the only sign of grace. A barren woman was
deemed to live under a curse. In England in the late 1670s, one man
claimed that 'Sterility or Barreness hath in all Ages and Countries
been esteemed a Reproach', a sentiment echoed in today's
technological battle against infertility, despite the world's over-
population. 'Real' women longed to be mothers, and if frustrated in
their desire would sicken and turn green.[6]

This older tradition of Puritanism combined all too readily with
political and economic contingencies of the Industrial period, so that
women's sole social status and purpose was easily located in their
mothering role. Not only childbirth but child rearing was held to be
a natural, God-given task. Looking after her children was a woman's
way to fulfil her best destiny and to bring her and them closer to God.
A treatise in 1739 claimed that 'The Care and Education of Children,
both with respect to their Bodies and Minds, is by Nature given all
along to the Mother, in a much greater Proportion than to the Father.'
The care of children, especially under seven, was regarded as
exclusively women's work: women's salvation lay in doing it dutifully
and well.

As industrial capitalism was more firmly established in the nineteenth century, this ideology of the mother intensified. Women were made for maternity. In both Britain and America throughout the Victorian period, the ideal woman was a good mother, her proper fulfilment the 'sacred calling' of motherhood and her proper place distinctly in the home. For the first time, then, in the sex-gender system introduced by capitalism, the home, family and child rearing became *one woman's* supposedly God-given and sole responsibility.

Moreover, if the mother's rightful place was in the family home, looking after her offspring, then it was only logical that *she* should be held responsible for all aspects of her children's welfare, including their character and actions. The mother was the child's social context, indeed its whole world, so if anything went wrong in the child's life, it was inevitable that *the mother* would be blamed. In Rich's words, 'the mother's very character, her status as a woman are in question if she has "failed" her children . . . in the eyes of society the mother *is* the child's environment.'[7] Delinquency, social mis-adaptation, crime, any form of deviancy in children must be *the mother's fault*. And it was from this period onwards that prejudice against the working mother grew: a mother should 'naturally' be at home for her children. Not to be there would (inevitably) open the door to damage, delinquency and moral decline.

When Ibsen's play *A Doll's House* (1897) offended the Victorian mystique of motherhood by defending a woman's right to leave, much of the outcry stemmed from this kind of assumption, that a mother's absence would be *bound* to have a damaging effect on her children. The English reformer Walter Besant wrote a sequel to Ibsen's play, indicating the usual view then and now of an 'abandoning' mother. In Besant's version, once Nora has left, her husband Helmer becomes an alcoholic, her son turns to forgery, and her unmothered daughter commits suicide! If a mother 'fails' her children, the children will turn into failures.[8]

This awesome notion carries heavily punitive implications for the mother *not at home* full-time, whether through working or being separated for whatever reason. It certainly carries a strong moral message to mothers who leave. Sarah, one such mother who left a physically abusive husband – and two sons – nearly 20 years ago, is still haunted by the personal and social effects. Both sons later became involved in drugs, petty crime and mental illness: the common consensus (impossible to prove, but nevertheless hard for her not to internalise) is that their instabilities have been caused directly by her departure. For Sarah to sustain her own life and second marriage in the face of this recrimination has been extraordinarily difficult. As mothers who've left, we soak up guilt very readily.

Because of this ideology of maternity from Rousseau onwards, women are never freed from motherhood in the way that men are exonerated from fatherhood. They carry the can for every kind of problem, whilst the father goes scot-free – as does the context or environment in which mother and child live. As Kaplan writes: 'Mothers are once again blamed, as individuals, rather than blame being placed on social structures and governmental priorities that steer funds in other directions.'[9]

In fact, Rousseau's construction of motherhood – and its promulgation as 'natural' – was to be far-reaching, spreading across Western society throughout the nineteenth century and surviving now as one of the dominant tenets in twentieth-century thought about the mother, part of a not-so-subtle anti-feminism intended to hold women in (private) child care rather than more (public) professional or creative roles.

Antipathetical evidence which suggests that mothering is neither instinctual nor biologically rooted has been simply ignored. This includes research by anthropologists like Margaret Mead, which revealed the practice of parenting in societies such as that of the Arapesh in New Guinea to be shared fully by men.[10] Likewise the findings of much modern psychology: 'The human male's relative lack of involvement in child rearing is essentially a cultural rather than a biological phenomenon . . . *mother need not be a woman.*'[11]

This covering over of evidence is part of the various shifts and manipulations in discourses and ideas about motherhood that have gone on throughout the twentieth century, as patriarchal thought has struggled to nullify the impact of feminism and the effects of two wars on women's position and employment. It is telling, for example, that during the Second World War, when women recruits were needed in industry – especially in munitions factories – and on the land, the rhetoric of mothering transformed into something much more fluid, and women's fulfilment and duty suddenly shifted to *outside* the home.

(In South Africa, under apartheid, there seems to have been no sense of inconsistency in condoning the removal of black mothers from their own children to nanny privileged whites. And in the past, female slaves were frequently forced to leave their children when slave families were split up and sold to different plantations.) [12]

Yet in post-war years, notably through the late 1940s and 1950s, the ideology of mothering conveniently shifted back again so that women – though still working in vast numbers – could be placed in positions that were ill-paid and no threat to men returning to civic life. Thus was born the 'feminine mystique' of motherhood and domesticity in America and Europe – promulgated through a spate of backlash films in Hollywood from the 1940s on.

It was the daughters of these 'feminine mystique' mothers who evolved the century's second wave of feminism in the West in the early 1970s and 1980s, and there was a temporary move forwards away from conventional roles for women and from their most 'meaningful' identification as mothers. There was some measure of legalised equal opportunity – in 1969 the Equal Pay Act was passed in Britain and in 1972 the Equal Employment Opportunity Act in the States (in the same year as equal pay legislation was passed in New Zealand) – but the counter-reactive backlash has recuperated and undermined much of this advance. Over the last decade, media rhetoric has once again been markedly pro-family in the most sentimentalising, regressive way and a removal of state-funded child care has compelled large sections of women back into mothering in the home. [13]

The current return to right-wing politics has inevitably meant a slide back to very traditional notions of mothering. Just as, at the beginning of the century, President Theodore Roosevelt condemned women who did not embrace motherhood – they were 'criminals against the race', 'objects of healthy abhorrence by healthy people' – and blacklisted mothers who did not identify with the role wholeheartedly – 'If the mother does not do her duty, there will be either no next generation, or a next generation that is worse than none at all,' so in the 1980s and 1990s right-wing movements have once more championed traditional motherhood. [14] In both Europe and (even more so) America, a pro-family lobby has held that social decadence and national decline can be arrested only by reasserting good old family values, again pivoting around the sacred role of the mother.

According to the New Right's old rhetoric, mothers leaving children – even in day care centres whilst they worked – were abdicating their true responsibilities and 'weakening the moral fibre of the nation'. Day care was dubbed 'the Thalidomide of the eighties', putting children's health at risk, though surveys have not only shown the incidence of child abuse as being almost twice as high at home as in institutions, but that the long-term effects of good non-parental child care are largely positive, making children more independent and sociable. [15]

Ironically, this most recent idealising of motherhood and family values coincides with an actual downgrading of women's social status and a removal of those nursery facilities and child care provisions that would make mothering easier. Since the 1940s, the number of women in employment in both the United States and Britain has increased enormously (the vast majority of women *are* in paid employment of some kind, albeit part-time or temporary), yet state child care provision has failed to reflect this rise. In the US in 1987, 5.6 million single American women were working and rearing children at the same time. In Britain, by 1985, 30 per cent of women with children under 5 and 60 per cent with children of whom the youngest was between 5 and 9 were employed. [16] Most of this employment was part-time and short hours, and often at very low rates of pay.

Britain hits the jackpot for its dearth of child care provision, with the lowest rate of state child care as well as the lowest allowance of paid maternity leave in Europe. Compared, say, with Denmark's publicly funded child care for over 40 per cent of children under 3 and over 80 per cent between 3 and 7, publicly funded child care in Britain is virtually non-existent. Recent cuts under Conservative policy mean these abominably low figures for state child care provision are still decreasing. More and more, women are left to cope alone. Less than 2 per cent of children under the age of 2 are given local authority nursery places and these are earmarked for exceptional cases, notably children from broken homes or single parents.

My own story provides ironic evidence of this. In Leeds, in 1974, I was unable to afford to pay for any form of private child care and I applied repeatedly and in vain for a place for my son in a state run crèche. Within a week of my departure from the family home, however, he was admitted. In other words, a nursery place *was* available, but it was reserved for picking up family casualties and not for helping pre-empt them. It was painful, too, to realise that his father's needs in having help in parenting could be met, whereas mine, the mother's could not – a mother should not *need* help.

The massive social mobility and deracination in our society has killed many of the extended family structures that previously helped relieve pressures on one woman's parenting. Instead of more collective, communal or shared forms of child care, we have the tiny enclosure of the nuclear family – and with the father's role being defined as outside the home, this means mother and child alone, imprisoned within it. This intense isolation of the mother-child unit is one of the worst effects of the modern institution of mothering. Rich even goes so far as to call it 'penal servitude': 'For mothers, the privatization of the home has meant not only an increase in powerlessness, but a desperate loneliness.'[17]

Research has shown a high incidence of female depression and breakdown to be directly related to this kind of social deprivation and isolation. 'Marital discord and maternal depression were both much more common among working-class women living in inner city areas.'[18] And contrary to popular thought, depression is *highest* amongst mothers who do *not* work outside the home.

All this evidence points to the damaging effects on *woman* of the mothering position. Ann Oakley admits it is 'hard to avoid the fact that there is something really depressing about motherhood,' whilst Adrienne Rich puts it even more strongly: 'female possibility has been literally massacred on the site of motherhood.'[19] Given the imposs-ibility of the maternal ideal (embodied by the impossibility of the virginal mother), there is bound to be a permanent discrepancy between the myth of mothering and the reality, the ideal Mother and the one we have had and are. The harder we try to get closer to the ideal, the more painful the failure.

Yet no individual woman *could* live up to the myth: by her very definition and construction, 'Mother' is an impossible ideal. She is not a specific human figure but a generalised abstraction, a function put together by intersecting political, religious and economic forces. This is the haunting image of the good mother we can never fully be, that 'patriarchal/ Christian construct of the cultural mother by which historical mothers are overwhelmed.'[20] No woman could ever get it right.

Mothers who leave are not exceptional aberrations, but signs that the modern institution of mothering has inherent flaws. We are simply fissures in the rock, those points at which its stresses and strains show through and the disparity between the mythical good mother and the real woman as mother becomes conspicuous. But there is no essential difference, nor is our love for our children necessarily any less profound. The wonder – given the conditions of mothering for the majority of women, its low economic status, the dearth of social or emotional support, the impossible and inordinate demands it places on the woman's body, mind and psyche – is not that some mothers leave, but that the number who do so is so relatively minute.

Causes: Why Women Leave

Take a look at it.
Take a look at that day.
Long day stretching from then
till now, myself the camera.

See – I am there
they are there
he is there
and everything's in silence.

Maggie Mountford 'The Unearthing'

Moving on to look more specifically at examples of particular women, leaving children is seen to have complex roots: it is rarely as voluntary or straightforward as it may appear from the outside. Different factors combine and inevitably overlap, so the following areas are not meant to be definitive categories, but suggestions of possible contributory causes.

Poverty

Despite mythical versions of maternal love, financial deprivation has always militated against good mothering. In early recorded cases of child abandonment in England and Europe, the major reason was dire poverty.[1] Foundling hospitals frequently took in children who had been left by mother or father or both, but this did not necessarily indicate callousness on the parents' part.

It has been argued that the constant presence of these foundlings in pre-industrial European societies is

evidence of maternal neglect, or indifference to the fate,
of their offspring who would be left to the mercy of
callous and uncaring nurses. However, a closer look at
the problem of abandonment in England shows that this
was not necessarily true . . . looked at from the mother's
point of view it may also have involved a heart-rending
decision to relinquish a wanted and beloved child.[2]

Causes for such action might be the child's illegitimacy, but as often
was to do with the father of a large family having died and the mother
having no other means of material support. Contrary to popular myth,
many foundlings were neither illegitimate nor babies, but *legitimate
children* whom the parents could no longer afford to feed – a thesis
supported by the fact that the average age of foundlings increased as
social hardship spread. And they were left by fathers as frequently
as by mothers. Poverty was the most common reason for leaving
children in pre-Industrial times: during periods of unemployment,
high prices and difficult social conditions, the number of foundlings
escalated steeply. In the late seventeenth and early eighteenth
centuries, the rate of child abandonment in London rose in direct
proportion to a sharp increase in bread prices.[3]

Records that survive support the view that the mother's motivation
for leaving children in this period was not any inherent heartlessness,
but sheer inability to provide. Notes pinned to deserted children tell
of the anguish of desperate mothers unable to afford to feed or clothe
them. In 1709, one such note admitted: 'I am not able to subsist any
longer by reason of my husband being dead & the times is severe hard
and having had much sickness . . .' A letter on the wrappings of
another, a one-year-old found on a gentleman's doorstep in London
of the same year, reads:

> This child was borne the 11 of June 1708 of unhappy
> parents wich is not abell to privide for it: tharfore I
> humbelly beg of you Gentellman however hands this
> unfourtunat child shall fall into that you will take that
> care that will become a feallow crattear . . . & pray
> belivef that it is extrame neseassty that makes me do
> this . . .[4]

Proof of the authenticity of these claims of extreme necessity lies in the fact that women often *reclaimed* their children as soon as their economic circumstances improved, usually through re-marriage or employment.

After the Poor Law Act of 1834, foundlings increased rapidly: Franks puts the estimated figure at 5,000 babies left per year.[5] Such children now went into workhouses to be brought up by female inmates, but it was still the children's *mothers* who took the blame for any social delinquency.

Today, with the rising number of parents and children in non-nuclear families, many mothers are once again caught in the poverty trap and MATCH cites poverty as one of the main reasons today for mothers relinquishing children. The pressures of single parenting in the poverty trap are particularly acute.

Hilary, a one-parent mother of two children who lived in a working-class area of Barnsley, South Yorkshire in the early 1980s, was unable to cope with bringing them up single-handed. Then 21, she lived in council accommodation on state support, and money was only one of many severe problems. There was no help from her family nor from the children's father. She suffered from acute depression and repeatedly asked social services for help, but whether due to bureaucratic error or indifference, they did not hear her distress in time. In despair one night, Hilary left both girls – then under three – in the house alone. 'I just walked out. I could no longer take any more.'

What followed was a nightmare of punishment for the crime, 'like mental torture'. Police breaking into the house; a police warning; children going into care; Hilary's access to them restricted to one hour per week, later to one hour per fortnight, then even less, sometimes being denied seeing them for months at a time. 'The social worker said my children would get confused and upset if I saw them more often, that it wasn't in their best interest.' After three months in short-term care, the children were taken by foster parents. 'Social services got the parental rights over my children. I have no rights at all.'

Soon after the separation, Hilary had to seek medical help for her depression, and has since spent many years trying in vain to get her children back. Despite her own wishes – and the foster parents themselves splitting up so the children were put temporarily into a home – and despite an attempt to regain them through the courts, Hilary has never had her daughters back to live with her. Although when she saw the girls alone they said they still wanted contact with her, the intercession of foster parents 'who did the talking for them' and well-meaning intermediaries resulted in her losing all access and eventually being cut off from her daughters completely. She complains her (male) social worker was prejudiced against her and affected both the court's decision and the children's view. Repeated court cases have all gone against her. Eight years later, in a more settled relationship, she had another baby but met with extensive suspicion and hostility from nurses and social workers, 'watching over' how she was mothering, defining her as a mother 'at risk'.

There are doubtless hidden complexities behind this story, but one of its central messages is that a mother without adequate means – whether financial, educational, emotional or psychological – is made to pay for her deficiencies. Whereas Ibsen's middle-class Nora (who was lucky enough to have nurses and nannies to take over) was turned into a heroine – even a role model – for walking out, less fortunate working-class women or single parents are seen as little more than criminals.

In Britain, where an estimated one family in eight is single parent, women faced with the prospect of bringing up their children on state benefits may decide – on separation or divorce – to leave them with a father more likely to have the means to provide a better material upbringing. Economic pressures on women in ethnic minority groups are usually even greater than elsewhere and there is a disturbing trend of such mothers losing children into foster care and homes. [6]

Economic privilege has always enabled some women to buy alternative child care – nannies, child-minders, au pairs, prep schools – at an early age. This respectable form of leaving children with surrogates receives little social condemnation, yet when less fortunate women have no means to carry out their mothering alone, they are defined as bad mothers, and severely punished. Economics play as much of a part as emotions when it comes to mothers leaving, and several of the accounts in Part Three will exemplify this, with social and class differences inevitably playing their part.

Abuse

In the 1980s, the fastest growing section of homeless people were women – almost half of these fleeing domestic violence.[7] Abuse within a marriage or long-term relationship – physical, mental, emotional – is one of the commonest reasons for a mother leaving. She flees alone to try to save her life or sanity and may be threatened with further abuse if she tries to get her children back. Out of Greif and Pabst's survey of 482 non-custodial mothers between 1983 and 1987, 43 (8.9 per cent) reported physical abuse as the main reason for their divorce and 44 (9.1 per cent) reported mental abuse.

Sandra, 45, lives in reduced circumstances in a tiny bed-sit in Chesterfield. She married at 25, mostly to get away from home and an overpowering mother, only to move into a terraced house next door to her mother-in-law:

I struggled for years through an unhappy marriage, so I was spared having to leave my children when they were young, but the events that led to me leaving still seem like a nightmare. I imagined marriage to be the answer to all my problems and I badly wanted to have children. My son was born a year after we were married, my two girls three and two years later. But it wasn't as I'd imagined. I was meant to do the house all day. My husband became critical. My mother-in-law condemned me for the slightest thing. It was a marriage of submission and humiliation. I was effectively a single parent, my children were my sole responsibility. I felt very alone and unhappy. My whole life was the children, but I was made to feel looking after them was nothing.

It was mental rather than physical abuse that made me leave. I had no support from any source, but I knew I had to leave. The first time I took my two girls, I contacted Women's

Aid and planned everything secretly. But I listened to my husband's blackmail and went back to him, then had to go through it all again. There were terrible rows. Finally he said if I wanted to do anything out of the home (I wanted to do an art course), I must leave on my own, without the children, as that was a single woman's career.

I had nowhere to take the children, no savings, whilst their father had a career, car and large house. But the mental cruelty was such that I decided I'd never go back there, living permanently on the edge of a nervous breakdown. It was a matter of self-survival. I couldn't take the girls to a refuge a second time, they were very sick in there with the dirty living conditions. But it was a terrible wrench to leave them with their father. For three months I was destitute. I went to refuges in Nottingham, Bradford and Sheffield. It was a terrible time: I saw them so little, I felt I'd lost them for good. Most women in refuges end up going back to physical or mental abuse because there's nowhere else for them to go.

Now I'm living on my own in this bed-sit, with very little. I'm studying on an Art and Design Access course. After 20 years of unhappy marriage I'm glad to have my independence. But the experience of being on your own away from your family, hoping a light will come at the end of a dark tunnel, is like no other. It takes a long time to pick up the threads of a completely different life. I have kept on seeing the three children in the most difficult circumstances and we do get on together, though it's usually for a short time.

Because women are reluctant or frightened to report it, the incidence of physical abuse within marriage is much higher than we suppose – and the intimidation of mothers from various forms of violence is likewise largely invisible. But violence against women is still widespread and works on many different levels.[8] Many mothers who have lost custody have felt intimidated, pushed out of claiming the mothering position, from whatever flaw the father can summon. When such women get angry at it being suggested they have any part in being separated from their children, it may be this is because it is so hard for them to move out of their intimidated, victimised role.[9]

Disabled or Problem Children

Until recently, emphasis has been focused on the *mother's* part in determining her relationship with her children, but there is increasing recognition that mothering is a *reciprocal* interaction and the child has its own effect on the process. [10] Many factors can interrupt or militate against a mutual bonding: premature separation in the first hours, days and months, as in hospital intervention; removal of the child; the baby's prematurity, illness or unresponsiveness. All these – through no fault of the mother – may make the relationship difficult. Children who are disabled, physically or mentally, add to the pressures with which a mother has to cope, and may become intolerable.

Liz married at 19, had four children quite happily and did not want any more. But she and her husband joined a religious group, the Mormons, who held abortion to be a sin, so when, at 30, she was expecting a fifth child, she felt there was no choice but to have it. The baby, Shaun, proved to be extremely difficult, and at 18 months was diagnosed as severely autistic.

With her husband working full-time and shifts, and with no additional emotional or financial support, Liz was alone with an unresponsive, uncommunicative child (as well as mothering the other four).

He didn't talk, he couldn't tell me what he wanted. He was frustrated, he'd scream, throw himself about, he wouldn't let you get close to him. I had to do everything: arranging, organising, running around. I had Shaun all day. I was tired. It wore me down. That was the biggest problem and it put the chink in the marriage. Realising you had a child that was never going to be as the others were. I grieved that. It was as if I had a son, but I didn't have a son, and I took on the guilt that maybe he was like that because I hadn't originally wanted him.

The marriage eventually broke down and Liz felt there was no option for her survival but to leave the family home and do some training for herself. She is now a mature student reading for a psychology degree. After not getting sufficient support for Shaun whilst she was at home, once she had gone he went to a good school for severe learning difficulties.

Ironically, once I'd left it was 'poor husband', the help suddenly appeared, respite care, lots of back-up for Shaun, he's now in a proper weekly boarding school. Everyone bending over backwards to help my ex, whereas there was no help for me. That really hurt.

Liz now sees all five children regularly and a more relaxed friendship with her ex-husband has evolved.

It seems that a child's being physically or mentally disabled only adds to the redirection of sympathy towards child rather than mother, as if she must be twice as monstrous to be able to leave someone with that double vulnerability and need.

Changing Circumstances

Just as there is not one 'type' of mother who leaves, so the individual mother can move between different kinds of relationship from one child to another. External forces may shift the pressure on the mother so that her bonding with successive children is affected differently.

Lorraine, in New Zealand, happily had two daughters in her marriage, but when the third came quickly after the others, she – and her husband – felt unable to cope with the additional pressure. When they moved away, the last daughter was left behind to be brought up by grandparents. All adults now, their relationships seem to be strong and open.

In the mid 1950s, Margaret left her abusive husband in London, taking her daughter with her but leaving behind her son.

Ages and sexes of children may influence the bonding. Mothers tend to have a more intense relationship with the first child, but may be easier and more relaxed with subsequent ones. Behavioural research points too to possible differential treatment of male and female offspring, with males being *more* likely to be abandoned.[11] Certainly the majority of younger children 'left' in Part Three are male. This may be coincidence, but it also links up with research suggesting that mothers are more likely to 'lose' sons than daughters to the father – and that, subsequent to separation, children are happier and better adjusted if living with the same-sex parent than with the opposite.[12] In addition it may be that an inner identification of mother and daughter makes their link harder and more painful to sever.

Adultery

One of the popular ideas is that women leave husbands and children to run off with another man. It is the kind of scandal loved by the media – 'Mothers who pay the price for another man' *Sunday Express*. In Franks' *Mummy Doesn't Live Here Any More* this is the first category of why women leave, and her language betrays some conventional moralising. 'Some mothers love more wisely than others or can put aside their personal needs with greater resolve . . . Those who succumb may be weak or foolish or selfish or all three.'[13]

But the reality is that only in a very small percentage of cases is the wife's adultery the main cause of her departure. Greif and Pabst's study of *Mothers Without Custody* found amongst the hundreds of women they interviewed only 4.9 per cent whose divorces had been caused by their sexual affairs, whilst 23.4 per cent ended with their husbands' infidelities. My own research suggested an even lower ratio, only around 1 woman in 12 being precipitated out of marriage by her own adultery. Paskowicz's survey of *Absentee Mothers* argues that rates of sexual infidelity amongst mothers who've left are, if anything, *lower*, than that of married women in general.[14]

Part of the welcome radicalism of Ibsen's *A Doll's House* was that he gave Nora no overt sexual motivation for leaving her marriage – a marked change from the pattern of *East Lynne* or *Anna Karenin*. And Nora's case is far more representative: adultery is *not* the primary motivating factor for mothers who leave.

But if sexual infidelity is part of the myth, this is because motherhood (*within* marriage) has been one of the primary means of containing women's sexual energies. Channelled into marriage and motherhood, female sexuality is permitted, but outside, it is taboo. The mother who leaves, shattering the myth of good mothering, also breaks this taboo and comes to be associated with unlicensed sexuality: she has to be 'fallen'.

Still, many mothers do leave because of the breakdown of their relationships with the child's father. According to Greif and Pabst's survey, as many as 46.2 per cent of divorces come about because of 'marital incompatibility'. So although this may reflect itself in the woman's being involved with a new partner, this is *effect* rather than *cause* of the marriage or relationship breakdown.

Lesbianism?

Some mothers who leave are involved in lesbian relationships, but as in the case of any third-party relationship, this is not the cause of their departure. Lesbianism *per se* is *not* a major motive for women leaving and it would be misleading to claim it was. For all the Freudian theory that homosexuality (female as well as male) is a mark of immaturity in psychosexual development, there is no evidence that lesbianism and good mothering are incompatible. Psychological studies have found no difference between the mental and emotional health of children brought up in lesbian households and those brought up in single heterosexual ones. [15] Lesbian mothers are as loving and responsible as any others and there is no higher incidence of leaving amongst homosexual women than heterosexual ones.

Indeed, it is simplistic to talk about lesbian mothers as a single category, for they arrive at their mothering – and lesbianism – by many different routes and are in no way a homogeneous group. 'They will come from a variety of social and ethnic backgrounds, hold a wide range of beliefs and attitudes about child rearing, and will have a diversity of identities and lifestyles.' [16]

Accounts in Part Three which include lesbian relationships show these happening *after* the various events that led them to lose their children were already set in motion, often *after* extensive marital abuse. Lesbianism was *not* the key motivating issue in their separation from their children, and it is *not* something that alters their role or identity as mothers.

But if lesbianism is not a prime causative factor it does affect social and legal judgements facing women fighting their children's fathers for care: many mothers in homosexual relationships have experienced difficulty regaining proper access or care.

Paddy, in London, is 40 and has been without her two sons for six years. Her lesbianism was suppressed during her early marriage, but when it finally manifested, her husband 'couldn't cope' and forced her to leave. She had nowhere to take the children. Homophobia and abuse – from husband and her own family – diminished her confidence to fight back and she was cut off from all contact. It was only when she was put in touch with GLAD – a gay and lesbian legal support group – that Paddy found a sympathetic solicitor and eventually won access of five times per year and some financial remuneration for the family home. But this was all to be conditional on not introducing her children to any of her lesbian friends or partners – 'I felt like a leper' – and despite encouragement to carry on the legal struggle, she felt the cards stacked against her. Her letters to the children were intercepted, her gifts destroyed. The five-times yearly meetings proved so unsatisfactory and distressing – being too infrequent, or suddenly cancelled by the father – that Paddy finally decided to stop them altogether. Apart from sending them cards at birthdays and Christmas, 'there is no contact now.' Their father remarried: 'he won't even tell me how they are.' Since then, Paddy has fought to construct a life of her own and has a successful professional career.

Susan, an Irish woman now working in counselling in London, has been struggling for years to regain her three children still living with their father in southern Ireland. She married at 20 but her husband became increasingly alcoholic, physically violent and promiscuous. At 27, to get away from him, she started to have a relationship with a woman, but in Eire gay sexuality was illegal and so she lost her children. She appealed to Mary Robinson and actions were set in motion to go to the European Court and to try to decriminalise lesbianism in

Ireland. Susan's access, dependent on her husband's good will, has remained sporadic and unpredictable, the children (and her lesbianism) have been used only too easily as weapons against her. Since first writing this, in fact, the laws on homosexuality *have* changed – on 7 July 1993, as President of Ireland, Mary Robinson signed legislation which decriminalised homosexual acts between adults of 17 years and over. (Incidentally these reforms leave English law standing, for although homosexuality was decriminalised in England in 1967, the age of consent for gay men is still deemed to be 21 *rather than 18, the age of majority).*

The Rights of Women Lesbian Custody Group was set up in 1984 to combat such discrimination, and the effect of the Childrens' Act, in England at least, may help make more acrimonious battles over custody a thing of the past. Moira Steel's excellent monograph *Lesbian Mothers: Custody Disputes and Court Welfare Reports* gives a concise summary of the research and background to the problems facing lesbian women separated from their children. Although legal judgements have not always gone against lesbians – more than half have won their rights to have major responsibility – widespread homophobia still operates, often making women reluctant to make their cases public. One judge would grant a child to a gay mother only when there was 'no other acceptable alternative form of custody'. In other words, lesbianism was seen as being only marginally preferable to putting the child in care. [17]

Feminism?

In 1912, in the film *A Cure for Suffragettes*, women who wanted the vote were seen abandoning their infants in prams on the streets to total strangers – in this case, policemen. The moral inside this comedy is still with us – feminism equals bad mothering. It continues in Franks' *Mummy Doesn't Live Here Any More* which implicitly associates the effect of feminism with leaving children, as if the two go hand in hand.

> And then of course there are the women who repudiate
> the discriminations and are prepared to walk away from
> the family home in search of self-development and
> personal freedom, on the basis that if men can do it, so
> can they ... How much is feminism or our 'selfish'
> culture responsible for loosening the ties of
> motherhood?[18]

She cites women who have deliberately rejected children, 'wilfully' living apart from them and putting their own 'cause or career first', amongst them the German terrorist Ulrike Meinhof, whose children were sent off to Sicily. George Sand and Shirley MacLaine would also fit this bill.

With the current reaction against the women's movement, the impact of feminism has to be seen as a negative one, and there is no better way of fuelling hostility than to suggest it works towards child abandonment. Franks, for example, identifies a new 'anti-mothering element in society', with 'motherhood an option' and 'some women [wanting] to be free as men are free, to find self-fulfilment, to seek social and career status, to eschew motherhood if need be.'

But feminism is *not* synonymous with leaving children, any more than lesbianism is, and we must resist its equation with child abandonment or bad mothering. None of the women I interviewed experienced their leaving as a feminist act. Indeed, most denied that it was consciously willed or entirely voluntary. Carol Findon, one of the spokeswomen for MATCH, insisted that 'To talk about options is misleading. As if women are choosing coldly between work and motherhood. It's not like that at all.'

Far from it being an *option*, being separated from children is experienced by mothers as being no option at all. None of them particularly wants to be without their children on a permanent basis but they are compelled to get away from the intolerable circumstances that are the context of their mothering. It does not feel like an option so much as Hobson's choice: either stay and lose oneself or go and lose one's child.

Adoption and Ruptured Mothering

One of the most common factors amongst mothers who leave is a history of broken or damaged parenting in their own lives. In her investigation of *Absentee Mothers*, Paskowicz identifies more than a third of non-custodial mothers as having been brought up by parents who were not the natural biological ones.

> Eighteen of the hundred women in my study had mothers who were actually absentee mothers. An additional eight had mothers who were absentee mothers in effect. That is, in one way or another, the mothers withdrew from actively raising their daughters in spite of the fact that they may have lived under the same roof with them. The mothers of another eight women in my group died while my participants were children. (The death of a parent is frequently experienced by a child as desertion.) A total of thirty-four participants were raised, in part or in whole, by someone other than their mothers. [19]

A similar ratio appears in Franks' sample, leading her to suggest that the early loss of a mother or mother figure can deeply affect a woman's maternal feelings when she comes to have children of her own. [20] Loss of an effective mother in early childhood or adolescence may lead to depression in adult life and to difficulties in bonding with one's own children. [21]

> Susan Cookson, a MATCH mother, has described a deep depression and her mothering being literally taken over by her own mother, so that she sank into deeper and deeper incapacity and despair, resulting in hospitalisation and ECT (Electro-convulsive Therapy). This then became further 'proof' that she was incapable of mothering. [22]

This broken parenting need not be external. As well as being caused by explicitly losing mothers or mother figures through adoption, death, illness or physical absence for whatever reason, it can be to do with having had mothers who were emotionally absent and so effectively withdrawn and unavailable. This unconscious patterning is one of the most crucial factors in affecting mothers' lives and I shall discuss it in greater detail in Part Four. But what this broken pattern means is that, in these cases, far from it being a willed or *conscious* position, leaving children is not a matter of *deliberate rejection*. It is more a conspiracy of a combination of circumstances through which the mother feels herself *ejected from*, unable to fully occupy, the mothering position.

Confirming this, a research project in Texas in 1984 cited as a major reason for mothers relinquishing custody – alongside the father's threat of a legal battle and financial hardship – their emotional inability to handle the children. [23]

* * *

The causes of mothers leaving or being apart from their children, then, are various. Greif and Pabst's survey in the 1980s found the main reasons to be: marital incompatibility leading to separation, the mother's *lack of money* then making it logical for the father to have the children; the *husband's emotional or physical abuse* which made it necessary for the mother to flee in order to survive; *children's choice* of the father as parent; the mother's *'inability' to mother*; her desire to *pursue a career* which necessitated leaving the family home or area. [24]

In a random survey of 20 such mothers in early 1990, the MATCH organisation found the following distribution of reasons for the separation of mother from child: two had children abducted, snatched or not returned by their father; two had violent husbands from whom they fled; three left highly unsatisfactory relationships; three lost children in the aftermath of marital breakdown; seven named their own mental or emotional breakdown and illness; one case was the result of the child's conscious choice to live with the father; one was unable to afford accommodation to take herself and the children; one lost a legal battle for care and control. More than half felt *they had no choice in the outcome*; the ones who appeared to have made choices had done so reluctantly and in a context of hostile circumstances.

Effects: Legal
and Emotional Aftermath

> The absentee mother is guilty of no more than the unusual, but because she has done the unusual (or simply finds herself placed in an unusual position) in an area of life our society treats as sacred, society responds to her as though she has committed a mortal sin or a capital crime. Because she is a product of a system that perceives her maternal status in this way, she herself believes to varying degrees that she is guilty of a wrong.
>
> Patricia Paskowicz *Absentee Mothers*

The Law and Mothers Who Leave

Women's legal position in relation to their children has changed enormously over the last two centuries. In England, prior to 1837, not only did a woman's material possessions belong by law to her husband, but her children did too. The father held absolute rights over all offspring, and if his wife left their marriage (for whatever reason) he could force her to return, refuse financial support and legally deny her access to her children.

Until the mid-nineteenth century, a woman who left a marriage had to leave her children too. Only after the famous case of Caroline Norton, whose marriage broke down after her husband's physical cruelty yet who was prohibited access to her three young children, was there reform in the custody laws, improving the (married) mother's rights of access.

A slow but sure progress towards fairer legal treatment of the mother continued through the nineteenth century. The Matrimonial Causes Act (1857), and various acts relating to married women's property in the 1870s and 1880s removed a man's automatic right to his wife's property and gave her more rights of access to children. But not until 1873 were women who had been proven to have committed adultery allowed to see their children (hence Isabel Vane's necessarily secret return in *East Lynne*) and only in 1886 did the Guardianship of Infants Act for the first time allow a woman – on her husband's death – to be the sole guardian of her children. The Custody of Children Act (1891) gave custody to the father only if the courts were satisfied this was in the best interest of the child.

But the law was still strongly against women who had broken their marriage ties. When Frieda Lawrence left her husband in 1912, she knew that her adultery meant she would not be able to claim her three children: the law was against her.

Women's access to the vote in 1918 in Britain and 1920 in the States finally put an end to some of their second-class legal and social status. Women had increasing right to plead for divorce on the same grounds as men and the important Guardianship of Infants Act of 1925 made the welfare of the child the first priority. Henceforth, in custody disputes, a father no longer had prior claims over the mother: indeed it was held that the mother was likely to be the best custodian. This tendency was reflected in the various laws affecting divorce, custody and child care over the next few decades, especially with the Matrimonial Causes Act (1973), the Family Law Reform Act (1987) and the most recent Children's Act (1989, implemented in 1991).

From 1973 on, at least theoretically, neither party in a divorce case was 'at fault', and laws pertaining to custody and access became much less punitive. Mothers at last had equal custody rights with fathers. (Though some religious groups hold different views: according to Muslim law, fathers still claim sole custody rights.) In the States, too, there has been progressive liberalization of laws around divorce and custody: in the 1970s many American states also approved 'no fault' divorce, though there is now a strong counter-reaction against these for hastening the death of the conventional family.

In England, The Children's Act makes a significant move towards equal parental responsibility and shows the vast distance the law has come from those unilateral patriarchal laws of the early nineteenth century. Even following separation and divorce, it holds no bias towards either father or mother right. The child should be with the person who will best look after it overall, whether mother, father, another relative, or some form of institutional care. It abolishes terms of 'access' and 'custody', instead proposing 'contact' and 'parental responsibility', which demands both parents (including unmarried fathers) playing a full part in the child's upbringing. Power is no longer conferred wholly in one parent, but mother and father are to have equal responsibility and rights over major decisions about education, religion, medical treatment, etc. In all of this, the child's welfare is paramount.

But this may not work as well as it seems on the side of a mother who may have left. For the Act defends a policy of 'only positive intervention' by the courts: an order will be made only if it is clearly preferable to making none and if it is beneficial to the child. This means that there is a likelihood the child will remain with the parent with whom it is already living, unless cruelty or abuse can be proved. So the tendency will be for courts to rule *against the parent who has left the home and children*, whatever the reason. In the majority of cases this is still the father, but where it is the mother who has left, the same reluctance to introduce change still applies. (The only exception is the case of very young children, where courts may still tend to favour the mother.) And evidence to date suggests it may be extremely difficult to *reverse* existing living situations: the parent who has 'left' finds it virtually impossible to get his or her children back. The new Act will tend to legislate on behalf of the existing 'residence' scheme. Also, it may be hard for a woman who is made to feel in the wrong, or is in a disadvantaged social group, to go as far as a legal dispute. An estimated 90 per cent of cases never reach court. And arrangements for visitation by the non-residential parent have always been hard to enforce.

What is interesting about the Children's Act from a feminist point of view is that the model of child care it embodies is one that upholds the *nuclear family* as the norm. The assumed ideal and natural unit is of the child being cared for by two parents, male and female, and any new arrangements try to emulate that model. The family may, in real terms, have broken up, but its invisible mould – a nuclear and heterosexual one – remains. There is no glimpse of alternative models of child care or parenting. [1]

More recent attempts to enforce both parents to take full financial responsibility echo this return to a nuclear ideal. The British government's Child Support Agency, set up on 5 April 1993, places the onus of child welfare on the shoulders of family rather than state. The effect is to try to negate the impact of one parent families (around 90 per cent headed by women) and restore a traditional family model in which father will provide (and save social security payments of £530 million in the first year). [2] Behind these various political and legal measures, then, is a desperate attempt to pull the disintegrating nuclear family back on course and reconstruct it as the primary, 'natural' model of ideal parenting, with father providing for (and therefore dominant over) mother.

Personal Aftermath

FOR THE MOTHER

When a mother leaves, concern leap-frogs to the children. We tend not to ask what happens next to *her*. Even Ibsen's *A Doll's House*, which defends a woman's right to leave a stifling marriage (to a lawyer), has no sense of the repercussions of her departure. What happens next? How would she survive?

Ibsen seemed unable to deal with the fact that Nora is also a *mother*. He had to rewrite the ending of the play for a German production, making Nora's maternal feelings blackmail her into changing her mind:

> Helmer: Go then! (*He seizes her arm.*) But first you shall see your children for the last time.
> Nora: Let me go! I will not see them. I cannot!
> Helmer (*dragging her to the door on the left*): You shall see them! (*He opens the door and says softly*) Look – there they are, sleeping peacefully and without a care. Tomorrow, when they wake and call for their mother, they will be . . . motherless!
> Nora (*trembling*): Motherless!
> Helmer: As you once were.
> Nora: Motherless! (*After an inner struggle, she lets her bag fall, and says*) Ah, though it is a sin against myself, I cannot leave them! (*She sinks almost to the ground by the door.*)
> *The curtain falls.* [3]

But Ibsen quickly repudiated this ending as a 'barbaric outrage' and refused to repeat the exercise. (Interestingly, there is a clue in this postscript to Nora's own broken mothering).

Yet by glossing over Nora's identity as a mother, and giving her *no* inner conflict over leaving her children, Ibsen makes such a scenario much less complex than it is. Her mothering is simply not allowed to be an issue: it does not enter the equation. In the list of the play's *dramatis personae*, the children are not even named. They are simply *'Helmer's* three small children' – a symbolic extension of the husband – with no identity of their own. And they are children like no other – always quiet, sleeping, unobtrusive – metaphors for their dead marriage.[4]

In such a simplification of experience, it is hard to see how anyone could *not* sympathise with Nora (especially since she has a nanny to take over). Ibsen makes of her husband such a patronising moron, even the most reluctant feminist would hardly urge her to stay. *The whole point of Nora's existence in the play is to leave Helmer*, to work towards the romantic freedom her leaving represents. As with Ibsen's other plays, there is an idealised rhetoric of liberation. It is as if the value and meaning of *A Doll's House* lies in its *ending*, its climax of emotional orgasm, that gets rid of the dilemma and releases the audience cleansed by the play's dramatic catharsis. There are no questions about what happens next, only a sigh of relief that the tension has been released.[5]

What *is* the postscript to *A Doll's House*? What *are* the social and personal *consequences* of a mother leaving her children?

> Sheila left her children when they were aged 20 months, 4 and 5 years. 'I sat on the stairs with them and said: "Your Mummy's got to go away." And I left in the clothes I stood up in. The next time I saw them was 15 years later. I never told people I had children because I knew what they would say.'[6]

Except in the very rare cases where a decision to leave is made consciously, with the agreement and co-operation of both parties – and with the children's understanding and knowledge – a mother who lives without her children is likely to go through varying degrees of emotional trauma, as we shall see, for example, in the case of John

Fowles' wife, Elizabeth, which is discussed in Chapter 23. When Elizabeth left her previous marriage and a daughter to be with John, she went through an immensely difficult period of adjustment. Diana Dors' autobiography, too, intimates terrible feelings of loss at not being with her children – feelings compounded by the desolation she went through when attempts to communicate with them were blocked by their hostile father and somewhat possessive nanny. They lived in the United States whilst she was based in Britain and for years, after her marriage to her third husband, Alan Lake, her approaches to them were met by silence or rebuttal. [7]

Feelings following the separation include loss, grief and guilt, problems with decision making, even loss of identity and memory. Anger is usually repressed and emerges only as frustration and hopelessness, a disbelief in the ability to control one's own destiny. Because of social misunderstanding, these feelings are compounded by secrecy and may lead to a form of paranoia. Franks noticed that many of the women she interviewed had entered a strange, withdrawn condition after they had been separated from their children: 'most appear to live in a state of siege, or in a kind of limbo.' [8]

There is a profound sense of disorientation. In some ways, the experience may be tantamount to bereavement, except that no public mourning is legitimate. There has been a death of sorts, but because the woman is assumed to have colluded with it, there is little sympathy. The mother herself cannot mourn because she is the one who has made the loss happen. These feelings – unacknowledged mourning, unacknowledged anger – perhaps account for the numbed underworld into which so many mothers who leave step.

Deirdre, in North Wales, lives with only one of her children, her ex-husband having the rest. Since she left four years ago (after a serious breakdown whilst she was married), she has been denied all access to the other three. She describes not feeling in control, cutting off from her emotions in order to give a pretence of normality. 'I walk around in a daze most of the time.'

Sophie: *Leaving my children was such a mind-blowing thing. I'd waited till my daughter's tenth birthday, till they were all*

in double numbers. It was terrible to do it on that day: it's
burnt into my memory. I'd thought I'd just take the room for
when I needed to get away from things, but I never ever went
back. That was a very depressing year. Floods of tears, deep
feelings of depression and guilt. I really went to pieces. Apart
from the one course I was doing at City University, I didn't
have any other life. I hardly saw anybody else. I used to go
back to the house and be on my own, sit on my own. I was a
hermit for a whole year. It was all I could cope with. My
children used to phone up and leave messages on the
ansaphone, I used to dread coming in and finding them on the
machine. Some tearful message. It was awful, because I knew I
wasn't going back. It's hard for people to hear that. I was
numb. At the time, I was in such a state I only felt my pain. I
never considered *that this might affect the children. Not really.*

Much of this book is an attempt to make sense of some of these difficult
feelings around leaving. But emotion recollected in tranquillity can
sound very different from the raw and painful experience itself. The
suffering of mothers living apart from their children can be very
acute – a particular form of suffering, hard to describe – and known
only by those who have gone through it. I do not want to underestimate
these emotional levels: my attention to theory and to a wider context
is more of an attempt to contain and understand, than to deny the
different feelings involved.

Part of the disorientation facing a mother without her children
comes too from the ambiguity of her social position. Is she a mother
or not a mother? If being a mother is defined *in relation* to the child,
what happens when that relation shifts and is physically distanced?
This profound ambiguity can add to the confusion of role and
identity – with resultant depression, anxiety, low self-esteem and a
sense of futility that comes from one's public role being so ill-defined. [9]

FOR THE CHILD

The more usual preoccupation is with the effect of separation on the
child, and as anxiety about this can add to the mother's guilt and
distress this too needs reconsideration.

In the 1950s, work of child psychologists – particularly John Bowlby's report for the World Health Organization in 1951 – emphasised the need for a continuous and loving relationship with the mother if the child was to grow into a mentally and emotionally healthy adult. From then on, any hint of a mother's absence (temporary or permanent) was linked to inner damage that resulted in the child's delinquency and future disturbance. The very term *maternal deprivation* has become a key phrase to intimate the suffering of children separated from their mother, but though it is important not to underestimate the effects of circumstance and environment in forming character, notions of a mother's absence have been misunderstood and very one-sided.

In *Maternal Deprivation Reassessed*, Michael Rutter has compiled available research of post-war years – including Bowlby's revisions – to show that although there *is* a clear link between child deprivation and emotional disturbances in adult life, the relationship with the biological mother alone cannot be isolated as the main determining factor. Deprivation covers a whole range of experiences – social and economic as well as maternal or paternal – and all contribute and interact to affect the psyche.

He points out that 'the very existence of a single term, "maternal deprivation", has had the most unfortunate consequence of implying one specific syndrome of unitary causation . . . [and] unfortunately it led some people [mistakenly] to place an almost mystical importance on the mother and to regard love as the only important element in child rearing. This is a nonsense and it has always been a *mis*interpretation of what was said in [Bowlby's] 1951 report. Nevertheless, this view has come to be widespread among those involved in childcare.'[10] What was valid in Bowlby's findings was that a child needs a *figure* with whom to bond. This can be seen symbolically as a mother figure, but it need not be the biological mother, nor a biological parent, nor even a female. 'Mother need not be the biological mother: she can be any person of either sex.'[11]

The vital factor is the *bonding* with another: this is the crucial element for the child's development and it is *not* just the relationship with the mother that is the most important thing. The strength of the bond and the *quality* of care and relationships matter more than the person giving them or the fact of separations. Thus separation from the mother is not *per se* harmful, nor is the bond with mother necessarily different in kind and quality from all other bonds. Significantly, Rutter discriminates carefully between *separation of mother and child and the actual breaking or disruption of the bond between them.* 'It is now clear that separation need not involve bond disruption and the two should not be regarded as synonymous.'[12]

If the bonding of mother and child is strong enough, it can withstand prolonged periods of separation. Also, it is intensity and *quality* of the mother-child interaction that matters, rather than its duration. All of this makes it possible to move away from the usual exclusive focus on the *mother* as the only one capable of being properly responsible for the child's well-being. Children need not suffer from there being more than one mother figure. 'It may be concluded that it is *not* necessary for mothering to be provided by only one person . . . if the mothering is of high quality, then multiple mothering need have no adverse effects.'[13]

It would be consoling to say that an authentically absent mother might be better than an inauthentically present one. But absence is absence and any child – unless so deeply defended it denies all emotion – is going to be affected by mother not being there. But *if* a sufficient bond has been established by the time of separation and *if* the aftermath is sensitively handled by other parent figures, there is no need for a mother's departure to be a major trauma for the child.

Nor for the mother. But many do experience emotional or psychological breakdown, their identities as both women and mothers become confused. Guilt adds to the isolation. The pain of not being with your own child makes it harder to be with other children, or to step-parent. Not surprisingly, there are high depression and suicide rates amongst mothers who leave. Paskowicz's research points to the proportion of absent mothers making suicide attempts being significantly higher than in the female population at large.[14]

These feelings are profound and it may take a long time to work them through – with other women; in therapy; by alerting ourselves to the social as well as personal dimension of what has happened to us: '(such) mothers may need assistance in dealing with anger rooted in their perceptions of the children's betrayal or desertion of them and with their acute sense of loss concerning the parenting role. Mothers may need to reconceptualize what parenting means in order to come to terms with the altered circumstances.'[15] To work through the many complexities of this situation, mothers who've left need just as much support as their children do, not added salt in the wound.

Yet we also need to be aware of the language in which our experiences are spoken. For the pressure on women to be *mothers* is so great that if we move away from that identification we are *supposed to* grieve, to feel incomplete if we do not try to change the situation or get our children back. Because of the pressure of dominant ideology – as we saw in the iconography of the mother-child dyad – a mother without her child is assumed to be only half of a whole, only half alive. The 1988 video and film of Sue Miller's novel *The Good Mother* shows the mother, Anna, being totally destroyed when she loses custody of her only child. Mothering is presented here as modern woman's only fulfilment – once the child is removed, the centre of the mother's life is a vacuum, with neither work, lover nor any creative activity to fill the gap. With this kind of cultural distortion in front of us, it is hardly surprising that we find it so difficult to overcome our real feelings, and not drown in a sea of apology and guilt.

Yet the stories in Part Three refute many of these negative assumptions. And despite there being many difficulties in forging relationships with children living in different houses, cities, even foreign countries, despite ambivalence about their new situations – often with stepmothers – mothers do forge positive links with them. Of the mothers living apart in Greif and Pabst's survey from the 1980s, a third felt content with their new lives, comfortable in their new role and did not experience guilt. The sample of positive stories in Part Three, then, is not unrepresentative. Mothers who leave *can* resist hostile projections and – eventually – survive relatively happily.

PART THREE

The Mother's Point of View

Gaining Ground:
From Gilman to Lessing

I don't mind who knows my history now. After all, it's not peculiar: it's representative of a lot of hidden experience.

Maureen M personal interview

There have been very few published works telling the story of leaving from the mother's point of view. The earliest and one of the most striking is that of nineteenth-century American feminist, Charlotte Perkins Gilman. She left behind some powerful writings – both political tracts and fiction – focusing on the difficulties of women's position. Her novel *The Yellow Wallpaper* (1892) is a brilliant fable of female breakdown, with madness becoming the last resort – a kind of counter-language to the crazy expectations of bourgeois marriage and motherhood – while *Herland* (1915) depicts a powerful feminist Utopia. Interestingly, much of Gilman's imaginative vision and her impassioned plea for alternative forms of parenting and gender relations grew out of her own highly troubled personal history, which included relinquishing her only child to its father and suffering all the abuse that such an act inevitably attracted in late nineteenth-century America.

Gilman had the courage not to make any secret of giving away her child, but this had nothing to do with abstract feminist principles. As we shall see in the personal histories of many, if not most, of the women who endure this kind of separation from their children, the roots of decision for such actions lie not in mere theories of liberation, but in their own specific psychological and emotional experiences of mothering. Gilman's case is extreme, but it is not exceptional – her leaving of her daughter is not something that happened in a vacuum, but was directly related to her own early experiences. What we find in Gilman's life story is a particular internal dynamic that recurs in the majority of women who leave children – a pattern of broken or damaged mothering during their own childhood – so that the later event becomes doubly painful in its replay and repetition.

Gilman's autobiography, though careful not to name too much, nevertheless reveals an early infancy and relationship with her own mother that was deeply scarred. Her mother forbade – indeed was terrified of – any physical intimacy, and rejected her children's need for reassuring gestures of affection. Well into her adult life Gilman recalls vividly her mother's unavailability:

> There is a complicated pathos in it, totally unnecessary. Having suffered so deeply in her own list of early love affairs, and still suffering for lack of a husband's love, she [mother] heroically determined that her baby daughter should not so suffer if she could help it. Her method was to deny the child all expression of affection as far as possible, so that she should not be used to it or long for it. 'I used to put away your little hand from my cheek when you were a nursing baby,' she told me in later years; 'I did not want you to suffer as I had suffered.' She would not let me caress her, and would not caress me, unless I was asleep. This I discovered at last, and then did my best to keep awake till she came to bed, even using pins to prevent dropping off, and sometimes succeeding. Then how carefully I pretended to be sound asleep, and how rapturously I enjoyed being gathered into her arms, held close and kissed . . . Looking back on my uncuddled childhood it seems to me a sad mistake of my heroic mother to withhold from me the petting I so craved, the sufficing comfort of maternal caresses.

Given this repression of love in her formative years, it is not surprising Gilman had difficulties with intimacy in her adult life, as both wife and mother. It was with much misgiving that she married the painter Charles Walter Stetson in 1884, and even on her wedding day she suffered profound doubt and depression.

The birth of her own daughter, Katherine, intensified Gilman's emotional withdrawal and triggered a series of psychosomatic illnesses – material she was to draw on for *The Yellow Wallpaper*. It seems that her experience of pregnancy, childbirth and nurturing an infant restimulated painful material around her own birth and infancy, producing a psychic crisis – one that can appear, to greater or lesser degree, in many women with histories of problematic mothering of their own, though it is usually sedated or suppressed. Gilman was well aware of the gap this crisis created, as she tried – but was unable – to mother the child she loved:

> Here was a charming home; a loving and devoted husband; an exquisite baby, healthy, intelligent and good; . . . and I lay all day on the lounge and cried . . . Absolute incapacity. Absolute misery. To the spirit it was as if one were an armless, legless, eyeless, voiceless cripple.

During this time, Gilman claimed her husband was loyal and supportive, her material circumstances were congenial, but still her damaged and depressed inner world prevented her from properly enjoying either. The result was that her daughter, whom she loved dearly, only brought out the pain and difficulty of mothering.

> The baby? I nursed her for five months. I would hold her close – that lovely child! – and instead of love and happiness, feel only pain. The tears ran down on my breast . . . Nothing was more utterly bitter than this, that even motherhood brought no joy. [1]

Eventually she left Stetson and took Katherine with her to live in Oakland, California. But the combination of external pressures, trying to survive economically as a single parent, and internal ones, trying to battle with a desolate inner landscape, resulted in her taking the only sensible course. The five-year-old Katherine returned to live with Stetson along with Gilman's life-long friend Grace Channing. Gilman knew that Stetson would be a good father and Grace a more than good enough surrogate mother, but even so the slander that hit her for evading her maternal role was enormous. She writes:

Since her [Katherine's] second mother was fully as good
as the first, better in some ways perhaps; since the father
longed for his child and had a right to some of her
society; and since the child had a right to know and love
her father . . . this seemed the right thing to do. No one
suffered from it but myself. This, however, was entirely
overlooked in the furious condemnation which followed.
I had 'given up my child'.

To hear what was said and read what was printed one
would think I had handed over a baby in a basket. In
the years that followed she divided her time fairly
equally between us, but in companionship with her
beloved father she grew up to be the artist that she is,
with advantages I could never have given her. I lived
without her, temporarily, but why did they think I liked
it? She was all I had . . . What were those pious
condemners thinking of? [2]

Gilman's moving story is an eloquent defence of all mothers whose
relinquishing of their children is read as delinquency. She gives a sense
of how reluctant a mother can be to give up her child, of how painful
is the aftermath, of how her action in no way diminishes the love she
still feels. And, happily, she was able to make use of her own struggles
and transform them to urge for changes in thinking around mothering
so that this kind of suffering need not be repeated.

Particularly in *Herland*, she argues for a revolution in social
patterns, fantasising an all-female society in which very few women
literally mother, but all have caring, loving qualities – a vision in
direct opposition to the increasingly hard, patriarchal world in which
she found herself, and compensating for her own sense of being
unmothered. [3] And, contrary to popular assumption, the solution to
mothering her own daughter moved towards this ideal – Gilman and
Grace Channing were not rivals for Katherine's love, but co-operated,
in their later lives even setting up home together.

Besides Gilman's, another major autobiography that gives a glimpse
into the life of a mother who has left is the more recent one of actress
Ingrid Bergman, *My Story* (first published 1980). I mentioned earlier
the notorious curse of the American Senate that fell on Bergman in
1950 when she left her first daughter Pia. What emerges in her

autobiography provides an interesting parallel with Gilman, in that Bergman's early mothering was also broken, and the three children – Robin, Ingrid and Isabella – whom she had later by Italian film director Rossellini were also eventually relinquished – after much legal warfare – to their father.

Bergman admits that she did not remember her own mother at all – she had died when Ingrid was only 2 – and was brought up by an aunt, who in turn died, 6 months after Ingrid's father, when Ingrid was 12. In the light of the mothering she was to give, this seems more than coincidental. It was perhaps her own interrupted sequence of parenting that made possible – or, even, shaped – her later unconventional and sporadic pattern of mothering: custody of all four of her children went to their fathers.

Bergman refused negative judgements of her actions. She compared herself to the true mother in King Solomon's court, who relinquishes her child rather than pursue vengeance in a way that might be destructive to it. To her first husband she wrote:

> I think you can just as well know that however you try
> to explain what are or are not my rights to Pia, I know
> as well as you that I cannot lose her. She is too old to
> forget me. The more you try to keep us apart the more
> she will desire to see me and be with me . . . In the long
> run you will only lose the child you try to take. It has
> been proved again and again.[4]

And reflecting on the battle with Rossellini over custody of their children: 'We were like the two mothers claiming the child before Solomon. I began to wonder how much of this was my fault. I could never abandon my children, but between us we were tearing them to pieces. Someone had to give way if we were to preserve their happiness.'[5]

So although Bergman's repeated legal abdication of her children can be seen as a reflection and repetition of her own (effectively absent) mothering – interrupted by the deaths of both her real and surrogate mothers – it can also be read more positively. As a result of her own flexible upbringing, she was able to embrace more unconventional options for her own children, too. For Bergman, a mother's physical absence need not mean psychological damage: despite the distance and time gaps, she fought for good relationships with all her children. There is evidence of passionate devotion, tenderness and concern, that eventually overcame even Pia's initial anger and hostility. Her relationship with Pia was gradually healed, and the bonds with all four of her children became very strong.

Margaret Trudeau's two-volume autobiography, *Beyond Reason* (1979) and *Consequences* (1982) gives another fascinating account of a woman struggling – and failing – to confine herself within the model of perfect wife and mother. Throughout the five years of her marriage, she was 'deeply unhappy', feeling herself to be trapped behind 'a glass panel', imprisoned in an 'artificial life' that 'was slowly crushing me to death'.

The features that make her story so exceptional – being so much in the public eye and held up as a moral example – also turn her story into allegory: Trudeau reveals the parts that are not contained by the myth. Although (inevitably) sensationalised and read by the media as failure, her desire for freedom and her need for independence are pointers to the repressive and masochistic cost of motherhood and marriage. The incredible outcry against her 'monstrosity' when she left premier husband, wealth and three young children is an index of the fear of female subversion, a fear (from men and women) of those elements that will not conform, will not fit.

Post-war women's fiction includes various examples of mothers feeling compelled to leave, whether temporarily or permanently. The final chapters of *A Proper Marriage* (1965), the second novel in Doris Lessing's *Children of Violence* series, tell of the heroine Martha Quest leaving a child as well as a stifling marriage. This sequence is based loosely on Lessing's own life and experience, drawn from the period when she left South Africa to come to Britain in the 1950s, though critics have tended to downplay or ignore this personal side of things, as if it would reduce her status or respectability.

Doris Lessing was born as Doris Tayler in 1919 in Kermanshah, Persia, then a British protectorate, where her father was employed in a bank. In 1925 the Tayler family moved to a tobacco and maize farm in Rhodesia, and the young Lessing attended a convent school in Salisbury. During the second World War, she was married twice, both marriages collapsing and when she left her first husband, she also had to leave their two children with him. Yet critical biographies have been somewhat coy about these details, glossing over the fact of the children she left behind in South Africa and concentrating instead on her second marriage, from which she took the name Lessing and her son, who travelled with her when she left for England. Thus a British Council pamphlet: '(Lessing's life in Rhodesia) led to marriage with a civil servant and the birth of a son and daughter. This marriage broke up and she married again. Her second marriage also failed, but out of it she brought with her to England in 1949 a son and her author's name of Lessing, which was her second husband's.'[6] Even women writing on Lessing – and specifically on the problematic issue of mother-child relationships – have glossed over this crucial aspect of separation from her children.[7]

One cannot help wishing that Lessing herself had dealt with this theme more directly, either in fiction or non-fiction.[8] But *A Proper Marriage* did break radical ground for its time by allowing an expression of acute ambivalence on the part of the mother towards her child. In a profoundly unromanticised account of pregnancy, childbirth and early infancy, Lessing gives a powerful sense of the cycle of alternate love, resentment and guilt that is such a large part of the maternal experience. Describing Martha Quest's frustration and tedium at a life structured around the implacable demands of a small child, she focuses on the contradictory feelings it invokes – tenderness as well as resentment, love as well as hate:

> And yet, during those three days while Caroline had been with her grandmother, Martha had slept, waked, gone about living as if Caroline did not exist, had never existed. Not for a moment had Martha felt anxiety; she had scarcely thought of the child. She came home; and again Martha was caught up into the rhythm of this other small life. Her long day was regulated by the clock to Caroline's needs; and she went to bed at night exhausted by Caroline's experience . . . Her whole life was a hurrying onwards, to get it past; she was back in the tension of hurry, hurry, hurry; and yet there was nothing at the end of it to hurry towards . . . her inability to enjoy Caroline simply filled her with guilt

> . . . Cycles of guilt and defiance ruled her living, and
> she knew it; she had not the beginnings of an
> understanding what it all meant . . . She was saying to
> herself, as she wiped off milk and grey pulp, Oh, Lord,
> how I do hate this business, I do loathe it so. She was
> saying she hated her daughter, and she knew it. But,
> soon, the hot anger died; guilt unfailingly succeeded. [9]

This is the same emotional spiral that Adrienne Rich identifies in *Of Woman Born*, where she talks of feelings of love and violence existing *concurrently*: 'the woman with children is a prey to . . . complicated, subversive feelings. Love and anger *can* exist concurrently; anger at the conditions of motherhood can become translated into anger at the child, along with the fear that we are not "loving"; grief at all we cannot do for our children in a society so inadequate to meet human needs becomes translated into guilt and self-laceration.' [10]

When Martha takes the (for her) inevitable step of leaving both husband and infant daughter, there is no great build-up of histrionics. For the first time in the fictional representation of mothers leaving, the event is dealt with quietly and realistically. Unlike the melodrama of *East Lynne* or the climax of *A Doll's House*, this is simply one important emotional decision amongst many, and does not bring life to a halt. Martha's leaving Caroline is not the end of the story for either of them: one of the radical effects of Lessing's writing here (as in *The Golden Notebook*) is that she resists melodrama or narrative closure – the novel is merely one section of experience and things will go on after it ends. Like the rest of us, Martha is a woman *in process*, and her story does not end just because she has left a family – the rest of the *Children of Violence* sequence shows just how much living remains for her to do. In direct contrast to Isabel Vane or Anna Karenin, Martha Quest is not punished for leaving and is not seen as needing to do penance nor be sacrificed. Her life is just as important as that of her child.

Published in 1978, the same year as the novel of *Kramer versus Kramer*, *Gaining Ground* offered a rather different version of a mother leaving children. Written by Canadian novelist Joan Barfoot, who was able to make a more positive response than Corman to the impact of the women's movement, *Gaining Ground* makes no apologies for a woman quitting the family home. Far from lamenting the mother's departure, here finally is a text that celebrates it.

The heroine, Abra, makes use of an unexpected inheritance to leave husband, children and suburban city life and sets up as a complete hermit in the country. In one way, this is an old tradition – a dream of a pastoral Utopia that is there in the Romantics and Thoreau – but now, with a woman – and mother – as the protagonist it takes on a new and more radical meaning. Abra's rejection of her former existence is a refusal of all kinds of patriarchal values embedded in her city life – family, the routine of domesticity and clock time, an identity constructed for her by others. She revels in her new-found isolation and self-sufficiency, so that even when her daughter Katie appears at the end of nine years to try to draw her back into social relationship, Abra resists.

There are problems with this kind of fantasy of retreat – it repeats the idea that women are marginal and have no significant place (the meaning of Utopia) in mainstream culture. It also gives a version of mothers who leave that is somewhat one-sided and at odds with the experience of most mothers who actually do leave – none of the dozens I encountered wanted a complete severance. On the contrary, like Gilman and Bergman, they devote a lot of energy to trying to maintain contact and to forge rich human relationships with their children. Still, as a feminist revision, re-working an old myth in an unsentimental way, *Gaining Ground* is a valuable, even subversive novel and stands on their heads many of the most traditional assumptions about women's role. [11]

Jane Rogers frames the various stories of *The Ice is Singing* (1987) inside the tale of a woman who has been driven frantic by the pressures of her domestic situation (single parent to baby twins since her husband left and her two teenage daughters went to live with him) and has temporarily left the twins with her sister. Like the woman's mind, the structure of the narrative is jagged and fractured, giving disturbing accounts of other women and parents in various states of crisis, as if her own experience is too awful to approach directly and can only be told obliquely and aslant. In between imagining these other stories, the woman drives through a landscape of ice and snow – a terrible mirror of her own state. It is a superbly written novel and even though the woman finally returns to her offspring it is with no romance or illusions. As in Lessing, life is not neatly sewn up into tidy seams, but goes on being contradictory and difficult. 'I am not returning with joy or hope in my heart, thinking it will be different. I am not thinking the twins will let me sleep, or think, or live . . . The earth won't stop turning for me. I am returning because I am not a story.'[12]

Ultimately, Rogers is distancing herself from identification with a mother who leaves and is relegating such leaving to the sphere of fiction. But women who leave are not stories, and the detailed accounts of their lives in the rest of this section will point to the disparity between their actual as opposed to their imagined, imaginary lives.

The Cost of Loving:
Frieda Lawrence's Story

What kind of an unnatural woman would I be if I could
forget my children?' Yet my agony over them was my
worst crime in his eyes. He seemed to make that agony
more acute in me than it need have been. Perhaps he,
who had loved his mother so much, felt, somewhere, it
was almost impossible for a mother to leave her
children. But I was so sure: 'This bond is for ever,
nothing in heaven or earth can break it.'

Frieda Lawrence *Not I, But the Wind*

Amongst the fragmented portraits of women without their children
this century, none is more poignant to reconstruct than that of Frieda
van Richthofen, wife of novelist D. H. Lawrence. Consigned to relative
oblivion at the side of Lawrence's 'genius', and neglected or defamed
by both men and women, Frieda Lawrence's life and writings
nevertheless give a moving sense of how it is once the doll's house has
been left behind. In the early 1900s, when Frieda left her first
husband, the reaction against women who broke marital and maternal
taboos was still deeply Victorian, and Frieda's behaviour met with
intense hostility. In addition to her husband's angry desire for
vengeance and much social condemnation, she was not helped by
Lawrence's impatience with her feelings and his jealousy of her bond
with her children in the early years.

Yet despite all this, Frieda managed to come through the emotional
devastation the separation caused her and eventually to sustain
relationships with all three children. Through her account –
reconstructed here through her letters, memoirs and autobiographical writings – we have a sense of what it was like then (and to
some extent now) for a mother when she chooses to leave her children

and make her own bid for life. We glimpse *her* pain and loss, struggling through with no external support and in a context of misjudgement.

Thirty-two-year-old Frieda van Richthofen was married to Ernest Weekley, an English teacher, when she met one of his pupils, D. H. Lawrence, in Nottingham in the spring of 1912. It was an eventful encounter. Only a month later, on 3 May, Frieda left her husband to go with Lawrence to Europe: they were to marry in July 1914 and their relationship was to last until Lawrence's death from tuberculosis in 1930. But it was not Frieda's first attempt to escape a marriage she experienced as repressive. Years later, she described Weekley as 'so cemented into his set ideas . . . he couldn't change. I remember when we first married and I slithered down those narrow stairs, he rushed out of his study and said "My God, I am married to an earthquake".'[1]

Some of these experiences went into her unfinished fictionalised autobiography, where an unhappily married woman, who 'longed madly for things she did not know, could not express', realises she is going desperately against the grain when faced with the unorthodox prospect of actually leaving her family. 'How could she stand all alone against all the millions of other people, their weight and power. She loved her children; they fascinated her, their difference of character . . . the fun she had with them . . .'[2]

And Lawrence warned Frieda that she should not underestimate the effect of the social hostility levelled against them. 'We are not callous enough,' he wrote in 1912, 'to stand against the public, the whole mass of the world's disapprobation, in a sort of criminal dock. It destroys us, though we deny it.'[3]

Frieda described herself as sleep-walking till she met Lawrence, but waking up to the intense love and life she found with him were to cost her dear. With the law and practicalities on Weekley's side, she had to leave behind with him their three young children, Montague (12), Elsa (10) and Barbara (8). Even on that first trip to Germany in 1912, she suffered at the prospect of not being with them any more: 'blind and blank with pain, dimly feeling I should never again live with them as I had done'.[4] Her intuitions were right: the separation was to become permanent and most of her remaining 44 years would be spent apart from her children.

Her correspondence following her departure points to the heavy price Frieda paid for her freedom. A letter to Edward Garnett describes a sad first Christmas without the children, when 'the tragedy was at its zenith . . . at that time . . . of course I was ignored by all my friends, the outcast.'[5] Believing himself more sinned against than sinning, Ernest Weekley took on the stance of the morally outraged self-righteous husband, punishing Frieda, as many men have done, by denying her access to the children. He even tried emotional blackmail by sending her a photograph of them, with the message she would never see them again unless she returned. Otherwise, they would be told to regard her as 'dead'.

She did not see them again until the following summer, 1913, but her return to England was preceded by months of anticipation, worrying whether they would be estranged from her and trying to make the intervals of not seeing one another as short as possible. (This was complicated by divorce proceedings which forbade Frieda and Weekley to meet.)

> I am trying to get Ernest's promise to let me have the children in the August holidays, then I will wait; if he *won't*, I shall come to England and try and see them, so please don't tell anybody that I will come, if I do! . . . Not a word about the children for months now, Monty will be 13 in June, so I must go on waiting, but we are coming to England; it depends on L's health now . . . So we are coming! I feel quite glad! It's like me, I ought to come in sackcloth and ashes and I feel only pleased at the thought of seeing the children![6]

When she did finally arrive in London, Frieda was faced with the daunting task of trying to locate the children. Weekley had moved the family to Chiswick, but Frieda had not been informed of the change of address. Earlier, she and Lawrence had identified with Anna and Vronsky in *Anna Karenin* and she had optimistically sent a copy of the novel to Weekley, hoping he might see how his treatment was as punitive as Karenin's, taking revenge for her adultery by keeping the children from her. But it made little difference. She was as ostracised as ever, and her frantic attempt to hunt the children down once she was in London could have been lifted from a scene of Victorian melodrama:

she wandered for days through the streets of that district in the desperate hope of catching a glimpse of the children. Suddenly, in the windows of a house, she recognised the curtains which she had once bought for their home in Nottingham. Without a moment's hesitation she entered the house and rushed upstairs. 'We children had been told,' Barbara recalls, 'that our mother had brought shame and misery on our family. And suddenly there she stood in the doorway of the nursery where we were having supper with our grandmother and aunt. She appeared to us children *like a terrifying apparition*, while granny and aunt jumped up in great excitement and hurled abuse at her, as if she were *the embodiment of evil*. I am sorry to say that we children joined in. Frieda fled, shocked and humiliated.'[7] (my italics)

True to his word, Weekley had effectively killed off Frieda. As an absent mother, she was now beyond the pale, having 'abandoned' husband and children and thereby revoked her claim to maternal rights. The metaphor of ghostliness here is a telling one – reminiscent of the apparition of the spectral bad mother in *East Lynne* – and reminds us that a wife who is no longer a wife, a mother who is no longer functioning as mother, has lost all social and family identity. She is a 'terrifying apparition', as unreal as if she no longer lived, with no right to exist. The metaphor is repeated in her daughter's memories of that traumatic incident of Frieda's return to the family home:

> . . . we saw our mother next as a kind of apparition on the day when, creeping by the back way into our London house, she entered the nursery and found us at supper with Granny and Aunt Maude. She put her foot in it that evening; the law was invoked to restrain her. And while she stood at bay before our relations, we children gazed in horror at the strange woman she had then become. The stuffy old show: yes, indeed.[8]

Yet Frieda refused to be defeated by Weekley's tactics or the general moral opprobrium. She persisted in maintaining contact with the children, devising extraordinary secret strategies to communicate with them. Her friend Katherine Mansfield acted as go-between, meeting the children in Hampstead and passing letters and messages to and from their mother. Edward Garnett's son David would 'hang round St Paul's School' with Frieda through long afternoons, hoping to catch sight of Monty.

On a few occasions, she was lucky. One morning she waylaid them on their way to school, and they 'danced around me in complete delight, "Mama, you are back, when are you coming home?" How I suffered not to be able to take them with me! So much of my spontaneous living had gone to them and now this was cut off.' But this only met more retribution, as the children were warned insidiously against her: 'When I tried to meet them another morning they had evidently been told that they must not speak to me and only little white faces looked at me *as if I were an evil ghost*. It was hard to bear, and Lawrence, in his helplessness, was in a rage.' (my italics)[9]

This conflict with Weekley was at its most intense in the months immediately after her departure, but it continued for years. He constantly thwarted her seeing the three children, and for long periods at a time she knew little or nothing of them. Even decades later, after Weekley's death, Frieda wrote to her daughter Barbara and complained at the injustice of it all:

> I am glad you children loved your father. When he was
> dead I tried to think of him with affection, but I could
> not. I don't think I can be fair to him. Of course he
> would hate me after I left him, but that he did not let
> me see you was not fair to *you*. I was your mother after
> all. If he had left me, I would have acted differently. But
> my leaving broke something in him. Had I stayed, *I*
> would have been broken; no compromise was possible.
> So grim is life.[10]

Frieda's emotional isolation was not made easier by an apparent lack of support from Lawrence. At the start of their life together, he was mostly sympathetic, as she admits in *Not I, But the Wind*:

> And always again the mail and the tragedy. I was so sure
> I would be able to be with my children but finally my

> husband wrote: 'If you don't come home the children
> have no longer any mother, you shall not see them again.'
> I was almost beside myself with grief. But Lawrence held
> me, I could not leave him any more, he needed me more
> than they did.
>
> But I was like a cat without her kittens . . . I felt the
> separation physically, as if something tore at my navel
> string. [11]

But when her grief refused to vanish, Lawrence became less tolerant.
Even on their first visit to Europe in 1912, when Frieda's feelings at
leaving her children were particularly raw, with Weekley still
pressurising, claiming he loved her 'madly', refusing to 'let go' and
saying her three children wanted her to return, there were frequent
arguments, with Lawrence remonstrating that she should stop grieving
and Frieda asking him what kind of an unnatural mother he expected
her to be.

> . . . we would be thrown out of our paradisial state.
> Letters would come. The harm we had done; my grief
> for my children would return red hot.
>
> But Lawrence would console me and say: 'Don't be
> sad, I'll make a new heaven and earth for them, don't
> cry . . .' I would be consoled yet he was furious when
> I went on. 'You don't care a damn about those brats
> really, and they don't care about you.' I cried and we
> quarrelled. [12]

He accompanied her to England, but took no part in her attempts to
strengthen the bond with the children despite her manifest suffering.
John Middleton Murry, visiting in London, said the mere mention of
her children was enough to cause Frieda to burst into tears. Others
besides Frieda – David Garnett, for example – perceived Lawrence as
unsympathetic to her grief, unable to identify with it and jealous of
her maternal love going elsewhere. As Frieda later reminded her
daughter Barbara: 'Don't forget how jealous he [Lawrence] was of you
children!' [13] He complained that nine-tenths of her love were not
enough: he would only be satisfied with it all.

One of Frieda's letters from February 1914 recalls that 'Over the children I thought he [Lawrence] was beastly; he hated me for being miserable, not a moment of misery did he put up with; he denied all the suffering and suffered all the more, like his mother before him; how we fought over this. In revenge I did not care about his writing. If he denies my life and suffering I deny his art . . . [but now] I have got over the worst, terrible part with E. and the children, so I shall enjoy L. writing.'[14] By the time of writing her reminiscence, *Not I, But the Wind*, this annoyance with the now dead Lawrence was mostly recanted: 'Lawrence was always cross when I had this longing for the children upon me; but there it was, though now I know he was right: they didn't want me any more, they were living their own lives.'[15]

Lawrence's poems from that period, most notably in the collection *Look! We Have Come Through*, certainly suggest preoccupation with his own feelings rather than Frieda's grief. Their self-pitying titles – 'Quite Forsaken', 'Song of a Man Who is Not Loved', 'A Bad Beginning', 'Why Does She Weep?' – indicate his resentment at Frieda's not being able to forget her past and direct all her love towards him. Frieda was in an isolated, no-win situation. Whilst Weekley – and his family and society – were condemning her for *not being* a real mother, only a ghostly one, Lawrence was blaming her for *being* one to her real children rather than a symbolic mother to him.

The worst of their many arguments were over the children: when Lawrence's male friend Koteliansky told Frieda she should stop grieving the separation and simply throw in her lot with Lawrence, she walked out and threatened never to return. Years later, in Mexico, when Frieda took out some old photos of her children to show a friend, Lawrence was 'out of his chair like a rattle snake' and tore them across.[16] Frieda had to learn to hide her more painful feelings from him and keep her mourning over the loss of her children to herself.

Lawrence's reaction was not dissimilar to Ibsen's in *A Doll's House*: the woman should transcend the trappings of maternity and be free – all limits to freedom, including children, should simply be left behind. Lawrence's poem 'She Looks Back', written at Beuerberg in May 1912, compares Frieda negatively to Lot's wife, condemning her for looking back to them instead of embracing the present with him. The poem climaxes with an outbreak of his jealousy, cursing her for neglecting him: 'the curse against you is still in my heart/Like a deep, deep burn./The curse against all mothers.'

Lawrence's short story on the theme of a mother leaving children, *The Woman Who Rode Away* – one of the fictions which feminist Kate Millett found most objectionable in her onslaught against Lawrence in *Sexual Politics* (1971) – shows a similar denunciation. Depicting the American wife of a Dutchman who owns some Mexican silver mines, it tells how the (nameless) woman rides away from her home and gives herself up to a ritual sacrifice by twentieth-century descendants of pre-Columbian tribes. The mother has absolutely no feelings for the son and daughter she has left behind and is single-minded and unloving in her pursuit of passion and death. Kate Millett condemned the tale as a piece of 'sadistic pornography', its ending malicious and gratiously punitive, sacrificing the female to 'Lawrence's phallic sect'.

The Woman Who Rode Away is usually interpreted as a vindictive attack on Mabel Dodge Luhan, but it could also be read as an unconscious expression of Lawrence's negative feelings towards Frieda's motherhood. For unlike the anonymous woman in his fiction, Frieda *did* care for her three children and could not so readily push them out of her mind after she had left. Almost as a way of dealing with the immense and intense jealousy which Frieda's love for her children aroused in him, in unconscious revenge, Lawrence here writes away that love entirely, denies it ever existed, and simplifies the erstwhile mother into a reckless and romantic figure with no ties nor divided loyalties. [17]

Lawrence's portrait of a mother who leaves may have emerged in part in angry response to her and the complexity of her emotional ties with her children. *The Woman Who Rode Away* is his (male) fantasy of female irresponsibility and romantic freedom and is in direct contrast to the more responsible and painful reality which Frieda actually embodied. In this sense, Millett's accusations of emotional sadism may be right: Lawrence loathed the strength of Frieda's maternal love for her three children, and – on an unconscious level at least, as his story reveals – would go to any lengths to try to tear it out of her.

When Frieda – knowing that her open expression of feeling only alienated Lawrence further – learnt to conceal her grief. He admitted his relief that she was 'getting better of her trouble with the children' and his writings of 1913 suggest that he lived in dread that on their return to England she might go back to stay with them. It is certainly hard to imagine what their future might have been had Frieda been

able to claim them. How would Lawrence have got on with the role
of stepfather on a day-to-day basis? Could he have coped with the
emotional rivalry, or with the changed physical conditions that living
in close quarters with three young children would create?

From that time on, Frieda's contact with her children was
necessarily sporadic and her love for them was largely forced
underground, but it never ceased. She worked hard at continuing good
relationships with them through letters and visits, and her
correspondence for the rest of her life is punctuated by references to
delight in their company and relief at their desire to be with her, even
though this often led to revivals of the old jealousy and resentment in
Lawrence. Extracts from her letters reveal this love sustained over the
years: February 1917: 'If we go to America I shall be in London . . .
I may see the children for a *whole* day – perhaps more.' September
1917: 'I shall see the children for half an hour at the dirty lawyer's
office: I am very glad.' To Lady Cynthia Asquith 1917: 'I saw the
children at the beastly lawyer's office. They were *so* natural and really
just the same. It left me with every hope. The boy is quite beautiful,
suddenly a youth, nearly six foot already. They *were* nice, I thought.
Otherwise I feel the world does *not* love L. and me very much.' 1926:
'yesterday . . . we met Monty . . . It was as if something had broken
through in him and there was all friendliness and love – all round . . .
Of course this is what I have always longed for . . .' 1928: 'we'll have
a connected life.' During the war, she met her son Monty, and was
appalled at his readiness to fight – even 'against his own relations' and
offered to hide him, 'but he was shocked.' In the 1920s she writes from
Italy: 'It's the most adorable Tuscan spring, and something in me just
insists in being blissfully happy! My daughter Barbara is here.' 'I shall
love having Barby here . . .' 'My daughter Barbara will come with me;
she is an exquisite creature . . .'[18]

All these personal writings attest to the deep level of feeling in Frieda
Lawrence and the sincerity of her attempts to mother well, although
in absentia. Yet even present-day women writers have not forgone a
tendency to vilify Frieda at the side of Lawrence and to construct her
behaviour in somewhat negative terms. Elaine Feinstein's *Lawrence's
Women: The Intimate Life of D. H. Lawrence* (1993), which once again
structures our view of women through their relation to male achievers
(Frieda is described unproblematically as 'the handmaiden of his

genius'), uses a rhetoric typical of the conventional treatment of a
mother who leaves. Once again we are asked to identify with the
children and family left behind – one chapter opens: 'The effect of
Frieda's desertion on the Weekley family had been devastating . . .';
and 'Lawrence was the one child she could not leave.'[19]

Frieda is represented here in a language that implicitly denigrates
and defames. Words like 'deserting' and 'abandoning' (not words
Frieda herself would use) effectively prejudice us against Frieda's
inner feelings and character. This effect is reinforced by deprecating
accounts of her domestic and sexual behaviour. We hear (without any
irony) that it was Lawrence who had to do most of the housework, that
he was chopping wood and cooking whilst Frieda stayed in bed
'smoking and reading novels until lunchtime' and '*lay about* being
pampered.' 'Lawrence began writing again in the mornings, while
Frieda *lay about and smoked*.' '. . . he treated her with gentle
indulgence.' And Frieda was 'more than a little overweight'![20] (my
italics). For a strong and powerful woman, Frieda is being represented
here in disturbingly patronising terms – and, moreover, being seen as
a woman of dubious morality. Feinstein tells us Lawrence had to learn
not to trust her sexually, that she had a catalogue of lovers, and that
'she behaved with some selfishness towards Lawrence's illness' in the
latter years.[21] This creates a very different impression of Frieda from
the one in her own account.

The bare facts of Frieda's and Lawrence's lives are not in dispute,
but what is interesting is the way in which they are being retold here,
again very much from a *male* point of view. The way events are
expressed and structured combine to give a portrait of Frieda much
more negative than her own, one that is still close to the
characterisation and plot of Victorian melodramas about mothers who
'abandon' their children. There is a disapproving undertone to
Feinstein's portrait of Frieda, as if Frieda had militated against
Lawrence's 'genius', slobbed around whilst he was trying to be creative,
and failed to match his morally superior stance.

Yet Frieda was a powerful woman. She was resilient enough to
resist the slander at leaving her marriage, and to keep on making
it known to her children that she loved them, in the face of heavy
opposition all around. Her letters are full of determination and
optimism: even in the midst of the Second World War she clung to a

vision of a more positive and humane future.

> Yes, the world is a chaos, but I feel curiously happy and
> hopeful, as if out of the chaos something new will be
> born. Surely humanity has lots of possibilities yet. The
> Nazis will die of their own horror and then if we are wise
> and follow the best in us, a wonderful people might
> come. It is so beautiful, this life, one seems to know the
> value of it more, with all the horrors going on. [22]

The quality that she most admired in Lawrence – 'I called it love, but
it was something else – *Bejaung* in German, "saying yes"' – was
something Frieda herself had in no small measure. She was a woman
who believed in life and – despite everything, including the painful
separation from her children – came through. In 1954, she could write
in celebration: 'Now it is all right between them and me, I am so lucky
(I touch wood).' 'I am a lucky old woman and love living, every moment
a gift.' From the 1930s until her death in August 1956 she lived with
Angelo Ravagli, an Italian whom she married in 1950 to save him from
deportation from the States. In a parallel version of her own story,
Ravagli left his wife and three children to be with Frieda, and their
years together in Mexico seem to have been happy ones, with none of
the perpetual (and mutual) abrasiveness that characterised her
relationship with Lawrence.

Not every mother who leaves children is so fortunate. With a wealthy
background in the German aristocracy, and a first husband with a
solid income, Frieda – like Ibsen's Nora – did not have to worry about
her children's material welfare. She knew that their nurses would go
on being there after she had gone, and that every aspect of their
physical welfare – education, clothing, money – would be amply
provided for.

Nor does every woman in a stifling marriage find such a good let-out
as Frieda: not only a love affair (however turbulent) that endured, but
extensive global travel, with spells in Europe and Australia before a
final home in Mexico, and the fame that comes from having as your
second husband a man who proves to be one of the most famous and
controversial novelists of the twentieth century.

Yet although Frieda Lawrence's circumstances were exceptional and
her life was, in so many ways, privileged, her inner story is not so

different from that of many mothers who have found themselves leaving children. She offers us a great example of the possibility of coming through – notwithstanding prejudice, slander and on-going misrepresentation – and of renewing relationships with our children, despite all the odds against us. In the chapters that follow, we shall see less famous women facing parallel struggles.

10

The Scene of the Crime: Dysfunctional Families

> a person who has consciously worked through the whole
> tragedy of her own fate will recognise another's
> suffering more clearly and quickly . . . She will not be
> scornful of others' feelings, whatever their nature,
> because she can take her own feelings seriously. She
> surely will not help to keep the vicious circle of
> contempt turning.
>
> Alice Miller *The Drama of Being a Child*[1]

Siobhan comes from a working-class background in Northern Ireland and spent her childhood caring for an alcoholic mother. So deeply did the pattern of her mother's dependency shape her that when Siobhan came to marrying she was driven to look after a man whose needs almost exactly reduplicated her mother's. The resulting knots became so destructive – especially when Siobhan was exiled in the husband's Third World country of origin – that she had to leave her children there in order to survive. She now lives once more in Northern Ireland, having returned to the 'scene of the crime' in order to try to come to terms with and move on from her own childhood injuries.

Siobhan's is a classic story of a woman trying to reproduce good mothering against the odds, against a personal history of utterly inadequate parenting. Her son of 13 and daughter of 9 are still in Jamaica and Siobhan has no idea when she will see them again. She and her husband are not yet divorced.

*The separation from my children was very involved and
complex, there were so many factors and events that seemed to
conspire to achieve it.*

I need to mention my personal history because I think it is

*due to the circumstances of my childhood that my life got into
such a mess. All my relationships have reflected, and to some
extent still reflect, the early ones I had with my parents. I feel
the whole scenario – the reasons for marrying the person I did,
everything – was directly to do with the person my history had
made me.*

*One thing dominated my life as child: my parents' unhappy
marriage. My mother started drinking when I was about 10
and during my teens gradually became a very destructive
alcoholic. I believe she had affairs: I'm sure of at least one. My
father, also unhappy and unable to cope with his feelings,
stifled his anger but let it out on his children – three of us – in
constant, humiliating and life-denying criticism. My sister, the
eldest, refused from an early age to be responsible for any of
our parents' negative feelings. She fought to be free of the guilt
and married early. Her marriage has been successful and she's
brought up a family of three.*

*My brother and I suffered most and consequently we're the
ones who've continued to suffer dysfunctional lives as adults.
My brother is alcohol dependent and though younger than me
has already been married three times. I have never had an
uncomplicated, loving relationship with anyone, despite many
attempts. I am 45 and alone now, separated from the only two
people I ever really loved without reservation: my own two
children.*

*I didn't have much of a childhood. I took on to myself all the
responsibility for my parents' unhappiness. I always tried to be
the best little girl I could, in the vain hope I might do
something to make them happy. From my early teens onward, I
became responsible for the family: meals, cleaning, washing,
looking after my mother and still doing my school-work and
getting excellent reports. My mother drank more and more and
cared less and less. We got her in and out of nursing homes
and clinics to dry her out but she was always back on the
bottle again before too long. When you live with an alcoholic
you don't have any life of your own – they're always the central
focus.*

I used to dread what I would find when I got home from

*school: would she be drunk again? how badly? Pretending to
other people that nothing was wrong, covering for her. The
whole thing's built on deceit and denial. There was no question
of 'what shall I do with my day today?' It's your whole life.
And on top of it all was my father's constant annihilating
criticism that crushed any spark of life left in me. For years, I
remember wishing they would end the farce of their marriage
and get divorced. I felt disgusted by that old lie, 'for the sake
of the children'. I was determined I'd never inflict that on any
of my own children.*

*By the time I was 18, I was already very depressed but I
didn't know it. I had wanted to go to art school but my father
wanted me to go to university, so to please him I did. I read
philosophy – much to my father's despair – perhaps it was some
mild form of protest at not being able to do what I really
wanted. After four unhappy years I graduated with an honours
degree, then took a teaching job for a year, but I got involved
with a destructive love-affair and became anorexic. I'd moved
away from home by then but was still bound up with it
emotionally, so I left Northern Ireland and went to London. I
drifted in and out of restaurant jobs and cleaning work and
did night school courses in life-drawing and sculpture.*

*I was 28 when I met George, my husband-to-be, then 24 and
doing an art degree at Goldsmith's College. After a series of
hopeless love affairs, I was on the rebound, very depressed,
frequently contemplating suicide and still experiencing the
eating disorders that had begun when I left home. George was
another suitable case for treatment. His own personal history
had created enormous psychological problems and he'd seen
several psychiatrists, both at home in Jamaica and in London.
Most pertinent to me was the fact that at 18 he'd consumed a
massive overdose of LSD from which he'd almost died. Since
then he suffered intermittent flashbacks, about one a year,
when he would be temporarily quite insane and need
hospitalisation and drugs. At other times, when 'sane', he could
be charming, funny and quite affectionate. He was very
glamorous and rather exotic: good-looking, with dark beautiful
eyes, hair in the Afro style of the seventies cognoscenti,*

beautiful Caribbean voice. And of course, with his minefield of unresolved emotional chaos, he was a magnet for me.

Later, I realised that what I'd found in George was a partner who resembled and replaced the mother I'd taken care of so devotedly as a child. Someone who had enough problems to let me continue burying my own. We'd been going out together for two years when George finished his course and wanted to return to Jamaica: he'd already inherited responsibilities as the only surviving male member of the mini-dynasty of a land-owning family. So I left my country, family, potential support system, chance of a career and meagre possessions, and went with this almost total stranger to an alien culture and country thousands of miles away. Initially I was to stay in Jamaica for six weeks, but George and his mother laid such guilt trips on me that I agreed to stay and get married. I had no idea that I had a right to my own feelings: it seemed natural that other people's wishes should come before my own.

The marriage lasted five years, but living with George was a different experience from seeing him only at weekends as had happened in London. I knew he was mentally unstable – I'd been with him through two of his breakdowns – but I was used to my mother's similarly self-destructive behaviour and thought I could cope. Indeed, I thought that was what love was, a total sacrifice of your own growth and well-being to try to nurse this human wreck back to health. But I very soon came to realise the depth of George's problems, which his family had kept from me. I began to understand how manipulative his 'breakdowns' were: if he didn't get what he wanted when he wanted it, he went crazy. Everyone wanted to avoid his craziness, so they were manipulated quite ruthlessly: he was unstoppable. His mother and two sisters crept round George's feelings as if they were handling high explosives.

Retrospectively, I realise that I married George because I felt so bad about him. It was a complete repetition of the experience with my mother. I thought it was my destiny in life to do the same for George as I'd done for her: he admitted he needed me badly and, like her, was very addictive. He'd been forbidden drugs or drink, even tobacco, in case they triggered an LSD flashback, but there was one drug he was still counting on: sex. It soon became clear that I was meant to be his 'fix'.

When my son was born, nine months after the marriage, things got worse. George had wanted a son. His own father had been killed in a tragic accident when George was eight, and that death precipitated the death of his grandfather in the same year. George was the only son, and the trauma of those deaths, combined with a fear he too might die young, had created a strong drive in him to produce a male heir to the considerable family property. The reality of a baby son, however, was quite different. George was intensely jealous of Daniel and couldn't adjust to the fact I spent so much time caring for someone other than him.

They say that when a woman gives birth she's very open, psychically sensitive, and it was like that when Daniel was born. I had the strongest impression of someone very ancient returning: as a child there was always a gravity around him, as with an older person, and the local Jamaicans nicknamed him 'Grandfather'. He was a sweet child and I loved him to the depths of my being. It was the first experience of love in my life. With his birth, I fell completely and utterly in love for the first time.

So I was less receptive to George, often tired, often not wanting sex and George reacted with tantrums and eventually another breakdown. It's easy to be deadpan about it years later, but at the time, in the midst of all that emotional turmoil, I was suffering too. I was smoking twice as much as usual, my health was poor and I was very thin. I felt sad and depressed much of the time and this manifested itself as tiredness. I think having a child had released in me many unresolved emotions about my own childhood and it wasn't so easy to bury them any more by looking after others.

I tried talking to George about how lonely and isolated I felt. I was frustrated being a housewife and wasn't adapting easily to Jamaican culture. Though I loved my child, I felt I was wasting my life: I was used to having art and books around me, but in the remote country where we lived, there was *nothing. I'd come from the metropolis of London to the backwoods of a Third World country where there was no culture, no like-minded friends. I suppose I blamed my unhappiness on the marriage, which was certainly deteriorating fast. George thought daily sex was the cure for everything. I couldn't help thinking of my parents' unhappy marriage and assuming the same fate might befall me, but I didn't want to do what my parents had done, let alone subject my children to a family situation like the one I'd suffered. So more and more I thought of leaving.*

When Daniel was four I had another baby, maybe a last attempt to salvage the marriage. By then, I don't think I knew what I was doing. I certainly didn't know what else to try. And I did want another baby. I loved Daniel so much, I feared for him too much, I wanted him to have a companion. But it was different with this baby. With Daniel, there was separateness: he was a boy, there was a difference in sex to remind me this was not me. This was a little girl, like me, and when I looked at her the merging was almost complete. She was a tremendously pretty baby, you couldn't help looking at her, and I remember looking into her eyes and her holding my gaze for minutes on end. Even more than Daniel she brought to the surface of consciousness emotions, feelings from childhood, that were impossible to contain.

I needed to be by myself to try to work out this unresolved inner turmoil and the desire to get away from George and his emotional demands became more and more pressing. For the sake of my own sanity, when Ruby was just three months old, I packed a few things into my car and moved out, taking the children with me. I had a job and had found a house to rent: I thought I would manage on my own.

Once again the reality was far removed from the dream. I thought that by leaving George I would solve my own unhappiness. To a small degree, I did – it was a relief to be on my own, I didn't have to be constantly thinking of him – but my job was very demanding and it all became too much. I had no experience of managing my own affairs alone in the world, particularly in a foreign country with two small children. The job hardly paid sufficient to support us all, plus the cost of a nanny who looked after the children. I did my best to manage on my own, but things deteriorated and eventually reached crisis point after about a year.

The rapid road downhill began when I crashed my car, writing it off. Unfortunately the insurance had just expired and I had no money to renew it. The car was crucial to my work: without it the job was virtually impossible, as public transport in Jamaica is a nightmare. Consequently, soon after the car crash I lost my job. And as my boss had lent me all the furniture in the house, including fridge and stove, that would go too. It came to a head on what was the worst night of my life, when I realised I had no job, no money, no support from George, no family of my own to help and, finally, no furniture. I had two small children and barely a roof over their heads. I felt I had failed utterly.

The night I came home after getting fired from my job, I was at my wit's end, I badly needed just to rest. Despite my begging, the nanny, who usually lived in, said she couldn't stay that evening. I was left with the two children, and Ruby was particularly unsettled. She just wouldn't sleep, I walked her up and down, praying she would settle but still she cried and cried. Eventually, something in me just gave way and I slapped her, very hard. I will never, ever, forget doing that to her. She was so tiny and vulnerable, but I couldn't bear her crying any more. I was in pain too: physical, mental, emotional. I don't suppose it was any worse than a lot of mothers do to children, but I can never forgive myself for that, not even now. I feared my cruelty. I think it was at that point that I decided I wasn't fit to be a mother.

It was very soon after that I packed the children's things and called their father to come for them. He had a house and job and was financially OK. I'd been worried about them not having a father and felt guilty at their being left with a nanny much of the time and as my money was barely adequate, I was anxious that the quality of their lives would deteriorate. All this conspired to make me feel I was failing as a mother and that their father would be able to give them better material care.

*At the time, I told myself it was temporary, I would get them
back when I got on my feet again financially. But there isn't
the same government support in Jamaica: when you go down,
it's all the more difficult to get back up. I also underestimated
George's capacity for revenge. He kept me from the children as
much as he could, eventually sending both of them to live with
his mother. She was much further away from where I was and
it was virtually impossible to see either of them at all. They've
lived with her ever since.*

*I went from job to job, trying to make enough money to live
and hoping somehow to get them back. But under so much
stress my health declined and eventually I found myself jobless
and homeless, in a foreign country, with no one to help. It
ended in agony. Reluctantly, I gave up on Jamaica and
returned to Northern Ireland. I always intended to go back
when I could. It's now been almost four years since I've seen
my children. I still have some telephone contact with them,
which I've kept up since I left, but my relationship with them
has suffered over the years. My daughter, the younger of the
two, never got to know me at all, so I'm almost a stranger to
her.*

*At every turn of events I blamed myself for what had
happened. Nothing in my experience of life to that point had
led me to expect or believe that I deserved anything better.
Maybe deep inside I felt I had been born for suffering and
deprivation, as if I expected the absence of those I loved and
had made a tacit agreement with the crazy law of nature that
decreed it so.*

*It sounds bleak, but basically it was. When I first came back
from Jamaica I cried all day and all night without stopping.
That was only the beginning of the suffering I have experienced
over the years, being apart from my children. But gradually,
I've begun to survive. I came back to Northern Ireland, to the
scene of the original crimes if you like, to work out my own life
at last. That's where I am now, trying to come to terms with
my past. I was a battered, neglected and deprived child: not
physically, but emotionally. I still am, inside.*

You can't just decide not to hurt your children the way you were hurt. The messages we've learnt inside us are deeper than that. It's hard to unlearn, to do things differently. People hang on to what they've got, even though it might not be very good. My tragedy was that I couldn't hang on any more, and I let go. Otherwise I'd still be passing on the same old stuff instead of trying to change. I think part of me was afraid to be a mother in case I passed on what I experienced as a child to my children. Perhaps I tried to avoid that by leaving, but in fact I did the same thing, only in a different way. You could say that I abandoned my children just as my mother emotionally abandoned me.

My experience is exceptional only in that it is extreme. I think there are many women – and men – who suffer enormously as adults because of their childhood. They just don't face the extremes as I did, they cope with their lives as they are. But I wanted to break the pattern of passing it on, break out of that cycle of pain.

So far, I've found it much harder than I thought it would be, though it's slowly improving. I'm completing a course in journalism. I've made good friends. We set up a women's support group two years ago, which is still going strong. I've done group work, rebirthing, one-to-one counselling. I've read books about everything: dysfunctional families, anorexia, compulsive eating, alcoholism, dependency, co-dependency. Women Who Love Too Much *gave me some insight into my own pain. And literature: one book that springs to mind is* I Know Why the Caged Bird Sings *by Maya Angelou. It's a portrait of a victim, but one who wins through in the end.*

Being apart from my children has forced me to try to repair my life and I do think that's a positive thing. I still feel desperate sometimes with longing for them – not a single day goes by when I don't think of them – I still cry over my loss. But now I also feel some hope. One day I'll find a way to get back to Jamaica: I believe when I'm healed enough I'll get back there.

11

Catch-22:
Physical and Mental Abuse

Leaving. Breaking up a marriage. Funny how it's always
the one that leaves that's the guilty one. The one who
accepts all the blame, all the failure. But when a man
walks out of a marriage, somehow he turns back to being
something like an eligible bachelor. Tea and sympathy.
With an interesting past. A woman walking out becomes
. . . Somebody that nobody wants to know any more. But
surely men must hurt the same way that women do at
leaving their children? I can feel on the edges of my
mind already how I'm going to hurt leaving mine, how
I will bleed. But there is no way I can stay here with
them and survive.

Sheila Holligon *House of Gingerbread*

Caroline lives in council accommodation in southeast London with her
partner Ian and their 20-month-old daughter Isla. She is divorced
from Christopher, with whom she had four children: two sons of 19
and 17, two girls of 13 and 10. Her ex-husband lives in Hull with the
girls and younger boy; two years ago he was given custody. Caroline's
sustained attempts to get the younger children to live with her have
been bedevilled by hassles around accommodation and legal battles.
Our meeting took place in March 1992, a few weeks after a court
hearing to discuss the issue of her contesting custody and legalising
access arrangements.

Her story seems to represent a fairly common pattern in mothers
leaving – a marriage featuring physical, emotional or psychological
abuse, her moving out to escape this, then being blamed for the
departure – problems compounded by insufficient income (or help
from social services) to provide suitable accommodation in which to
house the children. And as time goes by, so their living with the father

appears as a status quo that should be protected and preserved.

Moreover, for mothers without custody the father is frequently shown as blocking mother-child contact and as having turned children against the mother.[1]

I'll start with this weekend, as we've had the girls. I went to Hull for them. It's a three-hour journey there and a three-hour journey back. I literally went up on the 9.40 train, which gets into Hull at 12.30, came back to London on the 1.30. Fortunately there was none of the usual hassle over – are they coming? will he let them, won't he? – because I've at last got defined access through the court. That makes things better on one level, you can't be messed about with access, but at the same time, as soon as it's defined by the court it's rubbing it in that he's the one with custody, care and control, it's now defined that he's the one that has power, and I only have access. Eight weeks a year. So the emotions are very mixed: relief that something has finally been defined by the court and bitterness and resentment about it.

The reason that my children were left with my ex-husband in Hull in the beginning was because of housing difficulties in London. It's a very common thing. So though there's a lot I blame myself for, there's been a lot that's to do with circumstances and other people's negligence: my previous solicitor, for example, and the long, drawn-out fight with Lambeth Council.

I originally came down to London in 1986–7 to do a postgraduate teacher training course in further education. I didn't actually have a choice about where to do the course because it was the only one in the country. It was agreed I should come to London to do this course and then with that qualification get a job somewhere. Though the marriage had already deteriorated over the past three years to the point where it had become, at best, snipe warfare. There were differences that became greater as time went on: cultural differences (he came from a northeastern mining community). We moved poles apart, especially after we moved back up North. After my degree in fine art I wanted to do a Ph.D. and couldn't get a grant for it. I couldn't do it, I couldn't pay the fees. Christopher wanted to know why I hadn't done a degree in something useful like computer studies and where was this wonderful job I was going to get with all these bits of paper . . .

So I came to London on my own and lived in a hall of residence in Roehampton: that was a breathing space and, although the course was very intensive, it was also a time for sorting things out. Basically, Christopher didn't want me back and I found I didn't feel I could face going back. So although ostensibly the reason I came to London was to do this course, there were a lot of other things going on as well. I went back to Hull during the holidays, a month at Christmas, a month at Easter, and it got worse and worse. When I rang he wouldn't talk to me, he wouldn't answer letters. Towards the end of the course he said he didn't want me back – not unless I was going to be what he wanted me to be, on his terms, and his terms were not acceptable. I did go back for four or five weeks and the whole situation erupted.

I came back to London in August 1987, in a state of utter confusion and despair. It wasn't a question of thinking things out. He virtually threw me out of the house. Of course I could have said I'm not leaving, you go, and issued injunctions, made him get out instead, but that would have involved so much hassle: he would still have been there. I couldn't get a job in Hull anyway and I wanted to get away from that situation, which was really bad for the children, and for me, I was virtually cracking up.

I hadn't envisaged the housing problem being as bad as it turned out to be. I met Ian towards the end of my first year in London, so he was an additional catalyst and enabled me to make the break, but he wasn't the reason for it. We started living together in October 1987, and then had two to three years of living in sub-standard accommodation, various bed-sits where I obviously couldn't have the children to live. I was teaching part-time and working with Ian, who's self-employed, then for Southwark as a supply teacher in secondary schools. The difficulties over the kids went on and on. My solicitor saying he couldn't do anything about them till I'd sorted the housing out; I couldn't sort the housing out without the kids; Lambeth Council saying firstly they'd take the children into consideration then refusing to; all my money, such as it was, tied up in the house in Hull, which I obviously couldn't sell. The housing difficulty was the major problem.

I was also denied access to the former matrimonial home, even when I went up there to see the children. Letters were interfered with. Recorded delivery letters I sent to the girls were sent back to me. The only way I could see them was to travel 400 miles to my parents' house in Edinburgh. My mother would collect them, or they'd travel there and we would meet at my mother's. She was placed in a difficult position and was anxious not to alienate Christopher in case he stopped her seeing the children. Most of the communication with Christopher was through her – it was a messy triangle. During the first year there was some contact – the children came down to stay with us in London: one at a time because there was no room! Each one came for a few days or weeks in the holidays, and I'd go to Edinburgh to be with them all together. I was starting to get a better relationship with both my sons, though that sadly has since changed and Christopher has intervened between us.

Whilst this was happening, I tried to instigate divorce proceedings. My ex-husband said he didn't want a divorce, and stalled that. Then he met someone else, in 1989, and changed his mind. All along he's wanted to call the tune. He's used the children as a weapon against me. That's why he didn't want me to see them. It was part of his hostility towards me. There was no communication, he didn't even answer solicitors' letters. There was verbal abuse when I phoned. He'd like me to just go away and not bother him. But he's got an emotional hold over me, even now.

There were years and years of 'drip-feeding', telling me what an awful person I was, what a no-good mother, undermining me in any way he could, so that by the time I left I had no confidence in myself in any direction, as a teacher, mother, even as a person. He was even more hostile following my relationship with Ian, and having the baby.

Christopher's girlfriend sold her house when the divorce went through and moved in with him, with her two children, roughly the same age as the girls. But his new relationship only seems to have increased his hostility and resentment towards me. I wasn't even told about the divorce hearing, and he managed to push through a custody order without my being informed. I still haven't got to the bottom of what happened: the court says they informed my solicitor, he maintains he never received any communication from them. I wasn't receiving correspondence from the solicitors, so I wasn't fully in the picture. And the solicitor was sitting on things again because of the housing. We could have taken Lambeth Council to court, we had a case against them. Since then, having further information about that particular firm of solicitors, I'm kicking myself for not having changed them sooner. Their negligence certainly made the situation worse.

Then I got a good solicitor and contested custody. But I came up against res judicata *– which means you cannot challenge a decision made by one judge. I did finally get it back into court this year: it took 18 months simply for me to get a hearing.*

We moved into this property in October 1990, ironically, just a few months after Christopher had got that custody order. Up until that order I would have brought the children down when we got anywhere. Now, just when we had accommodation that was suitable, I couldn't do it. If we'd had even temporary housing before, we'd have been in a different position. I feel very angry about that. And now Lambeth Council were turning round and saying that as you haven't got custody, we won't consider the children in planning your housing. I've been caught in this catch-22 situation for four years. I feel like turning round to them and saying well whose fault is it I haven't got custody?

I was stuck with the old legislation until now. The Children's Act was introduced in October and because I'd started proceedings under the old law, I couldn't change mid-stream. Now it's all being swept aside and I can re-apply under the new Act. There's another hearing in April about ancillary matters, the house, my possessions there.

Some people might have given up, but I have too much of a sense of injustice. Not self-pity: injustice. Also the fact that one of my daughters is unhappy and does want to be with us. No one's listened to the children. The welfare officers had already made up their minds – they didn't even visit me in my home or when the children were visiting – they assumed the children were settled in Hull because of the length of time that had elapsed by then. It takes so long to get things into court and by then they claim the children are settled and it would be wrong to disturb them and upset the status quo. Another catch-22.

There's also some victimisation going on in Hull, certainly from the welfare officers, towards a woman who's 'deserted'. It's not like fighting in London – I'm up against a very parochial way of thinking. I felt they were very biased and I mind the unfairness of that. The whole case was prejudged and I was unable to say anything in my defence.

But the judge at the last hearing was very good. He decided to dismiss the case without prejudice, which means I can re-apply under the new law: it will get reviewed in another year, and the children's views will get listened to. But that's another year with their father, and ideas are put into them. I don't have influence over what they do, their lifestyle. The elder girl's now at secondary school and will be worried about changing that. A year of defined access. That's what I meant at the beginning about mixed feelings. It wasn't a defeat, but it wasn't a victory. The new law will help women in my position, it might make a difference, but it won't stop unreasonable behaviour or make others co-operate – you can't legislate for people's feelings.

Having the new baby has helped me tremendously, though she wasn't in any sense a replacement. It was to do with my relationship with Ian in its own right. And at the same time, because of all this, I'm terribly anxious about her. Everything has to be right. I have to be seen to be the perfect mother. Isla's 20 months now and I'm a full-time mother, I haven't gone back to teaching, though I could if I wanted to, I've got the qualifications and experience. For now I just enjoy being *with her, there's the pleasure of that, but also the pressure of wanting to get everything right.*

When the girls are here with me, I try too hard. There's a sense of unreality about it. There's so little time, I feel I'm just going through the motions of being a mother. The mother-daughter relationship's still there, it hasn't been too badly damaged by events, but I'm always trying too hard, over-anxious, being on my best behaviour all the time, trying to make up for the time in between. I can't say no to them. I wonder if that will go away. And when I take the girls out somewhere, shopping or swimming, I feel like bursting into tears, because it's such a normal thing to do. It looks like a 'normal' family unit, and it isn't. I've had to bottle up my pain about it so I could survive.

The girls have a marvellous relationship with Ian, and with Isla. They adore her. But there's a lot of difficult feelings. They weren't able to see her when she was born, I can't share her with them. So there's some sadness at Isla not being with her sisters, at her losing out. No one's considered her needs – she's a little appendage that came along later, the girls' relationship with her isn't seen as being important, whereas the one with their elder brothers, it is.

It's very awkward when you meet someone for the first time and they ask how many children you have. I find it very difficult to answer. I can't say I don't know. I can't say five, but ... but ... but ... but ... It's not a matter of wanting to justify yourself, but there'd be so much explaining, you tend not to start.

I always wanted to be a mother, but I didn't want to be a housewife. I wanted the children. They didn't just happen. But I suppose that adds to the guilt, even though I know I couldn't have stayed in a situation that was bad for the children and bad for me. I'd have cracked up completely. But having said that, there is always the feeling that it's not acceptable for a mother to leave her children, whatever the circumstances.

I don't think any mother actually leaves her children. She may leave her husband, she may leave a situation which has become unbearable and which because it's unbearable for her has become unbearable for the children, but she doesn't leave with the intention of leaving them. It's a desperate measure. A temporary measure. One leaves them where they are, for the time being, to sort oneself out or find accommodation. One leaves in a state of desperation, or one gets thrown out, but then it's all turned round and twisted against you, and it's made out that you're selfish and irresponsible. I did intend to leave, but I also intended to go back and get the kids. I regret leaving the children behind, I feel guilty about it, but I don't regret leaving that situation. It was finished. No, I don't ever regret leaving that.

12

Pennies from Heaven:
Marital Incompatibility

> All these years of marriage, I could see, he had been
> laughing at me, playing with me, using me and my
> money, and caring nothing for me at all. When he smiled
> at me it was to hide the sneer of derision on his lips;
> when he touched me and embraced me it was the worst
> insult of all, because he had to steel himself to do it. I
> knew he did. Because he touched me to keep me quiet.
> He lusted after someone half my age, and half my size.
>
> Fay Weldon . . . *And the Wife Ran Away*[1]

After inheriting considerable wealth and working for many years in
business, Daphne, now 42, is involved with healing work and lives with
her second husband, Terry. Until now, the four children from her first
marriage have remained with their father and his second wife.
Daphne's story points to some of the jealousies that can emerge in step-
parenting, and the way in which children can be turned into pawns
in post-marital games punishing the partner who has left. It also
emphasises how wealth is no anodyne for a mother who leaves.

*I was married in 1971, the marriage lasted 14 years. It was
basically fairly happy. Molly was born in 1975, the twins in
1977, Ben in 1980. Unfortunately, in 1978, I came into a lot of
money. I say unfortunately because my husband Brian had
great ideas of increasing it several times over, and each plan
lost us more and more. We set up a crafts business. It was
intended to be small, but it rapidly expanded, with 250 agents
nationwide and needing me to work full-time. After 18 months
Brian was taken into hospital with a heart problem: when he
came out I was left running the business virtually alone. It took*

all my energies. I was also doing up a little lodge for friends to stay. It was very hectic. The pressure built up and eventually broke up the marriage.

Emotionally and mentally we were very close, but increasingly I didn't look on him as a husband, more as a brother, friend, troublesome son, and after Ben was born we found ourselves drifting apart sexually. One reason was that Brian likes very slim women, which I'm not. He would say I looked fine from the neck up, and walk out of the bedroom when I was undressing. He'd need Playboy *on the bed beside him to get him aroused. He'd describe me as a fat frigid frump. It was terrible.*

Into all this came my present husband. He resisted getting involved at first, but we met occasionally over the four months from when we met till I left, and it became very intense. Brian didn't seem to mind, he had a girlfriend – my best friend – and said that would stop him being jealous. I was absolutely infatuated with Terry. His wife had died five years before and he was the first man for years who'd been physically attracted to me. But he was very aware of the children: he said there was no way he was going to take me away from them, so we broke up.

I was absolutely lost without him. On 10 January, I left the house and went to live in the little lodge I'd done up, a stone's throw away, and slept there. I still took the children to school, did the housework, spent time with them every evening before I went up to the lodge and we had a selection of different nannies. I never anticipated leaving the children.

Brian and I had a holiday in Corfu to try to get things together, but it didn't work. I was obsessed with Terry. It felt so right, I feel it was a karmic connection, I was sure there'd been a triangle between the three of us before, in a different life, in different circumstances. But I was torn. When I was with the children, I couldn't envisage being with Terry; when I was with Terry, I couldn't envisage going back to Brian. I'd originally intended to split up with Brian, but keep the children, but he said if he had to leave, the children and I would never see him again – he'd offer them no support and would drink

*himself into the ground. He cried, threatened suicide, I blamed
everything on myself. So I left them with him, thinking that
after a few months he'd grow tired of it.*

*I started to prepare a home they could come to for when that
happened, so after Corfu I bought a dilapidated bungalow
three miles away and the separation became more permanent.
It was a split life: I was still taking the children to school,
doing their housekeeping, shopping, clothes, doctor, dentists,
seeing them every day. It was still so close, I didn't feel I'd left
them. I was determined to maintain the closeness. Then Brian
interviewed a new nanny, Suzi, without my approval, and I
knew from the start he was going to marry her. She was slim
and blonde and fitted in with the social life he'd always
wanted.*

*I wouldn't say Suzi was a gold-digger, but she was certainly
on the up and up. I think she believed him to be a lot
wealthier than he was. Once she'd taken over, things changed.
I moved to a different house eight miles away and our home –
which I'd given Brian when we got divorced – went on the
market. He's always had delusions of grandeur and they moved
to a large house, ostentatious, ridiculous for his income. We had
joint custody, with Brian having care and control, and the
children came to me every other weekend and for a time each
holiday. Ben was five, the twins were eight, Molly was ten.
Thanks to my grandfather, the children were wealthy in their
own right, and originally Brian thought whoever had the
children had control of their money. I fought and managed to
get them some protection, but there was continuous pressure to
divert money from their funds into his businesses, he even
swindled and stole money from their trust account.*

*Brian and Suzi settled in their house and had a son, whilst
Terry and I lived in the old house I'd bought and Terry's
daughter Judy came to live with us. She was 15 when I met
her, antagonistic. I saw much less of the children once Brian
was married: his wife was very hostile about access and Brian
colluded with her. Quite quickly, everything reverted to her,
they saw her dentist, doctor, etc., till I was literally stuck to the
weekend meetings with them.*

That relationship, with her acting as stepmother to my children, has been quite fraught. I made great efforts to get on with her, but we do everything differently, especially with regards to the children. I felt she didn't look after them very well at times. I found it incredibly hard, hard being truthful to myself, because I wasn't sure of the truth at times. It was made doubly difficult by having my stepdaughter Judy living with us. She couldn't stand me, so the first two years with her were a nightmare. After six years, she's just moved out. The children remarked once how the complaints I made about Judy were exactly the same as the complaints Suzi had about them. That started me looking at it: I couldn't give to Judy what I gave to my own children, because she didn't want my affection. Though we did eventually manage a relationship that worked, and I got on better with her three brothers, who stayed with us at various times.

Social judgements were very hard. People thought I was the most terrible woman, to walk out on an ailing husband and leave four children behind to run off with the local carpenter! They couldn't understand it: they thought I'd gone from everything to nothing. Terry didn't own his own house, even his car was our second-hand one. It was very difficult. I believed what people said about me being an awful woman, so I gave in to Suzi, because I felt I was being doled out punishment for being a bad wife and mother. Even if the children were ill and asked for me, she didn't like me going in the house.

I had some valuable support from a woman cleaning for me in the house, we got really close. She had left her children 15 years before and later they'd come back. We found that our situations were very similar, though hers were even worse, more painful. We helped each other, worked through it together, read the same books. I was determined not to do it the same way as my parents when they split up. They fought for 10 years before they finally split up. They were never speaking, it was always chaos.

I was born June 1949, I had a younger brother and sister. My mother and father had met on holiday in Cornwall in 1947 and married three months later, after courting by post and a few visits. They had little in common. She's intelligent, career-orientated, romantic, into classical music. He liked drinking, nights out getting stoned. Sex didn't work out for them. Mother was unhappy with him for many years, she was always ill, crying, and as I was the oldest she took me completely into her confidence. I grew up thinking it was all my father's fault and that put me in awkward situations with him, it wasn't till years later that we became closer to him.

I knew things I wasn't supposed to tell him. For example, I was privy to the fact mother planned to leave. Yet unbeknownst to me, father knew anyway: he'd had a private detective on her for months and knew that she was going to South Africa to stay with her boyfriend there. Mother left on my 16th birthday. I arrived home from boarding school and she'd taken everything to her new place, thinking we'd be going there. Our house was massive, and now it was completely Spartan. That had such an impact on me that I knew I couldn't do that to my children. I didn't want them having that horrendous experience I'd had when I came home from boarding school and everything was gone. When I left, I left the house intact.

Also, my parents fought for six years over custody: my mother finally won it. That was the 1960s. But because my father pleaded poverty and couldn't afford to give her support, we actually lived with him most of the time. That fighting made such an impact on me too, I was determined not to fight Brian over the children.

Six months after my mother left, I had a breakdown and I was sent out to her in Rhodesia to get well. But the relationship with her cooled down when I returned to the UK, we drifted apart. She stayed in South Africa for a year – her new relationship didn't work out – and she came back to England. She lived not far from Dad, and the whole thing started up again. It was hard to stay close to her: she remembers only the grudges, the bad things. There's always been a great negativity in her, manifesting as constant illness, though she is making some efforts to combat it and we are closer now.

I've survived by working hard: hard work is a healer. When

I wasn't seeing the children so much, I would garden, work, do anything I could, keep busy, fill the time. In fact the relationship with the children changed. When I was with them full-time, I'd long for time away from them, quarter of an hour, an evening off. When I was limited to seeing them, I'd split the week so I was working towards their coming: their favourite meals would be cooked, everything would be ready, and the time we had together was quality time. We were really together, sitting, talking, chatting, watching TV, whatever we wanted. I was with them all the time. It became a much better relationship. Sometimes I'd drive miles to catch five minutes with them after school. I really worked on being close, fighting to get them one Christmas in two. It was damned hard work, in the face of Brian's and Suzi's opposition. I had to fight every inch of the way for every bit of spare time.

I don't have anything against Brian as a father – though he could pay them more attention – I just didn't want him as a husband. His last business went bust for a quarter of a million, and their big house was repossessed, so they've now had to move again, to rented property. The children wanted to come and live with us, but Brian did his crying act, as he had done before with me, so they told me they felt they had to stay. I don't want them to have divided loyalties. But my oldest daughter, who doesn't like her stepmother, has come to us, so she's with me again now.

I must admit there's part of me that regrets having all this inherited wealth. There must be something karmic to it: it's happened three times now. Grandfather left a massive will, a colossal amount of money, to my father's generation, then mine and my children's. Yet now I haven't got a penny of it left. Brian got through most of it, the rest went on buying the houses. My aunt then died and left me several million, but virtually everything that came to me through her has gone to the tax man. Father's just died, he's left me a small fortune, but they're putting a road through his farm, so we can't sell it, and I've still got to pay death duties. So there's an awful karmic tie between me and money. Money was definitely one of the main things to come between Brian and me. Interestingly,

Terry's got nothing. That's one of the reasons I like that relationship: it's free of that complex karmic bind.

As a way of healing this whole situation and myself, I've tried various forms of therapy. I knew I had to learn to love the people with whom I had to be in contact: the fact that they *were in my life was karmic and the sooner I learnt how to deal with that the better. I'm still coming to terms with that, even now.*

13

Children Having Children: Adopted Patterns

In my case, certainly, it was an infant who had given birth. Or at least the infant part of me was still in the ascendancy over a more adult part that had not found its chance to grow into a functional entity.

Nini Herman *My Kleinian Home*

Meredith is 37, unemployed, living in the British provinces. She was adopted at birth and experienced her surrogate mother as unavailable and uncaring. Virtually every childhood encounter she can remember is one of destruction and abuse and her adult life has reproduced, in an almost uncanny way, these earliest impressions of loss and bad mothering. On separate occasions she has 'given away' all 3 of her children: a 2-year-old daughter (now 18), a son of 8 and a baby a few days old.

These experiences appear to be deeply compulsive, as if an unconscious pattern has been repeated time and again, and there are clues to its origins in her own early life, where a cycle of broken mothering, abuse and destructive behaviour was established. Almost inevitably, this was mirrored and came to a head when Meredith herself was placed in a parenting role. Reading through her account, she was appalled: 'It looked so awful in black and white, one horror story after another,' but hopefully its re-telling will help give some sense to the experiences and stop them being re-enacted.

I was adopted when I was three days old. I was born at home and my biological mother had 2 boys – twins – who were 18 months older than me. She wasn't married to my father, who was about 20 years older. A lower-middle-class family, in council accommodation. Apparently she was very unhappy living with him and with life in general. She had a lot of mental problems, poor health and was too ill to keep me. That was 1954.

It was a third-party adoption, covered in secrecy: the families never met. My real mother didn't know where I was going. I was told about the adoption very young. My adoptive mother always said that I was 'chosen'. It sounded like a commodity that could be sent back. I was meant to feel grateful, lucky. I don't remember very much of my childhood. Things were difficult from the start. I wouldn't eat, I rejected food. I was physically cared for, with my own bedroom, but I have no memory of cuddles, laughter, light stuff.

My adoptive family consisted of a mother, her 11-year-old son, and his stepfather. I'd say it was already a dysfunctional family. Theirs had been a marriage of emotional convenience and I feel very strongly I was adopted out of guilt. My adoptive parents were first engaged in the late 1930s, but Mother broke the engagement to marry her childhood sweetheart. Almost immediately she became pregnant, but her husband was killed in the war. A baby boy, Peter, was born two months later in 1944. Meantime her mother had contacted the man she had previously been engaged to, and they met again and married.

Dad couldn't forgive her for leaving him for Peter's father, so he hated Peter and there was a lot of resentment and anger. They tried to have children of their own, there were several pregnancies and births but the babies failed to survive. One lived for a short time and the others died in utero. She didn't get on with her own mother, she had to look after herself from an early age. She's rigid, very efficient, dominating, disciplinarian. She stayed at home as 'Mother', but later – as a bet – went back to work, first in a pub, then a bank.

My mother developed classic illnesses of people who are controlled and afraid of their emotions. Feelings were displayed only through illness. She had migraines from a very early age and was often sick at school, she had sciatica, Bell's palsy, later a tremor in her head. She wouldn't react or let go, she wouldn't cry, she got impatient with any display of weakness, emotion or flappable behaviour. She'd squash it, call you a drama queen, when you were trying to say I'm lonely, I need somebody. There was no hugging, no touching, I was very neglected in that way. I realise their generation wasn't demonstrative, but still I feel they were exceptional in that they never touched or displayed any affection, either to each other or to me. The fact that she doesn't touch hurt the most – especially as I got older – so I overdo it now.

She was 34 when I arrived. I was the nearest Dad could get to having a child from her and I was the favourite. He loved me when I was little, spoilt me, but Mum kept a distance between us and in the end my relationship with him broke down. Then he might as well have never been. He was absent in all senses, like the wallpaper. There was always a heavy atmosphere, slow and tense, and though the house was modern, it felt gloomy and old. There was no warmth, joy, laughter. My brother was 11 years older, I was about 5 or 6 when he left home and got married, they had child after child. So I was brought up on my own. In the thick of it all, I did feel very neglected. It was quite lonely. I can still feel it, being very lost, in a world of my own.

My childhood memories are patchy. I was bullied at school, mainly about what I looked like and being 'no good' because I was adopted. My mother would dress me in old-fashioned clothes. About 25 per cent of mothers abuse their kids, but people hide it, there's this myth of good mothering that stops you telling the truth. I'm sure I was abused.

From an early age, about eight, I was the victim of sexual assaults. One man exposed himself to me, there was a mentally handicapped man who lived round the corner who would abuse me, another man made me look at pornographic photos. There was more at secondary school. It would happen quite frequently. I always seemed to be with some sort of pervert. Then Mum held a big party to celebrate her 25th wedding anniversary. I was 14 or 15. I'd been allowed a drink and was upstairs in my room when someone came in and attempted to rape me. It was him. My brother. Then my Dad came up, and I escaped. That memory's hard. To know what went on. It's very hazy. I don't know if things had happened before.

*I went to college to do nursery nursing. That wasn't my idea.
It was hers. I wanted to go to drama school, but she wouldn't
hear of it. So I ended up from 8 till 6 each day with a lot of
children and nappies. I really hated it, it wasn't where I
wanted to be at all. I was the youngest in the group, quite
small myself, looking after these children. I felt quite
inadequate, I had some sort of breakdown.*

*At college, I was obsessed with getting a boyfriend. My whole
self-worth was put into my sexuality: it was the only thing I
thought I had, from a very young age. I felt I was ugly and my
main preoccupation was finding a boyfriend. I was quite
promiscuous. I feel sick and sad about it all now, but it was so
compulsive. I hungered after touch, warmth, recognition,
attention, and went to anyone that showed the slightest interest
in me, mainly men. I wanted my Mum to stop me from doing
it, but I'd gone too far out and she couldn't cope. She can't
deal with grown children, she's the same with my daughter
now, I know things have happened to her too. You can see the
damage, it'll take years to undo. She's at college now, too,
doing business studies, but it's not her choice. It's my nursery
nursing revisited. She's going to be living round the corner
from my Mum, looking after her and she's just got engaged.
She wants to have a baby.*

*Mum would never hold you for the love of it, only to feed
you. So, as my daughter has said, you'd go to men for cuddles,
for holding, but they'd want something else. I was expressing
that sort of neglect through going to men, so I was promiscuous
round college, then I got into drugs. Sniffing Vick, smoking
dope, dropping acid. I left college and took a job with the gas
board, then a nanny job. The nannying was lonely. I was a
young girl, 18, stuck with this baby in this house. I didn't like
it, it was horrible.*

*Then I met Alan. We moved into a flat together and shortly
after I became pregnant. It didn't occur to me that I would get
pregnant, I didn't really care. I didn't think, it was mindless,
I'd slept around a lot and it hadn't happened before, so I
thought 'maybe I can't have any.' The pregnancy itself was all
right, I maintained myself. I instinctively knew what had to be*

done, managing to float into the right places at the right time, drifting to doctors and the antenatal clinic, making sure that I was looked after, but there was very little conscious thought. I don't think I'd been conscious through most of my teenage years. I didn't prepare myself emotionally at all. It was as if I was going to be pregnant for ever and there was going to be no baby at the end of it.

It was really hard. Alan was trying to study. We didn't have any money or food. Mum made clothes and went to jumbles and made the carry cot, like a mother hen, but it was all practical, there was no emotional support. I was scared of having the baby. I went into hospital too early, Alan wasn't with me, I was left alone a lot. There was so much pain, I couldn't believe how painful it was. I felt bullied, embarrassed, humiliated, out of control, very frightened. It was horrible, really horrid. She was born at 4 o'clock the next afternoon.

So the baby came. I was about 20 then, a young 20. When I woke, Mum was there by my bed and the nurse was saying how bad it was, children having children. So I had Chloe. She was a really good baby, and I breastfed her easily for nine months.

Alan had done a lot of drugs before I met him and we still smoked dope. I'd say now that I hardly knew him, we didn't take each other in at all and inside, I was all over the place. I was looking after Chloe and he was going off somewhere and I just kept thinking 'Is this my life, oh God, is this my life? What do I do now? I haven't done anything.' I was only 20, yet I felt older and very alienated. I wanted to be out clubbing it, anything except sitting in holding a baby. I was very low and afraid. At that time I really needed a mother for myself.

So then I was off looking for blokes again. I'd had a relationship with a man – a boy really – when I was at college. I slept with him again after Chloe was born – once – and got pregnant. I knew I was pregnant the minute I conceived. Chloe was only five months old. I was stupidly naïve, I asked the father to help me financially with an abortion, but he thought I was playing games. So I told Alan it was his. I had an abortion.

I spent some time trying to live properly, but I wasn't very *good with Chloe. I was still going out with anybody, still trying to express something. I was neglectful, I did things I wouldn't dream of doing now. Sometimes I actually used to put her in the high chair and go out. Anyway, in the aftermath of the abortion I got so depressed that finally I took an overdose: a couple of bottles of aspirins and Martini. My parents were due to come round, so it was more of a cry for help. I was taken to hospital and later went to see a psychiatrist. There was a lot of confusion with him, he broke the boundaries, and when he dropped my sessions I panicked and overdosed to get back. That happened several times. I found that experience of therapy very damaging, as bad as the original abuse I'd suffered. It was all a repetition of what had happened earlier. Each time I went to someone for comfort or attention, I would get abused. My mother knew about the abuse, but she colluded, she pretended not to know. I was just like a puppet, I'd go when men called me. There was a rape too. Everywhere I went I was the target of abuse. I had no idea how to protect myself. It felt like I was asleep or sleep-walking. I was always trying to get rid of myself.*

Till then, I still had Chloe, though it was half my Mum looking after her, half me. Then the doctor said I was off my head, so my Mum had her full-time. She wanted children, I didn't. I was in such a state, Chloe shouldn't have been with me. I can't believe what I used to do. Once I overdosed when she was there, a bit like Sylvia Plath, putting the kids to bed, giving them their milk, then killing herself. So in a way, I was relieved when Chloe went. She was about two then: it wasn't a conscious decision.

Then there was nothing to hold me. I was free. I moved to a council place in Hackney, and it was there I really got into drugs. Barbs, amphetamines, heroin, acid, dope, alcohol, the lot. I was well into it. Obviously to keep up the habit, I needed money. I didn't dare steal, but I had a body so I sold that. I ended up on the game. To do the game, you needed the drugs, and to get the drugs you needed the game. I met a man who became my pimp for a while and then took off on my own. I became a prostitute and a drug addict, as well as a mother apart from her child. Almost everyone I knew was either on the game or on drugs. A friend and woman that I worked with killed herself. Another woman lost custody of her two children. Most of the women I know that have been prostitutes have been incest survivors. They don't keep their kids. The few that I knew that did have children had great difficulty with them, I don't think they could parent them very well. I don't think someone who's gone as far out as that can look after herself, let alone children.

Mum was very repressed sexually; she lived through my sexuality. She knew I was on the game, she was even excited about the details, like I'd tell her about sleeping with a man who took his arm off - he had a false arm - and she'd think it was hilarious! She certainly wasn't stopping me, which is probably what I wanted her to do. But you're so high, so gone on drugs, you don't really see it as odd. There's so many weird things happening. There were transvestites, kids flying around, people killing themselves, it all came to seem normal.

Round about this time I met my real mother. I'd discovered their address and I turned up on her doorstep and introduced myself. I was thinking this is my Mum and that's my brother and his twin, but I had no real feeling. My Dad was horrified, that I just turned up. He wanted to know what I wanted, what I was here for. I got involved with one of my brothers, that was another repetition of the scene with Peter.

Then I met a man who was to become the father of my second child. He was an alcoholic and I was on the scrounge for drugs, so we made a pathetic pair. After a near-fatal overdose where I ended up in a coma, I decided I had to stop the drugs. Which I did. I got pregnant and Ted threatened to leave me, so I had an abortion, which in my heart of hearts I really didn't want. And I got pregnant again almost immediately. I think we both felt so bad that we decided to have the baby. I gave up everything - drinking, smoking, drugs - to ensure a healthy baby and had him, my second baby, in hospital. I adored him.

I really loved Joshua, but I felt I was a terrible mother, bad-tempered, inconsistent, I always thought I should be doing better. I couldn't parent. I still can't parent, because I haven't been parented. Which is horrible, because I've tried, I've really tried, but I was still searching for something that would make it possible. Yet all the time there was this terrible urge to get pregnant: Chloe, then the abortion, then the abortion with Ted, then having Joshua. I got pregnant again a few months after Joshua was born, and I knew I couldn't cope. That was my third abortion. Ted had a vasectomy, but by that time we'd left each other. The relationship was very strained, with his drink and drug problem. Things became unpredictable and violent.

After Joshua's birth I began to wake up to all sorts of feelings, I became aware of pornography and violence against women. Ted thought I was over-reacting, but I met a group of women, WAVAW (Women Against Violence Against Women) who were very supportive, they validated my rising consciousness. That was when my world started to change. I suddenly connected things, it all made sense. Porn, snuff movies, I wanted to get as far away from all that as possible. I became very sensitive to sexism and violence. Abuse, injustice.

Finally, my own needs took over and I left Ted and moved away. I desperately needed to find myself, I needed space to heal, but Ted pursued me through access to Joshua. Meantime, I'd met a young man, a toy boy, and we ended up in a relationship where I got pregnant and had yet another abortion. And in the midst of trying to keep Ted at bay over access, I discovered once again I was pregnant. I knew then it was the end of the road.

I had to make fast decisions as to what to do with my child. All the choices seemed blocked. My mother overwhelmed me with grandmotherly technics, telling me I should keep the baby whilst also telling me Joshua was out of control and I was a bad mother. Ted was blackmailing me for accepting his maintenance and not declaring it to social security. My daughter would come to see me and was jealous and hurt that we didn't have a good relationship.

I had the choice of having the baby adopted, or aborted. As far as I was concerned I couldn't have another abortion. I'd already had four and couldn't contemplate another one. I was then left with adoption, but I didn't think I could survive it. I'd been adopted myself and I couldn't dream of that happening to my baby. For many months I worried about it all and nothing became clear. A counsellor at an abuse centre said it was a choice between keeping the baby and working through things with my children, or having the baby adopted and working through my own adoption. I didn't know if I'd survive: I thought if I have the baby, I won't be able to cope, and if I have him adopted I won't be able to forgive myself.

I picked out the family through the social services and met them a few weeks before I had the baby. I was very confused and afraid. I didn't look after Joshua or myself very well in the final months. I had no contact with my family at all. My mother had hit the roof, she was so desperate for me to keep the baby, she even said my daughter could look after it. That was the last time I ever spoke to her. There were constant battles both with Joshua's dad and with the baby's father, who was threatening to go for custody. It all became too much.

I had a home birth. He was supposed to go straight away, but I was swayed by his loveliness and decided I needed to keep him overnight. Joshua saw him but was stressed and distanced. I gave the baby to his new mum and dad the next day with a grief that I cannot describe. Over the weekend I was desperate to see him and wanted him back. I phoned social services to tell them I wanted him back and back he came. But I knew I'd made a mistake. I just wanted to see him again to make sure he was all right.

In all of this Joshua was basically looking after himself, putting himself to bed, feeding himself, letting himself in and out of the house. Most of the time I didn't know where he was. I felt terrible. I knew that I would never be able to cope with two children on my own – especially with all the pressures that their fathers would put on me – and what it meant in terms of my mother coming back into my life. I had lived on social and men's money all my adult life. I didn't think I could give my children a proper life. They deserved better than I could ever hope to give them. I hated myself and my messed-up life.

On the Monday morning I cracked completely and phoned

social services to take both children away from me. They came and took the baby, made him a ward of court, and contacted Joshua's dad, after discussing whether or not to put him in a foster home for a while so I could rest. When this was mentioned, Joshua freaked and got so upset.

I remember it vividly, sitting on the bed with the baby in one arm and Joshua beside me, saying 'Are you going to send me away?' and I said 'For a little while' and he crumpled up. He said he hated all of us. I knew that he couldn't hate me as much as I hated myself then. I had betrayed his trust totally and was getting rid of him and his brother as if they were nothing more than rubbish. How could I explain the reasons why? I decided that it might be better that he stay with his dad. I thought it would be temporary. I packed a lot of stuff and his dad came the next day. I really didn't think that would be the last time I would see him. Then he was gone.

After a few days I phoned him, but Ted's family wouldn't let me talk to him. His mother said 'Why do you want to speak to Joshua? You don't want him. You gave him away.' I knew then that I had probably lost Joshua for good. Every time I tried to speak to him they said the same, so I stopped phoning in case I was upsetting him.

By this time the baby's father was being difficult and taking me to court to try to get custody of the baby. That court case dragged on for a year and whilst that was going on, Ted went for custody. I knew I didn't really stand a chance. I felt Joshua was settled – he lived with a big family, he was at school, his dad had a steady girlfriend, his own home and friends – what did I have to offer? Ted now had all the power and I let him have custody.

When I contemplated all the fights and battles and unpleasantness that would go on if I tried to see Joshua, I wondered if it was better that I had no contact at all. I swayed between disappearing from his life completely and risking seeing him. After some months I sent him a card and he wrote letters back, but they became more and more infrequent. Ted wouldn't let me see him. I've written several times but heard nothing. I find it hard to get in touch with him and I know he

*won't get in touch with me. I know he gets taken down to see
my mother and his sister, and that breaks my heart. It feels
like she has everything now: she even has my children.*

*I grieve deeply over Joshua. I grieve deeply over all the
babies I didn't have, but the grief of Joshua going is more than
all that. It's the grief of throwing myself away, almost as if I
can't forgive myself for being born. I love my children, all of
them, and if I had my time again I would keep them all. But I
know that's not realistic. Wanting to be able to look after them,
but not being able to . . . How could I have been a mother?
You can't give what you haven't had, and neither family
parented me. That lack of love and abuse go right into your
psyche. You're left so mangled. It affects your ability to feel
good about yourself or other people. The trust is gone. You get
a completely distorted view of life. You end up not knowing
what's real and what isn't and in any relationship your mother
gets in the way, your father gets in the way all the time. If you
can't love yourself, your own inner child, you're not going to be
able to love a child of your own. You're just a needy screaming
child, with no identity. So you've got nothing to give the child.
Your life's full of disharmony, dramas, crises, always in crisis.
It's a lost cause really.*

*Neither my real nor adoptive mum had very good mothering
either. It goes down the line, doesn't it? It makes me angry. But
the buck's got to stop somewhere. Now I've named the fact that
I'm a survivor of abuse, rape and incest and the honest naming
of these things and the fact that I am still alive and sane
means a lot to me. And then, I'm with women now. I need to
be away from men because I don't know how to be with them.
The games that I used to play, the seeking approval, I can't
play them any more. But it's a long process.*

*In a way, it's fortunate that I haven't got the children. I'd be
acting out, slipping into old habits. But on the other hand, it's
crucified me. People who haven't got any children say I should
have got over it by now but I'm still in grief over the kids
going, though it's over two years now. I really am divided.
Half of me thinks yes, it's best for them, and if I turned the
clock back I would do the same thing. And the other half says*

no, I wouldn't. I would keep them all and die here, not recognise myself. So it's either keeping them and dying or not keeping them and having to try to live. It's really that hard a decision. But women do, they walk off and actually get their lives together. I hope I'm one of them. I hope eventually I will be.

14

Out of the Stream:
Choice of Surrogate Mothering

guilt is a drag:
maybe just because i wasn't eager
doesn't mean i'm a lousy mother

Alta *The Shameless Hussy*

Shirley Glubka (her real name) was born in the US in 1942. She married and, aged 27, had a son, but the marriage disintegrated when the baby was eight months old and Shirley left, taking her son with her. A couple of years later, she took the unusual step of relinquishing her child on a permanent basis, not to the father, but to another woman – one of the teachers at her son's day-care centre. Her son was then three. Surrogate mothering is something we usually associate with debates around rent-a-womb or adoption at birth: in 1972 especially, such a voluntary choice of surrogate mothering of a *child* was very much against the grain, upsetting all conventional notions of how a woman should behave. Stereotypes were further confounded by Shirley obviously still loving her son and continuing to see him and sustain a relationship with him.

The emotions and events leading up to and following this 'giving away' of her child were complex, as Shirley expresses in the fascinating and compelling article she wrote about her experiences some years later. This piece, originally entitled 'Out of the Stream: An Essay on Unconventional Motherhood', was first published in the American journal *Feminist Studies* in 1983. It is reprinted here in its entirety.

More recently, Shirley returned to graduate school at the University of Maine to pursue creative writing and has had her fiction and poetry published in various feminist publications including *Conditions*, *Sinister Wisdom* and *Lesbians at Midlife*. She now lives and works in the Bangor, Maine area, where she writes and has a private practice as a clinical counsellor.

As I started this piece for the sixth or seventh time, I wondered how far back I would have to go to understand my unusual relationship to motherhood. Beyond my own life, I knew – to my mother and my grandmothers and aunts and great-aunts and generations of women behind them. I thought about those generations and was struck by a vision: I saw a swollen stream of women, all taking on the role of mother without the least sign of rebellion. I saw myself leaping out of this stream and landing hard, alone and disoriented, flopping like the proverbial fish out of water. Quite a sad scene.

Then I remembered reality. In my family there were plenty of good Catholic mothers with the mandatory five to seven children trailing them through the aisles of grocery stores. But there were also others: the one who never married, never had children, and cleaned houses for a living; the one who did marry, never had children, and worked in the college cafeteria; the one who had children and, when the last one came along, suggested to her husband that this child might be better raised by someone else, someone who was not tired of starting over with baby after baby. The husband would not hear of such a thing and the woman stayed in the stream of conventional mothers – but not without rebellion. These others stand in my personal history as surely as those women who seem to have taken on the role of mother without a qualm.

How peculiar, then, that I should have such a strong and immediate image that all the women before me were mothers, compliant in their role. On the other hand, how understandable that I should be assaulted by such an image. I, who left the conventional role of mother years ago, have no more protection from the myths surrounding motherhood than any other woman. In fact, I might be more vulnerable than most. Like the outcast, I sometimes imagine that all other women belong to an inner circle of mothers, a circle full of warmth and goodness, the locus of satisfying and productive activity.

I severed whatever connection I might have had to that imagined inner circle 10 years ago when my son Kevin was 3 years old and I was 30. At that time, Kevin and I were separated, by my choice. Kevin acquired a new mother in the form of Gretchen Ulrich who was a teacher in his daycare center.

If I believed in such things, I would regard Gretchen as one of the more enduring and beneficent apparitions of my life. She appeared as if by magic in my living room one day (actually, we were having an unscheduled parent-teacher conference) and by the end of several hours of conversation, we had come to an agreement. She would try being Kevin's mother and I would try something that was not quite not being his mother. He would live with her, I would live alone, and occasionally he and I would visit with each other. We determined a trial period which was to last one month; but we knew quite well by the end of our conversation that the arrangement would be permanent.

I had begun my experience with motherhood in a conventional enough way: inside the institution of marriage, a little haphazardly (through a failure of birth control that did not unduly distress either my husband or me – we had planned to have children eventually, why not now?) and, all in all, quite happily. When Kevin was eight months old, I left my husband, taking Kevin with me. For all practical purposes, that was the end of our involvement with my ex-husband. I had become a single mother.

I had also become a feminist, a critic of the status quo on many fronts, committed to finding sensible, humane, nonsexist ways to live. I tried communal living in what seemed to be an ideal situation – with other women from my consciousness-raising group, other children, and a few politically aware, thoroughly sincere men. We based our experiment on feminist principles. All work, including child care, was divided equally among us. The experiment was a success – for a year. The reasons for the disintegration of any living situation are, to say the least, hard to catch hold of. I could say we had personality conflicts; I could say it was extremely difficult to maintain a way of living that was unsupported by society at large. Both the purely personal and the social/political explanations would be true and even taken together they are not all of the truth. For whatever complex combination of reasons, our collective household split apart.

I continued to seek and find ways to break the isolation of single motherhood. I found excellent daycare, neighbors with

*preschoolers who wanted to exchange babysitting, friends both
female and male who volunteered days, evenings, nights, and
even whole weekends of their time caring for Kevin. Compared
with most single mothers, I was superbly supported; yet I felt
constantly burdened. It was becoming clear that I did not like
the role of mother. Specifically, I did not like the kind of work
involved in being a mother.*

*Having written this, I stop to think. And the voices come –
among them one that sounds suspiciously like my own: "You
didn't like the work? You left your child because you didn't like
the work?" And the images come of irresponsible mothers
abandoning their children for no reason: lazy, flighty, selfish, or
just plain bad women – loose women in garish green silky dresses
with long slits up the leg, tossing their babies into garbage cans
and going out for a good time . . . when my fantasy reaches this
height of stereotyped ridiculousness it becomes easier to deal
with. No mother separates from her child lightly. Yes, I left the
mother role because in a radical way I did not like the job of
being a mother; and because I believed that Kevin would be
better off if he were raised by someone who wanted to do that
kind of work; and because, by some miracle, that person
appeared in my life.*

*It would be a simplification to say that I liked nothing about
the mother role. That role is complex – and one of its
complexities is that it changes radically again and again as time
passes. I rather liked the work of mothering during Kevin's
infancy – all the holding, the nursing, washing him, even
changing his diapers was fine with me. I was good at it, I was
playing out a lifelong fantasy, and he was an "easy baby." When
I went to women's liberation meetings, I held him in my lap. If he
cried, I nursed him. When he fell asleep I put him down on the
carpet beside me and went on participating in the meeting. I
could write when he was a baby, too. He would play quietly and
I would type. When I took a break I would go and cuddle him –
then return to typing. Easy, I thought.*

*By the time he was a year and a half old it wasn't easy any
more. He didn't stay put. He was developing into a person who
would not be cuddled and ignored. He would not be ignored –*

*and I didn't want to pay attention. Much of the work of
mothering a small child (especially if you have only one) consists
in being present for another, being ready to respond to
emergencies, being ready to appreciate accomplishments, being
there for long periods of time with nothing, really, to do – except
watch and wait. During these times (which, if we were not in our
living room, seem always to have been in some park or other) I
would try to read or write, try to keep my mind active, try to
keep my sense of myself. But I never managed the trick of being
with myself and being ready to respond to Kevin at the same
time. I vacillated between two approaches. For a while I would
try shutting him out, focusing on my reading or writing or
thinking; and I would feel abruptly invaded by any small
demand he made. Then I would try the opposite tack and hold
myself in a state of dull readiness, trying to forget my own mind,
my own need to be with myself, trying to be ready for whatever
he needed without anger, without that painful sense of violation.
Neither worked well, of course. I was trying to do work for which
I was not suited.*

*Not everyone responds this way to the demands of mothering a
small child. There are women who amaze me with their skills.
Like jugglers (I have always been in awe of jugglers) they seem
able to keep track of many simultaneous movements. They can
balance their own lively consciousness with the activities and
needs of their children – without losing themselves in the
complicated, ever-changing pattern. On good days they even
make beauty and fun out of the juggle. I have often wondered at
least half-seriously if my simple inability to pay attention to two
things at once might lie at the core of my problems with
mothering.*

*I don't know if my difficulties with the mother role were made
more or less painful by the fact that I found Kevin to be the most
attractive child I had ever met. I liked him very much. He was
bright and beautiful. I liked being related to him, was proud to
be his mother. My affection for him was powerful, tender, and
could well up in tears easily and often. It was not Kevin I
disliked; it was the work of being his mother day by day.*

Many aspects of that work were difficult for me. I was

overwhelmed, for example, to find myself responsible for the physical existence of a little person who could suddenly move about under his own power. How could I know when he might step in front of a moving car, climb high and fall to his death, swallow poison? I could not lose the feeling that Kevin was at every moment vulnerable to a multitude of dangers. It was as if I were on guard duty, constantly vigilant, never fully relaxed.

Many mothers feel that when their infants become toddlers the job of being mother becomes easier and more rewarding – especially after the development of language and the completion of toilet training. In contrast, I felt the job expand into a complexity that I could hardly handle. Suddenly, for example, I was to pass on values to a malleable young soul. "Pass on" was, in my case, quite a euphemism. My own ethical stance and value system were still in the process of being reconstructed after the blitz of the late sixties. I felt absolutely inadequate to the task of building a strong structure for a preschool child. I struggled painfully with every situation that called for a decision about values: should I teach him nonviolence or the art of self-defense? Should I encourage him to question my commands or respect my need to have things done in certain ways? Should I demand that he maintain order in his room or allow him a measure of chaos? Every decision seemed to matter immensely – and to present unresolvable difficulties. I knew too much to opt simply for a highly structured universe on the one hand, or an existence that would trust to benign natural spontaneity on the other. And I was too confused to create a complex, workable blend of both.

The fact that I was now spending hour upon hour with a person who was verbal but not very good at being verbal was also difficult for me. I am the sort of person who can concentrate easily in the presence of jackhammers and roaring highway traffic, but let the most routine whispered conversation start up and I become totally distracted. When Kevin talked, whether to me or to one of his beloved stuffed animals, my whole mind swerved in his direction. But I was not good at child-level conversation and not particularly appreciative of the verbal gems of a three-year-old. I was, in fact, bored. I have often envied friends who take an easy delight in the speech of the very

*young. Not only do they enjoy the spontaneous comments of
children; they also have mysterious ways of eliciting the most
peculiar and interesting responses from them. Gretchen is one of
these people and in the last 10 years she has shared with me
many instances of Kevin's verbal brilliance. Oddly enough, I
have often taken special pleasure in hearing Gretchen tell me
what Kevin has said. It is as if her appreciation of his words has
provided a setting in which I can enjoy them.*

*Gretchen and I have always seemed to fit together like two
radically different pieces adjacent in the same puzzle. I did a
very good job of mothering during Kevin's infancy and then
entered the painful period that taught me I did not want to go on
with the mother role. When I looked ahead I saw the grade
school years as a severe challenge and if I imagined Kevin's
adolescence I shuddered. Gretchen, on the other hand, got
queasy at the thought of diapers and had no desire to be a
mother to a small helpless nonverbal specimen of humanity; she
liked a child she could talk to and she even, to my amazement,
liked the fact that the child would become a teenager; she
wanted to be a mother through that whole long growing process.
More specifically, she wanted to be Kevin's mother. And so we
made the change.*

*There is a stubborn, clear-headed part of me that has never
doubted the rightness of my decision. With that part I know that
Kevin, Gretchen, and I all have more satisfying lives because I
made that decision. With that part I have organized groups for
women who, like me, have left the mother role. With that part I
fight the demons of the night.*

*There are two of these demons, both expert tormentors. One
springs from reality, the other from myth. They are given to
impersonating each other, like clever twins. I have spent many
hours trying to pin down their identities, and I get a little better
at it as time goes on. The first demon is decidedly unpleasant,
but necessary. It is the caretaker of all the genuine pain that
comes from giving up a child. That pain rises and subsides
through the months and years. It feels demon-controlled because
it comes without warning, without apparent cause, and most
often in the middle of the night.*

*In the beginning, soon after Kevin and I separated, this demon
of genuine pain was quite distinct, not readily confused with the
second tormentor. I remember one night especially well. It was as
if all the pain had gathered to a single point in time and I must
experience it in a sort of purity. I felt as if Kevin and I had been
surgically separated. The pain felt physical, deep, radical – and
I knew it would lessen with time. That I had chosen the
separation and believed it was going to be good for both Kevin
and me must have determined the kind of pain I felt – pain that
could be so accurately described by the image of surgery. When I
think of the thousands of women who have been forcibly
separated from their children – because they were black and
slaves and sold in separate lots, because they were lesbians and
considered by that fact unfit, because they made their living by
prostitution and were therefore put in prison, or for whatever
reason – when I think of those women I imagine a pain that is
not the clean and chosen pain of surgery but instead the ragged,
uncontrollable pain of flesh torn at random which heals slowly
into an ugly scar and which hurts terribly even though new flesh
has formed.*

*The second demon is not only unpleasant, but also
unnecessary. It is the demon of myth and illusion and it is part of
what is now being called the institution of motherhood.*[1] *The
foundation stone of that institution and the constant message of
its demon is this:* children are meant to be raised by their natural
(that is, biological) mothers.

*I grew up in the all-white, working-class world of the small
town Midwest and went to Catholic schools in the forties and
fifties. I did not routinely encounter challenges to this basic tenet
of the institution of motherhood. On the contrary, I absorbed the
precept into my being. I imagined I would someday be Mother
Supreme. With infinite patience, good humor, and wisdom, I
would faithfully raise not 1 child, but 12. Having read* Cheaper
by the Dozen *and* Jo's Boys, *I had decided to fill my life with
wonderful, wacky children. I planned to have a few of my own,
but the majority would be homeless waifs, "abandoned" by their
mothers who were too poor or too ill to take care of them. With
me a child would have a secure home.*

That sort of self-image does not dissolve easily. In some very old part of my soul I still believe that I am a superior mother. I also still believe, with that same anachronistic part of my soul, that all children are best raised by their natural mothers. I have learned that neither of these beliefs is true, but in weak moments I forget what I have learned and thus open the door to the demon of myth and illusion. Like the demon of genuine pain, this creature comes most often at night. I know he has come when I find myself lying awake and nursing the terrible feeling that I have deprived my child of the most blessed of relationships; that my child is denied the special depth of bonding that could only come between him and me; that if I had stayed with him, he and I would have a full, clear, honest, tension-free relationship. I can remain in the grip of this demon for hours, colluding with society against myself.

But at some point I break free. I remember reality. I did not like the mother role. As long as I continued in it, I was doing something that aroused in me boredom, anxiety, depression, anger, and at times a fear that I would lose my sanity; it aroused in me also a deep fear that I would do violence to my child; at its best it turned me into a highly responsible, joyless, rather rigid person. Out of such things, great relationships are not made. I am not the best person to raise my child; only a powerful myth can make me think that I am.

The demon of myth and illusion has a strong grip which is not broken entirely by the act of remembering my own experience. I have also been faced with the task of sorting through distortions in my vision of Kevin's experience. The demon would paint the child as abandoned, damaged, a tragic figure. In my effort to correct this portrait I have sometimes drawn my own false picture: the child who moved easily from one mother to the next, happily relieved and blessedly unhurt. Somewhere between the demon and my own wishful thinking the truth hides. My memory, when it clears, tells me that Kevin's experience was as complex as mine, a mixture of pain and benefit.

I will never know all that Kevin felt during the time of transition, but two scenes come to my mind and I suspect that each is a hint and an essence, a clue to the nature of his first days and nights in Gretchen's house. One scene is painful, the other quietly delightful.

About a week after the separation I visited Kevin in his new house – our first visit. What I remember is saying good-bye. Gretchen held him, standing on the edge of the porch. I told him I was leaving and hugged him while she still held him. He got his arms around me like a vice, would not let go, and sobbed out all the loss, powerlessness, frustration, and pain that he felt. After a while we prised him loose from me and I turned and went down the porch steps crying and drove home crying. Gretchen called me a couple of hours later to say that he had gotten calm before too long and had had a quiet, happy game before bedtime.

The second scene that comes to mind was at the beginning of one of those early visits. Kevin and Gretchen were in their living room and had not heard me coming. For several minutes, which is a very long time, I did the thing that anyone in my position would dearly want to do: I spied on them. I was the mouse in the corner. I had the privilege of seeing my child and his new mother in a spontaneous moment. Classical music was playing on the stereo, one of those pieces of music that is subtle and engaging and moves like water in rough country with a swift clarity and little falls and still places following on each other over and over. Gretchen sat with Kevin on her lap and their hands pantomimed what I later found out were two alligators who talked and kissed and then fiercely ate each other up; which caused much laughing in Kevin and the familiar lump in my throat.

So he must have felt pain and he must have felt joy, too, in having a mother now who was as overflowing with energy for being his mother as I had been drained of it. It must have been confusing for quite a while to want to be with me and to be having such a good time with Gretchen. He got attached to her quickly. He began to express pride in the fact that he had two mothers – this made him special. But he was torn; he liked living with Gretchen and at the same time he wanted to live with me. Sometime during the first year he came up with the perfect solution for his dilemma: he proposed that we should all live together, he, Gretchen, and I. An intelligent idea, certainly; just

*the thing from his point of view. Needless to say, being only four,
he did not have the power to transform his idea into reality.*

*Mixed with the pain, relief, fun, and confusion Kevin felt
during those early days of the transition was at least one more
set of feelings: frustration, impatience, irritation, anger. Anger
was not a new thing in Kevin's life. His anger and mine had
mixed and grown together for some time before our separation.
Several months before Gretchen appeared and changed our lives,
Kevin found a way to express that building rageful energy: he
took a new name. He called himself Fire. With great seriousness
he instructed everyone he met to call him Fire, his name was no
longer Kevin. A month or so after our separation, he issued new
instructions: we were all to stop calling him Fire; his name was
Kevin.*

*Kevin's stay in the angry realm of Fire was relatively brief, I
think. The fact that he was separated not only from me, but also
from my anger, must have had something to do with that. But the
separation could not, by itself, have dissolved his rage. In fact, it
must have generated new anger. Gretchen's obvious abundant
good feeling about Kevin and about her new job as mother did
much to help him toward resolution of his feelings. In addition,
he had invaluable assistance from the staff at his new daycare
center (to which he was moved when Gretchen became his
mother and decided she should not also be his teacher).
Presented not only with his unusual name, but also with more
tangible evidence of his anger (biting, kicking, and so forth), they
reacted with intelligence and creativity – and patience. They
taught him how to be angry without being destructive. The
central character in this lesson on anger was Fred. Fred was life-
sized, stuffed, and beat-up-looking – with good reason, since the
point of his existence was to be an object of punching, biting,
kicking, verbal assault and any other manner of attack a
creative preschooler might invent. Kevin, I am told, learned to
use Fred as no other child in the center ever had.*

*The fact that Kevin was encouraged to express his rage must
have something to do with its disappearance. As far as I can tell,
he is not now a particularly angry person; and he does not seem
to have any resentment (at least at this point in his life) about*

having been required to leave me and adopt a new mother.

I can say this with some confidence because one recent spring (Kevin was 11) I found the precise mixture of relaxation, courage, and support from other people in my life that allowed me, finally, to ask The Question. The setting was an A & W Restaurant situated on a busy road along with K-Mart, G. I. Joe's, and quite a number of auto dealers. Kevin and I were having hamburgers and root beer. In the middle of my hamburger, I asked him: "So, Kevin, what do you think about the fact that I am your real mom and we don't live together?"

He was quite ready with his answer and considerably calmer than I was. He had a theory: he supposed that I had not been able to afford having a child and so had given him to Gretchen. (Other children in Kevin's situation have expressed similar theories. It seems that children who do not live with their parents are likely to come up with an explanation of their situation that absolves both them and their parents of responsibility for the separation. In Kevin's case it was lack of money; in another child's it was immigration laws that required the parent to leave. In neither case did the external force actually have anything to do with the separation.) I told Kevin that money had not been a problem and talked a little about the real reason for my decision. Then I held my breath.

His response was calm and thoughtful. He said it was a good thing I had given him to Gretchen, he was sure the job of being a mother would have gotten harder and harder for me, and Gretchen was a good mom. He added, clearly not ready to abandon a well-thought-out theory, that he supposed I would have had financial problems if I had kept him.

Before that day in the A & W, I had a recurring fantasy that Kevin would, sometime in his thirties, go to a psychotherapist and, hour by expensive hour, unearth his anger at me for "giving him away." Perhaps he will do just that, I cannot know. But the fantasy does not come to me now. I have asked the crucial question, which is really many questions: is it all right? do you hate me? were you damaged? And I have received the gift of a calm answer from a child who seems to believe his life is just fine.

Still, the demons come. Worry, guilt, romantic notions of what-might-have-been, a deep sense of loss – all mix together in the middle of the night. In the daytime, out in the world, I am bothered by another tangle of difficulties: I feel vulnerable to the judgments of others, isolated, different; I am afraid and I hide the fact that I am a mother; I cultivate a habit of cautious speech; I deny an aspect of my being. Any gay person will recognize this syndrome. It is called living in the closet.

I have lived partly in and partly out of the closet ever since I gave up my child. I told my family and close friends as soon as I made the decision, but for the first five years I did not talk about it with anyone who had left the mother role. I assumed there were hardly any of us. I did know of one woman, a friend of friends, but I avoided meeting her. Then I decided to do some intensive dealing with this huge fact in my life. I wrote my master's thesis on the experience of giving up my child. I organized a couple of groups for women who had left the mother role – groups that were a sort of coming out for me, complete with highs and lows, moments of clarity and confusion, and a sense that my life was changing. And I am still closeted. There are many people from whom I have hidden the fact of my motherhood: bosses, coworkers, neighbors, the families of my friends, any casual acquaintance. I feel the power of the institution of motherhood too clearly to take the revelation of my status lightly.

On the other hand, as the existence of this essay demonstrates, I feel compelled to tell the world about the experience of giving up my child. This is cathartic for me. Every time I wrestle anew with my mothering experience and get it pinned down for a while to a (somewhat) solid floor of words, I feel both relief and a fresh sense of control. I get my reward. But this is the most difficult writing I ever tackle, and I do not do it for pleasure. I do it because it needs doing and has been so little done.[2] In these days when the threat of a "Family Protection Act" hangs over us like some sharp and dangerous appendage to the institution of motherhood, it seems more important than ever to speak about alternative ways of raising our children. We must make it clear that many women cannot or will not be forced into the mold of happy motherhood; and this includes many women who already have children. Mothers – and fathers, too – who need to give up their children must be able to do so with dignity, without stigma, not only for their own sake, but also (and perhaps especially) for the sake of the children.

If ever I were to lose my conviction about this (and I could, in one of those sloppy, sentimental nights when a soft glow surrounds the image of Mother Supreme), the morning news would quite likely help me remember reality. In the past month my local radio station has reported the murders of two young children – one by the father while the mother looked on, one by the mother. These murders are hardly unusual. I happen to have the statistics from 1966. In that year, 496 children were murdered by their parents in the United States. I am convinced that if it were an acceptable option to decide not to continue in the parenting role, at least some of these children would still be alive. Some battered children, too, would escape the bruises, the broken bones, the burns. Other children, less obviously abused, would find themselves released from the subtle prison of their parents' tension, anger, and unhappiness. They would find themselves being raised by someone who wanted to do the job. And that, I believe, would make all the difference.

15

Motherhood and Destiny:
Work of One's Own

I have given away my son,
And all the years of patience and of love . . .

The truth is, I gave away my son
Being young myself, having ambition

To enter a harder race. I was not wise,
And harnessed neither burden nor remorse.
I stumble from success on to reverse,
And even if I win, you are my loss.

Kirti Wheway 'Success'

Alice, an American in her forties, was married to a man with very
definite ideas about woman's place being in the home. These proved
impossible to reconcile with her own need to work, and for various
practical reasons when the marriage broke down she left her four-
year-old son with her husband. Her career went from strength to
strength, and for the last nine years she has been living in England,
where she has established a successful consultancy practice in the field
of organisational development. Her son, now 22, is still in the States,
though he is no longer with his father and has strongly rejected the
father's traditional family values and expectations.

Alice has sustained her relationship with her son, but has had to
endure legal and social judgements against her – especially since her
son was adopted – and she has paid a high price, emotionally and
economically, for a life on her own terms.

*It was 1974 when I left. We'd been married in 1968, when we
were both just 19. It was high school romance, we'd known
each other for five years. It was an acceptable thing to do then:*

*our best friends got married when they left school, there was a
lot of pressure on us to do the same. No one said we were too
young.*

*I had three alternatives when I chose to get married. I could
go to law school, be an airline stewardess and I'd been offered
a place in a school of interior design in New York. Yet in the
end I did none of these and succumbed to the marriage
instead.*

*I'd been doing some training in the legal profession and
continued working as a para-legal assistant. The only reason I
was 'allowed' to work after we got married was because we
were saving up for a house: all my money went towards a
down-payment. We'd been married one year when we tried
having children: we didn't succeed. Doctors ran tests and said
it was highly improbable I would ever get pregnant with Ron,
so we started adoption proceedings.*

*It took us exactly nine months to 'gestate' an adoption. I
stopped work about a month before we had the baby. They had
what they call in the States a baby shower, where they present
you with gifts for when it arrives. Empire-style dresses were
fashionable, tight under the bosom, fuller lower down, and I
went to my baby shower with a pillow under the Empire dress,
as a joke, saying this is my kind of pregnancy. When they said
they had a child for us, I remember dancing around the
kitchen, screaming out 'It's a boy!' as if I'd given birth. So it
felt very much like a delivery, with emotional rather than
physical pain. There was a saying I thought trite at the time,
but that turned out to be true: that I carried him not in my
womb but in my heart.*

*I always resented anyone who implied it was different
because he was adopted. It felt just as real, I think the bonding
was the same. I was totally responsible for him. It wasn't
instant love, but that can be true with natural children too, it
took time to develop. They'd matched us on intelligence,
background, physical characteristics. His mother was a 'mature'
mother, a semi-professional pianist but not in a long-term
relationship with the natural father. Scott came to us when he
was five weeks old: he would have come sooner but for the*

paper work. I remember the day we picked him up from the family service centre, it was the first week in April. They had him dressed in a wonderful little outfit. Ron kept saying he's perfect, he's perfect. I was speechless, overwhelmed with the responsibility.

Once I'd stopped work, it became a very traditional marriage arrangement, where hubby was working and I was at home with the baby, making women friends that had other small children. I loved it for the first year or so, then I started getting very bored. It was difficult. I looked for things to do, like voluntary hospital work. I was about a year into the boredom, Scott was two, when I started talking about going back to work or university. I was regretting having broken the cycle of studying and wanted to do something career-wise with my life, possibly law. That's when the difficulties began in the marriage. For Ron, women going back to work was a real taboo.

It's a typical story of what happens when you marry so young: we grew apart in very different ways, primarily intellectually. Our interests split. Ron was very conservative, traditional, working-class. He had a strong work ethic, he'd turned down his own opportunities to go to university, and was a big union man. He wouldn't go into management: he wanted to stay a skilled worker. We lived in Akron, Ohio, the rubber capital of the world and he had a career with Goodyear, the big employer there. He had strong working-class values that cut across my wanting to have a career – it was completely unacceptable to him. The more I wanted to be stimulated, the more he wanted me to stay at home. His idea of a good evening was to invite over a couple with small children so the kids could play together till bedtime, then we'd sit around and play cards. My idea of a good time was going off to New York City for the weekend. The more he became a homebody, the more I exaggerated the other polarity and wanted to escape.

My father had worked for Goodyear too. He died when I was 16 and I went to work almost immediately, with white-collar professionals. I'd been very influenced by that world: attorneys earning high fees, private practice, nice cars, good clothes, country clubs. Now I realised I missed that and wanted a career. My rationalisation for leaving Scott with Ron was linked to that. I thought of myself then, in my mid-twenties, as a woman hell bent on having a career. I had a typically American belief that if I went for it, I could have anything I wanted. I felt ambitious, determined to make it happen, to get whatever university credentials I needed and throw myself into work to succeed. I reasoned that if that career woman was who I was, and I had to work full-time to support myself whilst I gained qualifications, then it was logical to leave Scott with Ron, who only worked eight hours a day and liked staying at home the rest of the time. It was fairer for him to be at home with a father who would see him more often than with a baby-sitter whilst I was working.

That became the rationalisation I presented to myself for leaving Scott with Ron, but I always knew there was a 'selfish' bit in there too, that if I didn't take care of Scott I could do a lot more for myself, promoting my career and having a different kind of life. I knew it was a turning point, breaking out of Akron, Ohio and solid middle-class America. I had no idea I would ever get to the point where I could say it was legitimate because it was about my fulfilment. It's easy to say now with hindsight, having done a lot of work on it, but I couldn't admit that then: probably because I didn't know it consciously, and more importantly because socially I needed heavy legitimate excuses, rationalisations, justifications for doing such an 'awful' thing.

It was very hard to do it. I can remember the day that I left. Ron was working nights, so we had to make arrangements for someone to live in. We found a woman, an old nanny type, called Mrs Bird. She knew I was going and arrived the night before I left, though Scott had met her and spent time with her. My plan was to get up very early in the morning, pack what I needed and leave, before Ron got back from work and before Scott woke up. It was important for me to get away without having to say goodbye to Scott again, which I'd done when I tucked him in the night before.

The memory that lingers is that everything was going to plan

*that morning: Scott was still asleep, I'd got ready, I'd made it
to the front door, and as soon as I opened the front door, Scott
cried out 'Mummy! Mummy, where are you?' That was the
moment of truth for me. I either walked through that door then
or I never walked through it. I'll never forget that moment. It
changed my whole life. It was one of those decisions when you
know whatever you decide will be right, but it will be your
destiny. It took everything I had to make one more step across
that threshold and to close the door behind me, with him
crying for me. The last thing I heard was Mrs Bird getting up
to go to him.*

*I got in the car and drove to the Western border of Ohio, to
stay with my mentor, the woman I worked with in the
prosecutor's office. She was the only one who accepted me non-
judgementally through all of this. I was also having an affair
at the time – I have all kinds of rationalisations for that too,
like boredom – and he was supposed to be making the drive
with me for some support, but he didn't, so I felt even more
alone. There was an overwhelming sense of total aloneness and
emptiness. I remember crying all the way and wondering if I
would ever get there. I was crying so hard that I couldn't see
the road. But I did get there and being with that woman was
such a relief: I didn't have to justify anything.*

*I didn't think of going to my mother's: we'd fallen out when
my father died and I found her very unsupportive. We were
close when I was little, but we've never made up that rift. One
of the earliest social judgements I had was from her. When I
told her, she said, 'How can you leave your new house and all
your beautiful things?' She didn't even mention the people I
was leaving! Interestingly, in my current relationship, my
partner is in a similar situation in that his ex-wife and their
teenage son live in Canada. The hardest thing for me has been
with his parents – for seven years they've been very judgemental
about me having left my son: What kind of a person could I be
to have done that? I feel they're still sitting in judgement on
something I did 18 years ago.*

*The first six months were traumatic. I was still being pulled
back, emotionally and physically. We talked about getting back*

*together, but it never happened: Ron wanted me to come back,
but only on his conditions, which were punitive. He wanted me
to sign an agreement that I would never leave again, and if I
did he would retain both custody and the whole house. So
though it was a fantasy for a while, I realised there was no
such thing as going back.*

*I had to support myself, so the first thing I did was set about
getting a job. Ron was keeping the house and giving me half
the market value, but there was no maintenance. Until I was
financially established, I shared a flat with a friend. She lived
near my mother, so it was easy to have Scott from there. I saw
a lot of him then, every weekend and some evenings during the
week: he was four years old, still pre-school. I got an exciting
job, doing administration at Cleveland Opera House and rented
a beautiful apartment in a community with a swimming pool. I
was beginning to settle down, then everything changed around
access and Scott.*

*The divorce was finalised in April 1974, but less than six
weeks later on June 1, Ron remarried! It was a woman whom
he'd dated briefly before, who had been married to the same
man twice and had one daughter, two years younger than
Scott. They formed another nuclear family, which fed nicely
into my rationalisation that I'd done the right thing, giving
Scott a stable family environment. Though again, unconsciously,
it gave me more freedom to pursue my own life.*

*After their marriage I moved away to Washington DC, taking
up my law career again. The relationship with Scott was very
close at times, but patchy – he'd started school and I came
home about once every six weeks to see him. It was strained
because he was being fed conflicting messages, told I wasn't
really his Mummy any more, that he didn't have to do what I
said, that he had a new Mummy, things like that. I didn't feel
jealous of her being married to Ron, but I did feel jealous of
her being with Scott more than I was.*

*They were married about six years and during that time
Scott went through a deeply disturbed period. He would
suddenly go berserk, not knowing what to do with his anger.
Guilt isn't one of my primary emotions, but that's one of the*

things in my life I do feel guilty about. I'm not trying to deny my responsibility in it all, but I do think Scott's difficulties were primarily due to Ron's marriage and what was happening there. Because I realised Scott was disturbed, I made a choice to come back from Washington to be closer to him. He was about 10 then. In fact, that problem with his anger has remained something of a life pattern for him, and as I'm very far away now, and he doesn't come to England very often, I feel rather helpless to support him. When he does come over, I pay for him to have therapy – which he asked for himself – and my hope is that he will come for a more extended period of time and do more.

Anyway, the wife had an affair, got pregnant by someone else, had an abortion, and the marriage broke up. Ron's now married for the third time. A pattern's emerged there. In the hiatus between marriages we get along fine: Ron's very friendly with me, we talk and communicate, take Scott to camp together, go out for a meal, very civilised. But as soon as he's married I become the other woman, a wicked, nasty person. It's a pattern that got established with his second wife and it made it increasingly difficult for me to see Scott. I had to go to court to petition for visitation rights. Ron countered by suing me for child support – which was very unusual then – me being the woman and the man having custody of the child. But he won, the bastard won. I was making good money by then and I never resented giving any to Scott, but I did resent the wife getting the benefit of it. Hearing of things she bought, a new swimming pool, all on my money! That's quite a classic thing when there are two families involved. And the pattern got worse. The third wife would even stop me talking to Scott on the phone. They'd hang up on me, though he was a teenager by then. Unbeknownst to his father and the family, I had to arrange clandestine meetings with my son.

There were some horrendous scenes for Scott in those two marriages, but as a result my relationship with him became closer: I was the only escape for him from his distressed situation at home. The more his relationship with Ron deteriorated, the more I was the person who provided sanity,

*some alternative for him. I hung on to that. To be able to
provide difference for him: a different way of thinking, a
different way of being in the world. So he and I have ended
up being closer than he and Ron, even though he lived with
him all those years.*

*When Scott was a child, he wanted to play the flute; his dad
wanted him to play the trumpet. That says it all. He wanted to
dance; his dad made him play baseball. When he went to
university, his passion in life was drama and art; his dad
made him do something practical, journalism, which bored him
to death. After a year of it, he left, at which point his dad
threw him out of the house, both for leaving university and for
having his ear pierced! Our relationship got even stronger then.
Ron's still the stereotypical male living out a very macho
existence and Scott didn't want that life. He didn't want the
traditional path, growing up, having children, getting a stable
job. He's a Piscean, very creative, artistic, and as he's grown
up he's seen the difference between my giving him permission to
be what he is and his dad wanting him to be an all-American
boy. He hasn't spoken to his dad for at least four years. He's
now sharing a house with friends, has some acting and
directing jobs, doing in a small way what he wants to do in a
big way. The nice thing about my relationship with him now is
that we can be with one another out of wanting to be together,
not out of a sense of obligation. That totally changes the
quality of our relationship.*

*My career went from strength to strength in the States. I did
what I'd set out to do, completed my university degrees at the
same time as working full-time, made a success of my career. I
was making more money than Ron. I decided to come to
England to do a Ph.D. but it meant selling all my belongings
and using up all my savings. I had to cut the golden handcuffs,
leave the corporate ladder-climbing and success of America.
Ron agreed Scott could come over every summer and every
other Christmas – if I paid his fare – but in the event he
refused to let him come and I had to take him to court to make
him fulfil his obligations around visitation. He was constantly
lying to the courts, and that time he won again. In the end, it*

felt as if the system was punishing me for having chosen to leave Scott with Ron in the first place: if you're a woman who can do that, then we're not going to rule for you. But acrimony led to more acrimony. Because the court ruled against me, I finally stopped paying child support.

I've done a lot of work on all this. Whilst doing my Masters degree, my work led me back into personal development, and I went into Gestalt therapy for a couple of years. That gave me an acceptance of what I'd done rather than trying to find a justification for it. I realised that it was the path I'd been on and needed to take; that, yes, Scott had some problems because of it, but everyone has their own set of issues to work on and that if you look at it in more esoteric terms, these were the issues he was meant to have in this lifetime: in some way he chose them. So I came to accept it in a different way.

The pain of not having had a child of my own went on for about 20 years, but I've had plenty of opportunity to work it through. Two years after we adopted Scott I got pregnant, but miscarried after 13 weeks. A year later I got pregnant again and exactly the same thing happened, we were told a successful pregnancy was impossible and we'd decided to adopt a second child when the divorce happened. I'm what they call an 'habitual aborter': I went on in my life to have seven more miscarriages, the last one four years ago. So after having left Scott, after having had two miscarriages in my marriage and seven since then, I've come to a strong belief that my destiny in this lifetime is not about mothering in the traditional sense. It's about something else which is related to developing new ways of being – for both women and men.

I'm not a fatalist in the sense of thinking there is only ever one choice, but I do think my path is one of destiny – that the work I've eventually got involved in and the decisions I was presented with and made that brought me here were destiny-laden. I feel the work we're doing in our partnership now is important socially and globally: working with underlying values and assumptions that determine behaviour in organisational settings, encouraging different ways of thinking and being in the world. It's rooted in new paradigm ideas about the world, a holistic rather than a Cartesian world view.

I always thought of myself as having a masculine energy. In the States I would find it easier to be with men than with women, especially in a work context. It was only when I came to Europe that I found my feminine side again, through consciously getting in touch with my spirituality, in a way that wasn't attached to any religion. The work I do now helps me blend the masculine and the feminine. It's to do with holding, supporting, nurturing, helping people through transitions – in life and organisations – working through blocks which are deeply rooted in childhood experiences.

I'm a Sagittarian, very future-orientated, into major change and transition. My work's all about change. Another reason for this drive is that I was never met as a child, never accepted for who I was. My mother had a series of careers, but she had been at home since I was born. I was a 'mistake', I was born when she was 41. My only sibling, my sister, was 18. I remember my parents as mature adults, not people I could play with. Everyone in my family was at least one generation older than me, so I couldn't be a child, I was always needing to be older and bigger. I had to grow up very quickly and be an adult in order to understand and be accepted. So I leapt through my adolescence, missed out on play and mess, matured very quickly, and in a way, that all made it easier to leave Scott: there was always a very deep impulse and motivation in me to move on, to seek major change.

I know there were lots of women who left their children in the thirties and forties, so leaving a child in the seventies wasn't really pioneering, but it sure as hell did feel like it.

16

The Dark Side of the Moon: Alternate Archetypes of Mothering

this is really . . . about choices. It is . . . not only about
the choice to parent from outside a traditional (and in
many ways outmoded) family structure, but about
choosing to see that choice as possible, positive,
energizing, brave, freeing, and right.

Harriet Edwards *How Could You?*

Ruth, who left her two children with their father when they were nine
and seven, refutes many of the usual theories about mothers who leave.
She has not been socially deprived, her husband was not abusive, nor
did she feel she wanted to pursue an ambitious career. She shares joint
custody, there was a minimum of acrimony during the break-up and
no legal wrangles. She has maintained regular and frequent contact
with her children and their relationships seem to have suffered no
damage. Ruth's account is unusually positive and optimistic, a
welcome contrast to some of the stereotypes and doom-laden myths of
guilt that prevail. She lives near a city centre in the southwest of
England and now paints full-time.

*I'll start with the time leading up to the separation. I was
married in total for 12 years, so then it had been about 8 or 9.
I appeared to be wonderfully happily married – to a doctor, a
GP – and we lived in the English countryside, with an old mill
house, four acres, a trout stream. We had lived in London and
then moved to the countryside together, but that was the
beginning of the end. My ex-husband was a delightful person,
but I became more and more frantic in my activities, desperate
to get away from the house. I love the countryside but I'd
always been a city person and I felt I was locked in this house*

*in the heart of the country, being nothing but a chauffeur the
whole time for the children.*

I was brought up on Hollywood and magazines and on the
surface it must have appeared I had the ideal life, a happily-
ever-after story. How could I have the cheek to leave this
perfect man and this perfect house and my perfect two
children? That was very difficult to deal with. To realise I was
that desperate. There's a wise saying that Ram Dass quotes:
'Freedom is not possible until you realise you are in gaol.' A
couple of years ago, in a writing group, I wrote about that
discontented phase at the mill and the whole piece was full of
terror and fear. I remembered how reluctant I would be to go
inside. I found it very difficult being in the house, I'd feel
under a great physical pressure. I preferred to be an outsider,
standing looking through the window, watching the family
inside.

So I got caught up in all sorts of frantic activities that would
take me away from home. I joined different courses, rushed off
to London, I'd drive for three hours to go to disco dance
classes! Paul was so nice, the thought didn't even enter my
mind of us separating. There wasn't anything I could pin-point
that he was doing wrong to make me want a divorce: that was
the difficult side of it. And of course I didn't want to leave the
children.

I'd always had a very free, exciting life. I was an air
stewardess for a while, and I spent 10 years living in America.
After school I went to teacher training college and did a year's
teaching in London – I would stand at assembly and there'd be
this smell of stale urine and I'd think 'this is not for me, there
must be something else to life!' So I seem to be the kind of
person who has to be free, or involved in something that's vital.
I always found it very easy to attract men so I knew I wouldn't
be on the shelf, I'd get married and have children. But I left it
as late as possible, partly because I was too busy and I didn't
really want to be tied down.

I feel I married Paul because it was time and he was a very
nice man, an appropriate father for my children. It was a
marriage worked out in my head rather than my heart. Having

children was part of the programming, part of the Hollywood image for a woman. I married quite late, so I didn't have my children till I was 38 and 39 and though after they were born everything still appeared gay and busy and I was going to the local art college for courses, there was that frantic quality to everything. Eventually, I couldn't help becoming aware just how extreme my behaviour was. I'm sure it was all part of trying to remain young.

Then I met a man who was younger, very open and free, with all kinds of interesting philosophy. It was playful, getting away from what I felt were my heavy responsibilities at home and we had a relationship, though my husband didn't know that. It was through many talks with him that the seed of the idea was planted that it was possible for me to separate and to leave the children. I started to think about that more and more, and whether it actually was possible for me. Eventually – after a couple of years – I said something to my husband about it. Paul suggested that I go to a psychotherapist and see if I could talk it out. I went for a while to a Jungian-based therapist in London, and that confirmed the fact that I really must get out of what I experienced as a trap. So I felt it was internal forces that made me leave, not external ones. I certainly didn't leave in order to be with the man I was having a relationship with – that had nothing to do with it. It was just a terrible desire to be free of the heavy responsibilities. Yet I was also torn because I felt I couldn't leave the children.

I read theories that by the time children reach seven, there isn't quite the same need for the mother, they're no longer in such a delicate formative period. So, everything put together, I decided that was the time to go. I organised for a housekeeper to take over and look after them when I left, we hadn't had one before. There would be stability: the children would still be in the same house, at the same school, with the same familiar surroundings and people, my ex-husband was still doctoring. So I went off and it was such a tremendous relief being away. Yet the actual parting was awful.

I have a very strong psychic connection with my daughter, and she seems to have been the one who was most strongly affected by my leaving. My son was always much closer to his father, my daughter to me. Even though it was implied I was just going away for three months for rest and rehabilitation, with the option of coming back, my daughter seemed to know that I was really leaving and that was it. There was a terrible scene with her, as she tried to hang on to me. I just felt I had to get away for a while: I didn't know at that time I was definitely going for good.

I went down to France for three months. And when I came back, there was no way I wanted to go back into the same domestic situation. Yet though one part of me knew I was doing the right thing, there was another part that was carrying an awful burden of guilt: what am I doing to the children? And so on.

My first meeting with them was very interesting: we got into the car to drive to the area where I was living at the time and immediately my daughter said 'Mummy, why did you leave us?' I told them – I suppose this was my way of working it out in my head – that I felt it wasn't them I left, but Paul, and that the circumstances were such that I had no way of providing them with such a good home, school, all of the comforts they had with him, because I was out without a job, staying in a bed-sit, on the dole . . . There was just that one question: why did you leave us? And they seemed very content with the answer. I don't think they wanted lots of explanations, only a simple answer.

Then I got into a routine with them. I would have them for half of the holidays, all of half term and every other weekend or every three weeks. I've always made sure I live within reasonable travelling distance of them. We'd crowd into my little bed-sit. It was an adventure for them, in a way. Often when people split off, children object to the new partner, but I was still with the younger man, and probably because he was so young and lively and such a clown, they loved him. They still talk about him very lovingly. I think that helped considerably: to have the support of someone the children really loved.

Even though I was wondering where the next penny was

going to come from, to eat – it was a luxury to have juice or fruit – I was so much happier and felt so much freer, I realised how terribly weighed down I'd been during the last part of my marriage. Gradually, I became more established. I set up a craft business on the Enterprise Allowance Scheme and bought this house of my own which provided better accommodation for them. We're still in that routine now: they're in the same place in the country and they come to me, in the city, every two or three weekends. That's a delightful balance. I can't go for more than three weeks without seeing them, or I get uneasy. When we used to have family holidays and Paul and I were together with them, they'd play us off against one another dreadfully. But this way, it's wonderful. I can be totally with them.

When I went back to the area where the family lived, I was surprised by the amount of support I got. I was wary of meeting parents of the other children, old friends, yet I got a tremendous amount of love and support from them. A lot of them said oh, how brave of you. The only disapproval was from the older generation. A bit from my parents, though not too much: it was mostly that they were terribly worried. There was I with a secure home, a doctor husband, material possessions and, as my father was an artist, things had always been precarious for them financially, so they'd wanted that security for me and here I was on the dole. And they were sad for the children.

My own home life: I was the only child, born just before the war, so I was sent down to nursery school at the age of 18 months, then to boarding school. So I went through the equivalent of boarding school from 18 months till I was 8. When some of this came out in my therapy, my mother's reaction was deeply defensive: she had to be in London, there was no way she could keep me there, and so on, so she obviously felt guilty. My mother herself was adopted as a baby. Her parents lived in South Africa and her father wouldn't accept having children, so her mother came to London and gave her up to adoption at birth, then went back to her husband in South Africa.

So my mother was abandoned at birth. I was abandoned at

*18 months. And I abandoned my children at seven years. I find
the repetition that runs through families, one generation to
another, quite amazing. I did think to myself well, at least it's
as if we're making the gap a little longer.*

*My mother's dead now, but I talked to her about it at the
time and when she was ill. The best talk I had with her was
when she was dying: I spent a lot of time with her then. They
were still living in the same flat where I was brought up from
the age of eight. She was sleeping in the room that I had used
as a child and I was in the room that she had been in as the
mother. We were very aware of how our roles had reversed.
Incidentally, after my mother died, my father married the
lodger – they were both aged 74 – and emerged from his shell
and is now gloriously happy. There wasn't that good a feeling
between my parents, I'd urged them to part many times, but
they felt it was their duty to stay together.*

*Apparently after I left there was a domino effect in the
community where we lived: marriages started moving around,
breaking up, partners moving here and there. Paul was
considered to be a highly eligible man in that area, and the
women flocked around him. But he was very hurt, very
unhappy for a while. I think it was extremely insulting to him,
as well as a shock, he hadn't realised how distant we'd
become. He tends to look on the positive side of things and
buries everything else underneath. Quite quickly another family
moved in with him, a girlfriend of mine, with her two
daughters. I thought it was wonderful – I had a friend in there
to make it easier to be friends with Paul – and the children got
on quite well, though she's since moved again, so they're
separate families.*

*But Paul has a very spiritual side to him and he was trying
to deal with it all in the best way. I feel that's why we've
managed to stay on reasonably good terms with one another.
Not that I follow any particular spiritual practice. After a
boarding school that was high Church of England, run by
nuns, I've always avoided formal religion, and though I'm
interested in various ideas, I'm scared of dogma. While we
were in London Paul got involved with a Buddhist group and I*

felt he drifted further away. There was a feeling of distancing because of the Buddhism and that may have contributed to our moving apart. Although there were wonderful things in it, I objected to it: maybe because at the time I was bogged down under piles of nappies! But we did both go to the Krishnamurti lectures and that was the beginning of my looking into the spiritual side of things, which has grown in the last few years.

After I left, Paul organised a divorce as soon as possible. There were some tense moments, but I was determined not to use lawyers. I said that if two people followed the teachings of Krishnamurti it should be possible for them to sort things out themselves. We organised joint custody of the children, though there was no way I could contribute much financially, I was having trouble supporting myself. It took a while to agree over some things, like a few antiques I'd bought before the marriage as insurance for my old age, but in the end, we worked it out.

There was one thing I found particularly consoling. Quite apart from all those theories about needing to be happy in yourself in order to relate well to your children, a counselling friend told me some interesting statistics about families that have split up. He showed me research that showed that children of parents who are separated reasonably amicably are much better adjusted than children in a family that has stayed together nominally but has all the tensions lying underneath. That was probably my greatest comfort during that time immediately after the separation: having a concrete statistic to hang on to.

It wasn't until my late thirties that I actually started to be creative, first with ceramics – whilst I was a stewardess, I did some art dealing, and dealt in oriental ceramics – then painting. I'd always avoided graphic art because my father was so good at it, but I started to paint when I was in San Francisco. So my creativity had already been starting to emerge when I got married, but it had to fit in between children and nappies, and though I managed to negotiate that fairly well in London, I couldn't in the country. It's funny how men just go for things they want, and don't let anything get in the way, but women find it hard.

It was as if I was in a complete dream during adolescence and only at 28, 29, that I started to wake up. Till then, I had no image of myself whatsoever, apart from trying to copy Hollywood images of women. I had no feeling of self-worth. I just accepted anyone, any man, that came along.

There's a book by Jean Shinoda-Bolen, an American psychologist, called The Goddess in Everywoman, *which discusses the various goddesses as images of different sides of yourself. And I found myself identifying with Aphrodite, the goddess of love. For some reason, I seemed to have an aversion to the mothering image: I don't want to identify with the archetype of the mother, there's something about it that makes me uncomfortable. Yet my mother commented to me that what she really loved to watch in my relationship with my children was how physical I was with them, how loving. I've always had a strong physical bond with them, which she never had with me.*

I was always really grateful to my mother for the amount of freedom she gave me. I was an avid tomboy and I never played with dolls, maybe that should have given me a clue! And my mother always encouraged me to go away on trips, explore, she was happy I saw so much of the world as an air stewardess. I think I may have been living out things for her, her own travelling for example, in the 1930s, in places like Hungary, that had come to an end when she became pregnant. And maybe it was her discomfort with mothering that I inherited. She was never the huggy kind of mother. She'd talk things through rather than cuddle you, so though there was strong support from her, it was distanced, at one remove.

And I can see I'm now doing the same thing for my children, being the kind of mother that stimulates and supports, giving them their freedom rather than holding them too close. I feel I'm now acceptable as a mother, but it's a mother of a different kind from the traditional archetype. And the children appreciate it too, as I did, they make very positive comments about it.

My son's at the age where he's becoming very interested in girls and recently, when I asked about his love life, he told me he wasn't intending to marry early. 'I'm going to wait until I find the perfect woman', he said, then paused. 'Like you, Mum!' I had to laugh. It sounded so neatly lifted out of the psychiatrist's text book. Yet what a gift. Here I was, a Mum who had deserted her children, being told I was the perfect woman. It was such a delightful absolution of guilt.

My daughter often asks for reassurance that I love her. On one visit, she asked if we could consult the I Ching. She asked a couple of vague questions, but they were just the run up to the real question she had in mind: 'Does my mother really love me?' The reply was along the lines of: 'Like the dark side of the moon, one shines although unseen. The waxing moon is not always visible.' We both immediately interpreted it as meaning my love for her was always shining for her, even though I couldn't always be there physically. She was the one who put it into words.

I appreciate now the combination of being without my children – the amount of freedom that gives me to get on with my art and my own life – and the wonderful love that I get from them. That's overwhelming, absolutely wonderful. So it's satisfying both sides of me. I feel that my ex-husband and I offer the children two totally different sides of life, and each is equally valid. My conclusion is that children love you no matter what you do. If desperation causes you to split up the family, then you must move on to your new life with total conviction.

17

Fatal Attraction:
Leaving by Default

... we will also gradually learn to realize that that
which we call destiny goes forth from within people,
not from without into them.

Rainer Maria Rilke Letters to a Young Poet

Charlotte's story is one of the most dramatic in this book. Her four
children were kidnapped by their father and – now teenagers of 19,
18, 15 and 14 – have been living in Costa Rica for the last decade,
where Charlotte has been allowed no physical access to them. Her
attempt to regain them legally led to imprisonment. Added to the
physical violence inflicted on her during her marriage and her
difficult early circumstances, all this might have conspired to make
Charlotte define herself as a victim, but she argues passionately
against such a position. It is her conviction that we have to take full
responsibility not only for what we do, but for what happens to us.
So even though her children's abduction was against her conscious
will – and she has strongly resisted it – she acknowledges that we may
play an unconscious part in shaping the events in our lives.

So although Charlotte's account is one of leaving by default, it throws
light on many cases of mothers separated from children and insists that
we look at the whole issue in a wider perspective, one that does not
simply put the blame 'out there' on husband or social pressures. Now
happily settled with her partner in the southwest of England, Charlotte
has a successful private healing practice, working with Chinese
medicine and shiatsu.

*I met Tim on my first day at university. Fatal attraction, it was.
I was studying Geography, he was reading Spanish and
Portuguese. That was 1969, we lived together for a while. It*

was complicated, but basically after two years we both dropped out of university and got caught up with a group that was then known as Children of God: the Jesus people.

It was a hippy, Evangelical American religion, where you surrender all your money and possessions to them and they pay for and control everything you do. You live in communes and convert other people to Christianity, to the group. It's a form of brain-washing. The aim is to convert the world.

It seems inconceivable now, but in the climate of the late sixties and early seventies, with everybody dropping out of tight social structures, it seemed a good alternative. Ironically, most of the people drawn to the group were very intelligent. So Tim and I joined and under their leadership, we got married – I'm convinced we would never have done otherwise – first in the group, then at a registry office. They wanted to send us abroad and you had to be married for that. We were sent to the States, then to Central America. By this time we were both totally under their control and it was extremely difficult to get out. They don't approve of or practice any form of birth control, so I got pregnant almost immediately and we had our first child a year after we got married, in Costa Rica. Fourteen months after that, I had the second one in Colombia. We were still with the group, but things were getting dire. There was a lot of coercion, dreadful treatment, and whatever Christian faith I had before soon went out of the window. Some of the experiences I went through were horrific.

If I questioned what was going on, they'd tell me I was possessed of the devil. At one stage, when I was pregnant with my first child, they took me to a hut in the middle of the jungle in Costa Rica and left me there for two weeks, on my own, with no food supply, to purge me of the Devil! I laugh about it now – there was nothing to eat – so one day, I caught a frog. It took me half a day to catch a frog and then I couldn't eat it! I just ate leaves and whatever there was. I was really very ill. But I'm a resilient kind of person. It didn't change me. If anything, those experiences hardened me. I still continued to openly question them, argue with them, though I wasn't allowed to mix with the rest of the group.

In the end Tim and I both felt we had to leave, so in 1974, when the second baby was 10 days old, we borrowed money from the British Embassy and returned to England. We found jobs as residential social workers, then heard they needed a married couple to run a drugs project in the southwest. It was run by a charity and had a strong Christian element, so we moved down here and had the other two girls, in fairly quick succession. That was a conscious decision. I wanted them, because I love children. It wasn't for Tim.

The marriage started to go wrong before the birth of my last daughter, though for a long time it had been a question of sheer survival rather than happiness. Between 21 and 27, I'd had four children. We were constantly in dire straits, no money and my parents had disowned me since I joined the group. Tim and I rowed most of the time. I'd never really loved him. Initially it had been total infatuation, then there was the group involvement, and you end up on a kind of roundabout, wondering how you got on, but not knowing how to get off. During my final pregnancy I was ill and had to go into hospital for over a month. On my first night back, after the baby was born, Tim told me he'd been having an affair with my best friend. That finished the relationship for me.

It was around that time too that he'd got drawn back into the organisation again. As well as being called 'the Children of God', they were called 'the family of love', and they'd altered their premises slightly and were now advocating prostitution to get converts. It was all over the papers, in about 1977–78, women being used sexually to win converts. Tim used that ploy as an excuse for going to bed with my friend, then with other women. We'd bought a house and he invited members of the religious group to live there with him: there wasn't much I could do. I refused to sleep with him any more, so we had a period when he frequently raped me within the marriage and beat me up, late at night, when the girls were in bed. Several times he knocked me out; once he strangled me till I blacked out; another time he put me in hospital with a very badly broken nose.

This went on for about 18 months after the birth of the last

child. I was desperately unhappy, at a very low ebb. I would
abuse any substance that would put me out of my head:
alcohol, drugs on prescription, morphine, to blank out what
was going on. In the end, because of all the mental and
physical cruelty, I had a breakdown. One Saturday afternoon,
Tim was out with the girls. I couldn't see any point in living. I
took 150 paracetomol, went unconscious. I only survived
because a friend of mine had sensed something was wrong and
broke in. I was in the general infirmary for 10 days then I was
taken to a psychiatric hospital. I don't remember the first
couple of weeks there: I was on heavy-duty drugs. When I
became lucid, I wondered what the hell I was doing in a place
like that, but it was very difficult to get out. They suggested we
have family therapy. We had two sessions. The psychiatrist told
me it was Tim who had all the problems, but as he hadn't
done anything, they couldn't treat him. Tim was very
inadequate: a Mummy's boy, he slept in his mother's bed till he
was a teenager. I think that was why, in the end, he couldn't
let go of the children, he just couldn't cope without them. And
they all look like me: he's living with four constant reminders
of me.

I was in hospital for two months. When I came out, Tim
wanted a divorce and to take all the children to South America
with him to rejoin the group. I refused, he taunted me, saying
it was a pity I hadn't succeeded in killing myself and to try
again. I couldn't cope with the abuse, so I went back into
hospital for another 10 days. Meantime I consulted a solicitor,
who told me there was a very good chance I would get custody
of all the children. When I next came out of hospital, Tim said
he was taking the eldest two girls away on holiday to visit
friends. I objected, but he beat me up again, quite badly, and I
couldn't stop him taking them. They just disappeared. The
eldest was eight and the second one six.

I saw a solicitor then, protected the youngest two by making
them wards of court and got interim custody. But I discovered
Tim had taken the eldest two to Costa Rica, where he'd joined
the group again. I didn't realise that was where they were
going. He wrote and said God had told him to do that. You

*don't argue with God! So for about three months I had the
youngest two on my own: one went to nursery school, the other
started school, I was back working, we got into a good routine.
At half-term, I decided we needed a holiday and took them to
Majorca for a week. We had a great time, but whilst I was
there I had what I can only describe as a vision. I was
walking with the children on the beach and I remember my
heart pounding, feeling I couldn't walk any further. I suddenly
knew that Tim was going to come and take the youngest two
children away. Reason said it was totally illogical, he was
abroad, I had custody, they were wards of court, but my heart
knew.*

*We came back and on one long weekend they went to see
their grandparents, Tim's parents, as they did quite regularly. I
was due to pick them up on the Sunday evening. At lunchtime,
I had a phone call from Tim at Gatwick airport: they were all
about to board the plane, he said I wouldn't see the youngest
two children again. His parents had been complicitous in the
whole thing. I immediately contacted my solicitor, but by the
time all the calls were made, the plane had taken off.
Subsequently I received another letter from Tim, saying God
had told him to take those children too. He gave no other
reason. The version he gave the children was that I was
mentally ill and couldn't look after them. So they all went to
live in Costa Rica in 1981.*

*It took about six months for it to sink in. I was just left
numb. I didn't believe it was actually happening to me. I've
been on automatic pilot ever since. I'm not a person for tears,
I've never cried about them going, not even in therapy. It's a
strange feeling: a full-time mother one minute and nothing the
next. It's totally disorientating. What is your role in life? Where
are you going? What do you do?*

*At first I went from one disastrous relationship to another, not
wanting to be alone. Then on 1 January 1982, four months after
the kids had gone, I met Kate. I hadn't had a relationship with
a woman before then, and wasn't specifically looking for one,
but it felt right and natural and we've been together ever since.
It wasn't a conscious or ideological decision, it wasn't a matter*

of turning away from men, I have a lot of good male friends, though I know I couldn't have had this same kind of partnership with a man.

If people know I live with Kate, they invariably assume my husband took the kids because I'm in a relationship with a woman, and then there's that implicit assumption of blame. So they avoid the subject, or they hold back from asking me how the children are because they don't want to upset me. It triggers people's distress. Especially with women who are mothers, there's this immediate identification with what they assume is my distress, imagining I must be suffering to a point where I can't manage. 'I've got children, I don't know how I'd cope if something happened to them . . .' But I'm happy to talk about them.

The relationship with Kate affects the story of trying to get the children back, for she was very supportive and helped me financially. After a television programme about a similar case, we hired the same private detective to trace the children and reclaim them, though it was made difficult by the great distances involved between here and Central America. It was an administrative nightmare: the amount of paper work was incredible. But we did finally locate them and a year after they'd gone we too went to Costa Rica – the detective and his assistant, myself and Kate.

The plan was that whilst Tim was away on business in Panama, we would get the children. It sounds very simple! They were ultra-sensitive to the presence of foreigners as, coincidentally, Ronald Reagan was visiting that week, but Tim had connections with the police in Costa Rica and was probably tipped off about our arrival. The police suddenly raided our motel and the four of us were arrested for attempted kidnap, and thrown in gaol.

We were taken to police headquarters and locked into separate cells. There were no windows, no lights, no bed, just the floor. After about five hours I was taken out at gun-point to see the chief of police, with an interpreter. They had our papers, and I asked how I could be accused of kidnapping my own children, but the chief kept saying the papers were false and I'd be in gaol for 8 to 10 years. I know it sounds melodramatic, but that's exactly how it was. I couldn't believe it was happening to me. We were kept in that gaol overnight, then the next day Kate and I were taken together to a women's maximum security prison and the detective and his assistant were put in the men's equivalent. There was still no charge.

The prison was quite humane, run by nuns, though with armed guards outside. We pretended we didn't understand a word of Spanish so we didn't have to co-operate with any of the cleaning. The food was terrible. It was a nightmare in that prison, the conditions and atmosphere. There were a lot of terrorists there on heavy charges. Eventually, through another prisoner, we got a female lawyer who managed to get us out.

One of the conditions of our release was that we had to leave the country immediately. I was allowed to see the children for three hours, with their father and lawyer present. It's hard to describe that meeting. It was very difficult, such an abnormal situation, but I tried to be as normal as possible. We'd just had two weeks in gaol, in terrible conditions, then we'd been plunged into this sudden meeting and didn't dare do anything that would risk re-imprisonment. The children were bemused – the youngest one was only three – and upset, having been told by Tim that I was mentally ill. So despite the extraordinary situation, I had to act normally and convey to them that I wasn't. There was no melodrama, no histrionics, no tears, nothing like that.

It was then I made a subconscious decision never to attempt to try to get the children back again. I felt it wasn't fair on them to get involved in a tug of war situation. If I had tried again, Tim would simply have moved them on, and this would have been unsettling and unfair. We learnt that Costa Rica and other Latin American countries don't recognise British law, so the custody order and wards of court made no difference. Also, men's rights over children were more dominant there.

After our return, contact with the children became sporadic. I used to write to them, but it was impossible to tell how much Tim interfered. Sometimes their letters didn't reach me for months. That's gone on for almost 10 years, though it's improved enormously since they're old enough to write and post letters themselves. I telephone regularly on birthdays and Christmas, but anything more is too expensive. Twenty minutes, half an hour, it's £40 or £50. I taught myself not to think about when I was going to see them next.

I'm legally separated, but I never got divorced because a judge would have to be satisfied with arrangements for the children, and I refuse to say I'm happy with them being where they are. For all I know, Tim might have divorced me in Costa Rica. There's still a warrant out for his arrest here because of his kidnapping the children, but he could easily sneak into Britain. He's now left the Jesus group and is running his own translating business. He was living with someone, but I never ask the girls about his relationships with women: I don't put them into that role. I don't speak to Tim. I have no desire to.

I'm not a quitter. Not long after they went, I realised I could let Tim destroy me, which may be what he wants to do, or I could get on with my life. So I decided I had to do something positive. I went to university and read Geology, which was what I'd originally wanted to do when I was 18. It's as if I've had two lives: the first was my mother's script and lasted until the children left. Then I started again on my own. It was as if it took such a drastic measure to release me to my own life and go on from there. I got my degree, then a Ph.D., but at the same time started to qualify in Shiatsu and studied Chinese medicine. I also went into psychotherapy for four and a half years and that changed my life. Till then, I'd always suffered from depression. The situation with the children had made that worse, but it pre-dated the kids.

My childhood was extremely unhappy. My relationship with my mother has always been fraught, I don't like her very much. She worked from when I was four and I was left alone most of the time, or looking after my younger brother. My mother was unavailable physically and emotionally, she couldn't give affection to either of us. I'd spend hours at school rather than go home, I couldn't wait to get away. By the time I went to university I was so unhappy I'd crave affection from anybody, I suppose that's why I was so easily seduced by Tim and the religious group. When I was in therapy, I had a vivid dream about being physically abused by my mother when I was a child. I'm sure it was true: it makes sense of why I can't bear being alone with her, the terrible discomfort of being in the same room. She knew when I had my breakdown, but she never visited. When I lost the children, my parents claimed to be devastated, but neither of them came to see me.

There's no emotional bonding between me and my mother at all. But the important thing is that the pattern has changed in relation to my own children, and with them it's totally different. I was always there for them, they went everywhere with me, we did everything together. I was so aware of what I hadn't had, I gave it to them. So there has always been a very strong bonding with them, even despite what's happened and the physical distance. I know I'm a really good mother. The paradox is that although the day-to-day mothering's been disrupted, my bonding with my children is very profound, and I'm a much better mother to my children in absentia than my mother was to me.

And the children know, they haven't forgotten. The letters I get from them are overwhelming. The eldest ones remember the tiniest things, films I took them to when they were four. They make me little presents, cards, pictures which say 'I love you' on them, totally spontaneously. And that love has never stopped: if anything, it's increased as they've become more aware and independent. We've got an incredible rapport. They write and tell me about falling in love, clothes, problems.

It's important to see how these things are inherited from one generation to another. My mother was a battered child. Battered by her own mother: twice she had her arm broken by her. My father was in the police force. He didn't actually batter her, but he had a violent temper and wouldn't speak to her for weeks on end. My husband battered me. So the mothering from my mother to me didn't happen, or rather it was abused, and the mothering of my children has been abused.

I don't feel anger about it. It's hard to describe, people think I'm mad seeing it like this, but I actually believe it was right that they went. Because if I was going to break that destructive cycle I'd inherited from my mother, it needed something as extreme as that to do it. It was very painful, but it was right, the whole negative cycle that gets reproduced between mother and daughter had to be stopped. I believe that's why these events had to happen. Otherwise I would never have responded and changed. I would never have been happy. The separation made me a better person. In my thirties I've been able to do what I couldn't do in my twenties because I had the children. I've enjoyed it. I don't believe I would have sorted myself out in the ways I have if the children had been with me all the time. I wouldn't have had time to change career direction, which I know has been the right thing for me to do. I feel very strongly that they were partly taken for this reason, and that I was destined to do what I'm doing now.

Chinese medicine has helped me see that a lot of these issues are inherited, particularly from our mothers. We go on carrying things they've handed down: we inherit our mothers' anger, we inherit our mothers' depression. I believe this very strongly: there's evidence of it all the time in the work I do now. Negative patterns and emotions that have been passed down from generation to generation. So many women are carrying their mothers' stuff, and our mothers were carrying their mothers'. We have to see that, to see we can finally stop it and not take it into ourselves. This isn't just to do with social conditions or political issues. It's a deeper knot of mothering, as if it's subconscious material that's inherited, emotions and complexes passed down in a deeper way. The important thing is to recognise something can be done about it now, the pattern can be stopped before it's passed on by us to our children. Undoing that cycle is part of the changing times, part of people's healing.

The work I do with people – physical and emotional healing – is very intuitive, and I don't think you can do that unless you've been through suffering yourself. The experiences I had took me further and deeper than many people ever go, and that was part of their meaning. I believe that we create our life circumstances, that in some way I created my own script, set up the circumstances that would lead me to working in a healing capacity. So I don't go for that line about our being victims. I believe that the situation with my children was created by me in some way: I created it in order to work on that inherited pattern, to break out of it and change it. I subconsciously needed those events to happen, so I could change. There's nothing passive about it: it's my destiny, subconsciously I made it. We have to take responsibility for writing our own scripts, we have to understand that it's in our own hands to make and change our circumstances. And because I created it, I know that when the time's right I'll see the children again, and that it will be fine.

I know people won't see it like this. Many mothers who lose their children resist seeing their lives in this way, and of course the media keeps them stuck. Most of the representations of women in circumstances similar to mine are that they are – and should be – utterly obsessed with getting their children back. Their lives come to revolve totally around children that have been gone for years. I get so angry with that kind of depiction. I've never seen a television or newspaper story of a woman who's been separated from her children and not been totally dominated by it. The media wants mothers who've lost their children to be obsessed with getting them back and mothers who've left their children to be obsessed with guilt. As if they've got nothing else. But it's not like that: there are a lot of women who do lose their children and just get on with their lives, do something positive with them.

There are such fixed notions of how women are supposed to respond in these extreme situations. I feel I'm expected to behave in very stereotyped ways. I'm meant to collapse and need loads of support. I should break down and cry and be completely useless and helpless. But I'm not that type of person. Of course I miss the children and it's hard when I'm with other children that are at ages at which I've never seen mine. I get pangs of wondering how it would have been, sometimes I feel deprived of part of their growing up, and I realise I've missed out. But it's how it is. It needn't be desperate.

I'm planning to go over and see them at Christmas. I feel it's right to go back now, just to visit. Tim can't keep them after they're 18 and as they're all completely bilingual and have expressed strong desires to come over here, they may come to live, or go to university. It will be more than 10 years since I've seen them, but I know that when it happens it will be fine.

Alma Mater:
Finding a Voice

Mythology offers many variations of the mother
archetype, as for instance the mother who reappears as
the maiden in the myth of Demeter and Kore; or the
mother who is also the beloved, as in the Cybele-Attis
myth. Other symbols of the mother in a figurative sense
appear in things representing the goal of our longing for
redemption, such as Paradise, the Kingdom of God, the
Heavenly Jerusalem.
Carl Jung 'The Mother Archetype' in *Aspects of the Feminine*

Leonie is a professional singer and voice therapist and has also
published autobiographical writings. At the time of our meeting, she
was living in a provincial British city with her male partner, a few
hundred yards from the home of her only child, Elizabeth. Elizabeth,
then aged 10, was living with Leonie's ex-husband, Francis.

Since the interview, though, Leonie has moved into the country a
few miles away. This reopened the issue of separation from Elizabeth,
who was given the option of choosing where she would prefer to live,
with her father or with Leonie and her new partner. After some
indecision, an educational scholarship in the city where her father
lived tipped the balance in his favour. Leonie describes this whole
episode as a turning point for them all, clearing away a debris of guilt
on her side (for this was her daughter's conscious choice, not hers)
and dissolving any doubts in Elizabeth's mind, for now she knew that
her mother wanted her to live with her and would have been prepared
to fight legally if that had been necessary. They now see each other
regularly on a weekly, sometimes fortnightly, basis.

As a prelude to our interview, Leonie shared with me some
photographs of an Indian female saint, Anandamayi Ma (1896–1982),

whom she regards as her spiritual mother. Her explanation of the central importance of Anandamayi Ma in her life throws interesting light on the whole question of the mother. For whereas a psychoanalytic tradition of thought, from Freud through Melanie Klein, would hold the quest for the good mother (including Leonie's) to be based in the personal unconscious – a nostalgic desire for a lost unity and wholeness with the mother – Leonie turns this idea on its head. Along with more transpersonal thinkers such as Jung, she takes the ideal of the good mother to be an image of lost spiritual wholeness. In marked contrast to an ego-based psychology which insists that the idealised mother figure is a lost personal goal, such transpersonal psychology holds her to be an image of lost spiritual perfection. Leonie's account is deeply informed by this more archetypal level of thought.

Elizabeth was born in 1982. At the time of her birth, my marriage was already very much under question but I was still under the thumb of my own conditioning. Unlike any relationship I'd had before or since, the marriage was very conservative, I think out of my great wish to please my own parental heritage, to come back into the fold. So there was a combination of deep unease and a wish, at some level, to make the marriage work.

My experience of the everyday world of matter – mother, Mater, the material world – was virtually nil. I was totally up and out of the body. But there was a very strong call to have a baby. The centre of my consciousness seemed to be focused on it, and that combined with my own conditioning to make me feel I ought to be having a child by now. I was all of 28. I think the wish to have a baby was something to do with the unconscious calling me down. And her birth was certainly the first real physical experience I had – save a remarkable first love affair which awakened my sexuality – there was something about the birth itself which really did awaken me to the pain and beauty of being on this planet. It was a rude awakening.

When we first met, when she was born, that was the first shock to my system. The shock of seeing her and being aware of her foreignness. I'd clearly had in my mind some expectation that she was going to be utterly familiar. So though I put my all into it, it was a surprise not to feel truly bonded with her as a baby. I breastfed her till she was 13 months, I loved breastfeeding her, I did everything according to my own natural response to her life. But the shock was realising that she hadn't come into my life to smooth over the edges and make everything all right but to really awaken me to the conflicts and tensions that were so alive in my unconscious, and of which I'd been sublimely – literally sublimely – unaware. I'd been living in another, almost 'angelic' realm. Elizabeth's birth burst into that. In astrological terms too, it was the time of the Saturn return. There were whole areas of myself that I wasn't acknowledging, wasn't really living, or allowing myself to live and Elizabeth brought them home to me even more clearly. Her arrival clarified and enhanced the weaknesses of my marriage rather than the strengths.

There was very poor communication in the marriage. Francis and I had never discussed how we were going to bring Elizabeth up. We had very separate ideas. He thought I was going to be the housewife and bring up Elizabeth full-time, whilst he would be the university teacher and go to work. So there was shattering disillusionment as a result, particularly on my part. We were also living in a house which was under construction. So there were all these different levels of disruption and re-creation.

I was also out of sync with my own mother and I wouldn't allow her to come near my daughter. That was very painful. I could not let her anywhere near. It's a long-standing difficulty with my mother, a very uncomfortable relationship. My mother is a very complex and conflicted soul. She was married to someone a lot older – my father was a bishop, he's retired now – we were a big family. She was required to bring up five children virtually single-handed with little money. We had no private income. And against her unconscious nature, against her very passionate, artistic, intelligent soul, she submitted her life to her husband. She's lived under that doctrinal, authoritarian, patriarchal stamp, she's really endeavoured to be obedient to authority. I have memories of being in church

*with her and her bowing as he walked up the aisle – the
archetypal priest, the high priest, so to speak. That connects to
her father's relationship with her, which was very powerful and
has never been consciously dissolved.*

*My father was rarely there, he was always writing sermons.
Basically, he was absent, mentally very alive and interesting at
that level, but out of his body and physically shy. I completely
idolised him and projected my love of spirit onto him. They
were Protestant, self-denying, austere. I took refuge in things
spiritual, particularly music. Music was my mother. My mother
was not a musician, so we couldn't communicate through that
either. She'd come to concerts where I was performing and I
knew she'd be crying. She's very much governed by the
emotions in a way that hasn't been cathartic for her. I feel
there's a fear of madness in her, actually. And I don't feel her
sexuality has ever been met. She's very much the little girl and
I was never able to entrust myself to her. I don't remember a
bonding, though I'm aware of her difficulty in wanting that. So
my mother feels unformed, very unformed, as a person.*

*There were five children, all girls, and I was in the middle,
the cross-carrier trying to make things all right, fearing my
mother's emotional atmosphere. There was a lack of trust there
that still exists. As to physical affection, hugs, I remember them
very little. My memory of what it was like to be with 'mother',
my experience of mothering, came largely through one of the
nurses we had. One particular one, Margy, gave me the first
sense of what it was like to be* mothered, *to feel that nurturing
mother. I must have been five or six. I was also much more at
home in nature, which was my other experience of mothering,
in the universal sense, a nature that instilled joy rather than
fear.*

*This mother-daughter pattern has gone one stage further now,
so that with Elizabeth there's a sense of history repeating itself,
in a much more overt and unconventional form. Our
generation has allowed for that, for things being manifested
rather than hidden, but of course the pain of it all is
accentuated too. I've been in psychoanalysis and done a lot of
analytic work myself on all this. Now I'm beginning to be able*

*to express my feelings more directly and honestly to Elizabeth:
how sometimes she has a constricting impact on my life, but at
the same time communicating to her my great love for her. It's
more like a friendship than a mother-daughter relationship.*

*[Then Leonie showed me a beautiful pastel portrait of herself
and her daughter. Elizabeth faces directly forwards, staring
wide-eyed at the viewer, whilst Leonie is in half-profile in the
background, her eyes focused out of frame.]*

*If you look at the two people in this portrait, they seem to
bear no relationship to each other. One is dreamy, looking out
and away, whilst the look of the other, Elizabeth, is direct. It's
here, immediate: she's very much like that. She can be very
demanding of life, of me, of people, she's competitive, right
down here, interested in whatever's happening, at school,
music, she's got to master it. She's unapologetically on the
earth.*

*I've always spiritualised things. I've protected myself with an
all-convincing spiritual cocoon. So in terms of my relationship
with Elizabeth, we have an enormous amount to learn from
each other. It's like a marriage of spirit and matter, another
opportunity to look at how those two worlds can meet. And it
goes through the generations: she's called me back, she's woken
up the thing that was sleeping in me – the thing that was also
asleep in my mother and that I took on – as if the pain can't
be escaped any more, things have to find form, come into
expression. But the other question in the light of that, which is
still an open but crucial question to me, is why I left her with
her father? If we have this important work to do together, how
could I leave her behind?*

*Because my mother was so enmeshed in the family scene, she
couldn't find herself. There wasn't enough* hara, *enough
intention she could generate on her own in that context to help
her. So, looking at the question in relation to my relationship
with my own mother, I know I had to leave. The first thing was
the horror of acknowledging that I might have to live in that
marriage for the rest of my life. I remember the loneliness of
that, thinking 'My God! Is this how it's going to be for the rest
of my life?' Lying in bed at night, next to somebody with whom*

you experience this immense *loneliness. I know it's common amongst a lot of women in marriages they try to see through. But I'm not attacking my ex-husband. Everything I say is said with a wish to be honest about this kind of story and it's in the context of a friendship which remains. I do respect him, Elizabeth's father, enormously. He has many fine qualities. He has been, and is, an extraordinary father. He's very steady, physically very healthy, active and caring. He's much more formed than I am at the everyday level, he manifests very well at that material level, and that's a great gift he's given Elizabeth.*

If I could have let myself be provided for, created a beautiful atmosphere in his house, looked after my daughter there, with all these sweet well-meaning friends, and been a pillar of society, a sort of spiritual inspiration . . . but I just couldn't do it. Francis was very upset when we separated, deeply sad and I'm not sure he's got over it. He's still angry. And he was very clear about Elizabeth not going with me: he refused to be a weekend father. That was the most powerful reason for Elizabeth staying at her father's base: he insisted on it. He needed her to be there, and he has learnt to father her well in many ways. She's got an immense sense of loyalty to him. Nothing short of confrontation and court struggles would have changed that and I wasn't strong enough to challenge him there.

Also, if I had taken her, I would have had to return to a more conventional way of life, which something in me didn't want to have to do. It would have been an enormous struggle. I had to leave Elizabeth in order to find myself. She was three and a half – very little. But the interesting thing was I couldn't go more than two hundred yards down the road! I knew it was important for her to know she wasn't stranded. It was so bizarre – my body would only go two minutes' walk away. It's as if I've created an illusion of still living with Francis, giving Elizabeth the feeling I'm still so close.

Before I left, I was desperate and profoundly lonely. Two years prior to Elizabeth's birth I had a physical stroke, a relapse in which my whole body seized up. All through that time, my unborn self was desperately crying out for help, not knowing where to get it. Paralysis from the neck downwards was my response. My head was the only thing left. I had to be carried around for three months. I think it was my way of expressing anger and despair. For many years my voice couldn't utter it.

After the paralysis, I took on a complete new lease of life. I went on a theatre-in-education tour, I accessed enormous resources and stamina, which hadn't been tapped before. I was so enthusiastic about working out in the world again, doing something imaginative that empowered me. Then I was involved with the peace movement in education and had an office in the house, which was very disruptive for Francis. He was wanting a settled home in which his wife would live and bring up the children. That's fair enough, it's the way a lot of people do it, but for me it was the ultimate imprisonment. So then I became increasingly depressed again, my soul ached, though on the surface I was still struggling to make the marriage work.

I wrote a lot, I cried a lot. I wrote poetry to try and maintain some sanity. There was also, if I'm honest, something quite exhilarating about the prospect of leaving the marriage. The feeling of excitement that comes with moving into new territory – the idea of breathing again, expanding out into the world, starting a new life. And I do remember a sense of relief following the separation. At the same time as torrents of guilt. You can feel guilt in the air, and that has followed me. Guilt about betraying Francis and my commitment to him, to our vows. We'd had a very beautiful Quaker marriage service. The power of the institution of marriage is quite extraordinary, a very real power when it's authentic. We were legally separated from 1985–1990 and divorced after my return from India. Francis was given care and control.

I've been doing more interior, spiritual, meditative work for the last 10 years and working with the interface between vocal expression and listening. That's been fascinating to me, probably because of my own lack of that experience – listening and expressing oneself authentically, without the double messages and social trappings that were there in my upbringing. Working with the voice is absolutely essential to me now. People finding their own voice. Of course the mother is the instrument for that: if you find yourself with the right mother, that naturally occurs. I know it's a very rare occurrence in the West but it's there in the much more instinctual way that the mother, say the African mother, will nurture and hold her offspring, completely without condition. It's very physical. Holding without conditions.

Where there is that experience between the child and mother – or where that holding force and presence can be provided elsewhere, as in therapy – it inevitably gives rise to something new. There's a chance for the person to dis-integrate and rediscover something out of the chaos behind their own conditioning. Everyone has a voice inside which is an absolutely natural expression of who they are. It's nothing dramatic, except it might be the first time the person's connected to it. They've forgotten what it is, who they are. But through the vehicle of the voice we can discover that matter and spirit are one and the same thing. Now I'm trying to make a real living from my singing and have just made an album.

It was music and silence that carried me across the threshold of my divorce. Plus a few important female friendships. I had a brief love affair with a woman prior to leaving, which connected me with the power of my female body. That was a very beautiful relationship, which has since matured into a loyal friendship. It gave me a lot of strength and self-confidence. Also I set up a women's group at that time to be a protective network.

Occasionally there's been a voice asking if I should go back. Particularly following the experience of being in India, when I became so completely unconcerned about 'personal development'. I realised that the outer karma doesn't really matter at all – you might as well just live out what you've come here to do, whatever's required. It's all unfolding, and all we have to do is let go of our attachments and aversions. All this personal questioning and change is just the activity of the ego! Trying to get beyond ego to the impersonal Self. That's really what my journey seems to be about. Yet I know that if I had gone back, I would be lying to myself, at my deepest level.

Psychoanalysis has been enormously helpful to me. It enabled me to start speaking my truth to Elizabeth, to tell her why it was I found it impossible to stay and not covering things up with an artificial sweetness and light. It empowered me to start taking my singing very seriously. Also, it's made me realise how my unconscious has created the very conditions I need in my life.

But it was my meeting with Anandamayi Ma in India a few years ago which has really seen me through. For the other side to it – which I've learnt from India and which is where I depart from psychoanalysis – is that the soul clearly has work to do. It chooses a context in which to come, a context which creates a certain kind of suffering, a particular sequence of painful events. If there's enough creative will or intention on the part of the person in those circumstances, they can realise that the situation provides the very conditions that they need to work on themselves. So I now see the situation with Elizabeth from that point of view. It happened in order to awaken me to these things.

I can't imagine having any children now, I can't see there'll be enough time, this time round. There was a dream I had last year in which Elizabeth was directly present. I was saying 'You are mine' and being very proud of it, very unapologetic about it. Not possessive, but a sense that we are of one flesh, really welcoming being her provider, her protector, her nurturer, her mother. Marion Woodman said to me at the time, 'Are you perhaps talking about your own inner girl?'[1] And of course they go together. One's own daughter is a manifestation in some way of where one is internally, either of what's unrevealed or of what's required. Children are the ultimate mirror, really. Elizabeth certainly is for me.

Grist for the Mill:
Long-distance Mothering

and what I know now is nothing
can abduct you fully from the land where you were
  born . . .

. . . there is no erasing this:
the central memory of what we are
to one another, the grove of ritual.
I have set my seal upon you.

I say:
you shall be a child of the mother
as of old, and your face will not be turned from me . . .
                    Robin Morgan *Lady of the Beasts*

Maggie is another woman who has fought hard and successfully to wring value and meaning out of the experience of having (unwillingly) left a child. She has two sons: Paul by her first husband and Joe by her current partner. Maggie was separated from Paul for many years, when his father kept him living abroad. The following account describes their separation, its personal aftermath and how it has added meaning to her work. Her writing has been widely performed and published.

My elder son is now 27 and at last living in England, so we're in more constant contact with each other. But when we were separated we lived in two different countries and the viewpoint was entirely different. The whole saga spans thousands of miles.

Paul was six or seven when my parting from him began. I'd been married for some years to his father, and he was my only child. Although my ex-husband was and is a liberal man, giving me a lot of scope for personal development, I still found it very difficult to be in a conventional marriage situation.

For a long time I'd been straining at the leash of the relationship, branching out in different directions. Looking back now, it's clearer what I was trying to get at, though at the time it was very muddied. I thought I wanted sexual freedom, to be able to indulge in as many relationships as I wanted. But now I realise I wanted to liberate myself in a more profound way. I wanted my own space. I wanted to find my self, and that's linked with my creativity. I've now been writing – as a profession – for 17 years but I wasn't writing then. I'd been thinking about it ever since I was a child but hadn't realised it in any concrete way. So retrospectively, it seems I was seeking out my own creative energies, trying to find expression for them, but they were only emerging in a wild, mad way, which wasn't at all satisfying.

The crunch came when I got involved in a relationship with a younger man. It was much more intense than any of my previous relationships had been. Now, after therapy and prolonged thought as to all the patterns, I don't think it was much to do with the young man in question. Rather I was projecting on to him what I wanted for myself, in myself, and investing him with it. But it developed into an amour fou which neither of us could resist, one of those heightened, fatal relationships, the stuff of opera and Greek tragedy.

It caused enormous conflict in me, thinking I would leave my husband, then changing my mind. I was working as an actress in a community centre and all through the rehearsals I'd toss decisions backwards and forwards, first going entirely for one option, then the other. I was half crazy, in a maelstrom, and I wore myself out, at one point I completely broke down. The result was that after a great many tragic – and sometimes comic – occurrences, including the attempted suicide of the lover, I decided I had to put an end to all the madness and stay with my husband and child. My son at that time was eight. So we evolved a plan to emigrate, and off we went, three thousand miles away.

But I hadn't worked out what was going on and when I got there, I pined to come home again. It was an exaggerated version of what had been happening all along. I starved myself. I lost an enormous amount of weight. I never slept. Eventually, I was so strange and ill I simply couldn't stay. At the same time, my husband met someone else. I don't regard that as the major factor, but it gave him a firm footing for our separating, particularly since the other woman came from a conventional background and didn't want to be involved with a man who was still married. His reasoning was that I should go back to the younger man in England, while he stayed there.

The mistake I made was allowing myself to be persuaded it would be better if I left Paul behind while things got sorted out. So back I went. And, of course, that was a fatal error. As soon as I was gone, my husband began suing for divorce, citing desertion, which was exactly what it looked like, and indeed, in cold fact, was what had happened. As soon as I got back to England I changed my mind again and wanted to be back there, but by then it was too late. So I sat it out, in the most terrible state.

I tried to make the best of it, set up home with the young man, but I was pining for Paul and beginning to realize the enormity and implications of the situation. I went back for the divorce, and lost custody. This is nearly 20 years ago, and my behaviour didn't look too good in court. I looked like a scarlet woman, and I couldn't defend myself. I didn't speak the language, I had no friends nor relations there, not even a lawyer and in that country, the law favours the man anyway. I remember standing on the steps of the divorce court, in brilliant sunshine, and thinking 'what shall I do now?' It was a chastening set of circumstances. I was alone in a foreign country, having ended my marriage, lost my child, and with no home, no money. It was extraordinary, as if I was floating in space.

I stayed on there, but for a period of a few months I was totally distraught. I appeared to be carrying on a normal life, working and seeing people, but I was completely out of control. I'd be sitting on a bus and suddenly it was as if someone had

*turned on a tap. Tears would just pour in sheets down my face.
Or in a class learning the language and I'd keel over on to the
floor. My brain just couldn't take it. And so it went on . . .*

*I saw Paul, though to begin with, it was madness. I was
hysterical. My ex-husband was remarried by this time and I
couldn't go into their house. I used to tear things off the wall,
smash plates, scream and yell, create mayhem. They banished
me. So Paul had to come to me, and my circumstances were
minimal, which was shame-making for him. It was a hard
country to be in on one's own, enduring not only this but other
things, including war. I couldn't make a career for myself in
writing because of the language problem and after about two
years, I knew I couldn't drift on with my life on hold, vaguely
hoping things would improve. I had a vision of myself as an
embittered old lady who'd given up everything for her son,
laying all that guilt on him, and gradually I became aware the
best thing for me to do would probably be to come back to
England.*

*It was obviously not a decision I made quickly or lightly. I
returned to England to see how I felt, and was fairly sure that
was what I wanted to do. So I went back there again to tie
things up and break the news to my son, which was very
difficult. It was made clear to me then that any arrangements –
financial and otherwise – for my continuing contact with him
would be all down to me. No one was going to help me to see
him. So I came back to England knowing that was the case.*

*Leaving was probably the most difficult thing I'll ever have
to do. I knew that when I got back to England, a lot of other
things would descend on me and I wanted to be in a neutral
place to consider what had happened, so I came back via
Greece and stopped on the Greek islands. I had nothing to
come back to. I wasn't coming back to the relationship – I knew
that – I wasn't coming back to a job. I didn't have any idea
what I was going to do, except committing myself to keeping
contact with my son and to see him as often as I could. In my
own mind I thought I'd try to see him twice a year. So I knew I
was going to have to get a job that paid quite well.*

Greece was a wonderful time, in a way, all the pressures and horrors that had gone before seemed to fall off me. I like my own company very much now and I was beginning to then. I wandered around on the islands, with very little money, living quite simply, till I felt ready to go back. Eventually I came back to England, selling my blood in Athens to get enough money to catch the magic bus overland. My parents didn't recognise me. I was so thin and brown, ragged and shabby. I'd left as a proper married woman with a professional husband and child, and I returned as a waif and stray, a madwoman.

I quickly got a professional job, which paid what seemed to me a king's ransom, found somewhere to live, and began the next phase, committed almost entirely to seeing my son as often as possible. At the same time, I became involved in a loving and supportive relationship with the man who is still my partner. I think I believed that if I had somewhere good to live and a proper job, I might redeem myself in the eyes of the law and reclaim custody. But whether that was merely an idea or a real possibility, it receded as time wore on. It didn't become feasible for a few years anyway, and by then, I don't think Paul wanted to come here to live. So it didn't feel right to make him the centre of a battle for custody. Gradually I became acclimatised to the fact he didn't live with me.

I saw him approximately twice a year. He usually came here at Christmas and sometimes I went there, in the summer, for six weeks. If I was feeling affluent, I managed another trip. We settled into a rhythm: it even became quite pleasurable. I enjoyed going there, I made friends there. And, a strange development, from being the outcast in the home of my husband I became an intimate friend of his wife: it developed into a genuine friendship. She and I still correspond. I like all that: it appeals to my sense of the unconventional.

So those years passed. But in spite of the free-wheeling aspect of it all, and in retrospect it's probably more romantic and fun than it was at the time, I would never want to minimise the internal agony of it all. It was deeply agonising. It was great fun to go, lovely to be there, but it was agonising to come away. Paul and I made a deal with each other. We had a saying: 'No crying at airports.' Neither of us could bear that overt show of emotion, and we agreed always to withhold our crying till after we'd parted company.

I didn't hide what had happened, but I didn't particularly go public with it. I perhaps devised a form of explanation which cast the best possible light on myself, the way one would in self-defence. I did find that almost without exception people condemned my situation, without ever attempting to penetrate the pain of it, or the price of it. Or, while seeming in some way to agree with or approve of it, they subtly condemned. They saw it as a bid for freedom. Which, to be truthful, it was. I felt it was my prerogative to be free, I wanted to be free to express myself. But they didn't see the other side.

People could be extraordinarily spiteful and insensitive. Some assumed it had been my decision not to have my child with me and assumed I'd gone along with it very gladly. What they didn't take into account was that for years I spent my life trying to hide from where there might be children of a similar age. I couldn't stand outside a school. I couldn't go to a supermarket or anywhere there were likely to be children. That makes for a very warped life.

Strangely enough, the most difficult time was when Paul came to live in this country when he was 21. It was a period of readjustment for us all. He had a relationship with a girl in a different country – a third country – and at one point he was going to live with her, to move elsewhere again. I was as traumatised by that as I had been by the rest.

I've got another son who's now 12, and when he approached the age my elder son had been when I lost custody, I began to experience all kinds of irrational feelings. I withheld emotion, I was afraid to be too involved with him, as if afraid he too would be taken from me. It was very difficult and painful, and I knew I had to get some help. I had counselling for a year, then psychotherapy, to look at the reasons for the whole thing developing in the first place. I also did Tai Chi. Within the safety of the therapy, for nearly two years, I went into a kind of controlled breakdown and came out of it feeling a lot stronger, more aware of what had happened. It was enormously constructive.

The relationships in our family were very difficult. I grew up in a conventional working-class Jewish family. Mother had very traditional expectations for us – my one sister and I. My sister was anorexic for many years. Academically, I was very clever, a high-flyer in certain spheres, extremely developed intellectually and I went to university, but my parents hoped I'd get married. I did, even before I left university. It wasn't that I was pregnant, it was under parental pressure. I was only 19. Very soon after the marriage I began realising it wasn't what I wanted, but before I knew where I was, I was having a child. I can remember pulling against it, feeling life has got to have more to offer than this, though I wasn't married to a repressive man, quite the opposite. So that was behind everything.

Even now, though my parents are supportive of my work, I have the feeling I can't quite do the right thing. There's a residual sense that I'm a disappointment somewhere along the line. I was always afraid of being smothered by this pressure and have spent most of my adult life rebelling against it, defying them and the world. I never wanted to live in the middle. I was always very wild, mad, on the edge. People used to call me the gipsy: I don't know how I was contained.

I've now managed to find an equilibrium between my creativity and my personal life so I can lead something which approaches a 'normal' existence whilst still expressing myself in a satisfactory way. I feel proud of this, it's something I never thought I'd achieve, though it's consistently difficult. I feel I've survived it all quite strongly, but I've paid for it. Every inch of the way. I think we both did: Paul paid too. We both continue to pay.

Paul and I get on incredibly well now, we communicate well, like a two-man show, it's hard to pull us apart. I'm sure we're so close as a result of these experiences. But there are residual difficulties. I watch him like a hawk. Whenever things go wrong for him, particularly around relationships, I blame myself. And I am incapable of denying him anything. Nobody else can make such a call on my emotions or time or energies, in the entire universe he's the person who has the strongest hold on me. I'm helpless, at the drop of a hat I'll do anything.

*I would like that to change, I'd like it to be a more equal
situation.*

*When I'm being very positive, I portray it all by saying yes,
there are different kinds of mothering. I didn't bring up my
child, we were separated, we only saw each other twice a year
and now he's a grown man, yet we have this extremely close
relationship, much closer than most mothers and sons. We're
open with each other about discussing our feelings and he and
my other son get on very well, so it proves you don't have to be
with a child all the time physically etc., etc. . . . And in one
way, being positive, I do believe that.*

*But speaking honestly from the other side, I also know there
is something rather neurotic involved, and I don't think we'll
ever work that out. Mostly though, it feels very rich. He's a
very creative person and when we work together on a project,
which we have with some of my writing, it's magical.*

*People often ask me if I regret it, if I had my life again
would I do it differently. I wouldn't. I do feel responsible for
things that have happened to Paul subsequently, but I don't feel
guilty. That's a different thing. So I don't regret it, not for a
second. Firstly because what I did, when I did it, was all a
necessity, something I had to do. It felt as if I didn't have any
option. I remember feeling that if I didn't do these things, I
would die. It wasn't a choice. It was like oxygen.*

*Secondly, given the richness of what followed, the complexity,
the pain, the fun and pleasure and interest, I don't regret
anything. Taken over the whole spectrum, it's given my life
something it wouldn't otherwise have had. Certainly, from the
point of view of being a writer, it's given me plenty of fuel. I
don't mean that in a callous way, but rather in the sense that
maybe that's why it happened. It's all part of me: who I was,
am, will be. In Buddhist terms, it's part of the mandala, part of
that complex pattern that makes up the life we're in. And
Buddhists believe in karma, so I might also say that these
difficult and painful things are set up in some way and have to
be worked through.*

*I certainly don't think I've been a victim or that life has done
me down. I have a very good life, very creative. I'm in a*

supportive and rewarding relationship. My work's in demand. I feel true to myself: what I'm doing is what I want to do. I'm conscious of the fact that many people have very impoverished, thin lives, and mine has been very rich, complex. It's been difficult, sometimes incredibly painful, but rich. And I'm grateful for that. I was really fortunate to have those experiences.

As I started to write and get some recognition, I could see some kind of equation. I began to see that all this was justified. My life hadn't followed the pattern that everyone had laid down for it, but the outcome of it all was this. How could I have been expected to have a 'normal' life if I was going to start writing in this way? It was all grist to the mill.

PART FOUR

*Inside Story – Making
the Unconscious Conscious*

Fantasy Mothers:
Shadows, Fears, Projections

> In your awful hatred you've formed a picture of me,
> but is it true? Do you seriously think it's the whole
> truth?
>
> Charlotte Andergast in Ingmar Bergman's *Autumn Sonata*

The widespread hostility towards mothers who leave children comes
in large part from their offending a social institution which some hold
to be sacred. But the persistent negativity of the images found in
literature, film and popular culture and the emotional hysteria which
so often informs reactions suggest a level of response that is more than
the sum of social conditioning. It is not merely *conscious* prejudice
about women being kept in their proper place in the home and family
that darkens the views of such mothers, but more profoundly rooted,
unconscious fears and fantasies.

For other women, mothers who leave are acting out their own
(forbidden, denied) desire to do the same. We represent unadmitted
feelings and impulses. We manifest forbidden possibilities that are
usually deeply repressed – dreams of leaving an impossible situation,
longings to get away, hunger for freedom or a fullness of life that
women have been led to believe lies in marriage or motherhood, but
which they may discover is not held there. No matter what the reason
for her departure, the woman who leaves transforms into a figure who
is the 'good' mother's double, her repressed other – the 'bad' shadow
side.

Feminism has at last made it possible to name some of the
ambivalence that surrounds the experience of mothering. In *The
Second Sex* (first published in English in 1953), Simone de Beauvoir
gave full vent to her doubts about women's motivation and behaviour
as regards motherhood (an experience she chose to know only from

the daughter's point of view). Noting the distortion of mothering that comes from 'the religion of Maternity', De Beauvoir shatters the myth of the saintly or good mother:

> For while maternal devotion may be perfectly genuine, this, in fact, is rarely the case. Maternity is usually a strange mixture of narcissism, altruism, idle day-dreaming, sincerity, bad faith, devotion and cynicism.
>
> The great danger which threatens the infant in our culture lies in the fact that the mother to whom it is confided in all its helplessness is almost always a discontented woman . . . [and] She will seek to compensate for all these frustrations through her child. [1]

The second wave of feminism has taken further this questioning of the myth and confessed to mixed feelings about motherhood. Like Adrienne Rich's exemplary study *Of Woman Born*, Jane Lazarre's ruthlessly honest autobiographical account of childbirth and child care, *The Mother Knot* (1976), expresses the *essential ambivalence* in any full or truthful version of mothering.

What Rich, Lazarre and others have dared to admit is that, far from the positive experience pushed by the media, mothering can be partially or even unremittingly negative. Social and personal circumstances can become so intolerable that only desperate remedies are possible. Faced with appalling pressures – outer, inner or both – and not knowing how to negotiate a way out of them, many mothers are driven into depression, madness, suicide, even murder. [2] Compared with these violent alternatives, the option of leaving children would seem a relatively sane, wise and rational one. It would be far better to have heard of Sylvia Plath walking away from her young children than sticking her head in a gas oven.

Yet denial has become such an accepted part of the maternal process – with women denying any dissatisfaction, resentment or lack of unconditional love – that the sudden manifestation of a mother who has actually *left* her children may still seem as disturbing as a figure from outer space. Like Jung's idea of the shadow side as personifying everything that the subject refuses to acknowledge about herself, the mother who leaves is ostracised because of her uneasy closeness, her

(denied) familiarity. She is that part of the self of which women feel
they ought to be ashamed.

As one MATCH interviewee, Sophie, put it: 'I think I've done
what many women are scared of doing. I think there's hardly a
woman in the country who wouldn't want to leave their kids at
some point, quite honestly, only they won't admit it. They've
swallowed so much for so long.'

It may be that the more outspoken the condemnations – '*I* believe in
putting the children first,' 'I'd never leave *my* kids,' – the more stifled
and intolerant of their own feelings are the women who make them,
retreating from any subversive possibilities into unassailable (and self-
righteous) good mothering positions. In Adrienne Rich's words:

> Reading of the 'bad' mother's desperate response to an
> invisible assault on her being, 'good' mothers resolve to
> become better, more patient and long-suffering, to cling
> more tightly to what passes for sanity.[3]

The absent mother, then, becomes something of a scapegoat,
functioning as a shadow figure who takes to herself a collective female
negativity. Acting aggressively against one's own unwanted parts is well
known as a classic mechanism of psychic defence, and so such women
are ostracised – not because of their difference but because of their
similarity, the fact that they represent part of an inadmissible drive
which the personal or collective female psyche finds hard to accept.

Psychoanalysis has also played its part in making it possible to
understand more fully some of these different – and more difficult –
aspects of mothering, for it has given us the means of *naming some*
of the fantasies about Mother that we tend to carry, and in this sense
it may help undo the myths rather than reinforce them.

Freud's daughter Anna, who worked extensively with infants, had
eventually to admit that any idea of perfect parental love was an
illusion. 'No child', she acknowledged, 'is wholly loved.'[4] But this
inevitably imperfect side is still something hard to bring into the
mother-child relationship (as in all relationships) and is something
women are particularly loathe to admit. They dare not say they do not

love their children fully or consistently because they are terrified of being cast as (or felt – by their children – to be) 'bad' mothers. Yet the more the mother represses her own feelings, her own needs, her own unadmitted or unresolved aggressions, the more likely it is that her expressions and actions of love will be muddled and misleading to the child, if not hypocritical.

Child analyst Donald Winnicott knew only too well that there are many cases in which the mother may simply *not be in a position* to give the child the unconditional love, or even the 'good enough' mothering, it needs, and that this is *not* the woman's *fault*. In one of his papers – unusually focused on the mother rather than on the child's development – Winnicott draws attention to the position of the *mother* herself and enumerates some of the difficulties that might arise for *her* in developing a positive bond with her offspring. And he is not talking here about exceptional or damaged mothers, but about ordinary ones. What he reveals is that alienation and ambivalence are not the monopoly of neurotic or psychotic women, but an intrinsic part of every mothering process.

To show how natural it is for a mother to have ambivalent feelings towards her child, Winnicott produces a striking list of specific reasons why a mother may actually experience feelings of hate towards her baby. Amongst these are:

> The baby is not her own (mental) conception.
>
> The baby is not the one of childhood play, father's child, brother's child, etc.
>
> The baby is not magically produced.
>
> The baby is a danger to her body in pregnancy and at birth.
>
> The baby is an interference in her private life, a challenge to preoccupation . . .
>
> He [the baby] is ruthless, treats her as scum, an unpaid servant, a slave.
>
> She has to love him, excretions and all . . . He tries to hurt her, periodically bites her . . . he shows disillusionment about her . . . His excited love is like cupboard love, so that having got what he wants he throws her away like orange peel . . . he does not know at all what she does or what she sacrifices for him.

Especially he cannot allow for her hate.

He is suspicious, refuses her good food, makes her doubt herself . . .

After an awful morning with him she goes out, and he smiles at a stranger, who says: 'Isn't he sweet?'[5]

And so on. He admits that these feelings may be further intensified if the woman's relation with the baby's father is at all difficult, for the child is an extension of the father and so will symbolically carry any negative associations with it.

This remarkably unromantic appraisal, admitting it is only natural that 'the mother hates her infant from the word go,' is one that many women would rush to deny. But Winnicott stresses how dangerous it is to deny or repress negative feelings: only a relationship able to own fully and acknowledge any hatred can both contain it and develop into something that is authentically nurturing (as opposed to the cleaned-up and sentimentalised version of mothering so many promote and practice). Mothers who claim they *only* love their children are less likely to be giving them real love than mothers who can fully own and accept their ambivalence, for love based on denial or repression (or fantasy) is bound to falter and lead to damaging the child in other ways.

Children are bound to arouse in their parents negative as well as positive feelings. Anger, frustration and hatred are as real and valid emotions as affection, protection or love. Yet the prohibition against experiencing, let alone expressing, both sides, a taboo linked up with the romanticising of the child and the sentimentalising of mothering, make for a repressed and therefore potentially dangerous relationship.

What Winnicott suggests is that awareness of feelings and authenticity of response is the most important thing: better some element of (contained) hatred than a false sentimentality which attempts to cover and disguise.[6] He is not, however, suggesting a blind acting out of these emotions, but his arguments do alert us to the dangers of *false mothering*: *the pretence at presence* that many mothers assume. It is a warning that comes strongly to the defence of the mother who loves but leaves.[7]

Sophie again made these feelings explicit: *'I have to say I don't always like my children. I love them, but often I don't like*

*them and I wouldn't want them to come and live with me now
. . . I don't want to cook and clean for them. Why is there such
an assumption I should be good at nurturing? If I was a man,
it would be different.'*

Even the 'best' mother is also a person with her own developmental
needs and with an emotional life affected by her history, by her
relation with the father, by social and economic pressures. Thus there
are bound to be shifting and complex feelings that are intrinsic to the
process of mothering – resentment as well as love, doubt, anxiety and
envy as well as delight or altruism. These make it impossible for her
to be eternally the same one figure that the idea and myth of Mother
conjures up – that one stable, omnipresent, never-changing entity.

On a deeper level, what the figure of the mother who leaves summons
up in men and women alike, and accounts for the widespread
hysterical reaction to her, is one of the most primitive of all terrors:
the fear of abandonment. This is why immediate unconscious
identification tends to be with the child or children left behind and
not with the adult woman.

A terror of being abandoned operates at some level in all our
psyches, even in people with the most 'normal' and protected
childhoods. For as psychoanalysis has shown, having to come to terms
with being left by mother is a crucial – and often terrifying – part of
any infant's early development. From a state of being totally at one
with the mother – first by being incorporated in her body, then by
being an extension of it, attached to it for feeding and nursing – the
infant has to learn to endure progressive separation. At this time, the
mother's physical absence may be experienced as an intolerable and
incomprehensible state of affairs, completely threatening the
dependent child's life with extinction.

Winnicott's term for this sense of abandonment in the child was
'primitive agony' – the most primal, painful state imaginable. And
unconscious processes attach themselves – in the child's mind – to the
mother who has left the infant in this state. The real mother, in fact,
gets split in the child's unconscious mind into a 'good mother' (who
does not actually exist except on a fantasy level), who is the all-
nurturing, ever-present loving one, who should never leave, and a 'bad
mother' (who also exists only in the fantasy world of the unconscious),

who is her total opposite, secretly plotting the child's torture and prepared to leave it to die in the pain of its primitive anguish.

It is these fantasies that help explain the deep prejudice against women who leave children. It is as if an irrational response is triggered and the same kind of primitive splitting occurs as in the infant, as if *one were placed once again in the uncomprehending position of the child who cannot rationalise mother's not being there – so that the mother's absence is assumed to be the same as abandonment and is beyond reason.*

This splitting between two kinds of mother, two kinds of parent figures – good and bad – has been mapped out further in the work of child analyst Melanie Klein. She found that during the early inner life of the infant, a severe splitting occurs on a fantasy level. To protect against its own ambivalence towards its parents, its own anger and aggressiveness, the child splits off any negative feelings and projects them outwards on to external, often persecutory figures. Aggression towards the real mother (which in the child's fantasy would leave her dead and hence would leave it, the child, without any source of support) is dealt with by denying it and trying to hang on to an idealised, perfect fantasy mother. Thus there is a splitting of inner parents – especially mother – into two polarities: the good, which the child tries to internalise, and the bad, which it tries to push away. The Bad Mother, then, is a manifestation of all the child's innermost primitive feelings, hostilities and aggressions.

Since these processes happen to a greater or lesser degree in all our psychic development, we are all familiar – at least on the level of unconscious fantasy – with potentially nightmare images of avenging, persecutory parent figures. In the inner world of unconscious fantasy – which is timeless and can therefore be triggered and reactivated at any point – there still floats this monstrous, destructive and avenging female – the fateful Bad and abandoning mother.

This accounts for the incredible symbolic charge with which 'abandoning' mothers are invested: their association, on an imaginary level, with witches, demons, vampires, even death itself. No matter how, as adults, we try to think rationally about mothering and mother roles, these early unconscious fantasies are still lying in wait and they cloud the judgements of much popular opinion. Just as in the infant's fantasy life, where a woman who is not the idealised image of the ever-present good mother, surrounding the child with wholeness, must be a persecutory bad one, wanting to rip things apart, so in the collective unconscious a mother who leaves is transformed overnight into a monster who cannot possibly wish her child any good.

From a Jungian perspective, what is being activated is the negative side of the Great Mother archetype. According to Jung, all archetypes have their positive and negative aspects, and the archetype of the Mother is no exception: Jung defined her ambivalent attributes as those of the 'loving and terrible mother'. On the positive side she is the goddess, Mother of God, virgin, maiden, beloved, evoking 'all that is benign, all that cherishes and sustains, that fosters growth and fertility' and 'representing the goal of our longing for redemption, such as Paradise, the Kingdom of God, the Heavenly Jerusalem'.

On the negative side, she becomes the 'terrible mother', ominous goddess of fate, witch or Lilith, and is represented symbolically by devouring animals, dragons, graves, demons, vampires and death itself, 'the abyss, the world of the dead, anything that devours, seduces, and poisons, that is terrifying and inescapable like fate'.[8] In Greek myth she appears as Medea, ready to sacrifice her children, and in Hindu lore as the goddess Kali, reputed to have fang-like teeth and a protruding tongue that drips with blood.

Hence the difficulty of talking about the subject rationally. A mother who leaves is no longer apprehended as an actual woman, but as a fantasy figure, with archetypal qualities projected on to her and putting her outside the real. She is the Bad Mother, the threatening, uncaring mother, akin to the stepmother in fairy tales, who has replaced the (longed for) good mother, pushed away the protective father, and secretly plots the child's death. Common projections turn the woman in flight from 'true' motherhood into precisely such a fairy tale witch – the disobedient hag whose very *capacity*, assumed to be a capacity for destruction, is feared.

It is these projections that make it so hard to get at the reality of mothers who leave, for these many layers of myth that have accreted round the 'bad' mother have first of all to be stripped away. Archetypal images have invaded and surrounded actual women, transforming them into symbols – Frieda Lawrence the unwanted ghost, Margaret Trudeau the monster, Ingrid Bergman defamed as 'a powerful force for evil' from the heart of America. Such mothers have been overlaid with layer after layer of myth and fantasy, making it hard to think about them – about ourselves – as real people, with specific histories.

One could say that the very division into Good and Bad mothers, the very positing of an archetypal Great Mother is not helpful – another abstract and fantasy construction. But Jung stressed that it is not the archetype itself that is the problem, so much as the projections that arise from it. We do not necessarily have to destroy the archetypes, but to dissolve the projections – to stop investing others with our own unconscious material.

Some women, though, have questioned the very construction of the idea of the Mother that we carry in our unconscious lives. For not only are Good and Bad Mothers constructions carried over from our unconscious formation in childhood, but the very notion of Mother and *motherhood* itself can be seen as being deeply invested with specific unconscious associations, feeding further into the fixed positions of women who occupy the maternal role.

As I shall explore further in Chapter 24, the very notion of 'Mother' has come to be one that summons up a fantasy of wholeness. It is the dream of Mother as a state of original unity and bliss, a time before separation, language and culture, that lingers in the imagination and colours our views of real mothers. The imaginary Mother represents a vision of perfection, of totality. She is the Paradise we have lost, the innocence that preceded our human experience. Mother is the lost domain, a barely remembered Eden. [9]

In this respect, it is no wonder that mothers who leave should be so resented and condemned. For this is their real shadow side, that they threaten to wake us out of such a collective dream. They unsettle what is perhaps the deepest of our nostalgic fantasies and remind us that this ideal Mother does not, after all, exist. Through them, we see that when all the projections and archetypes are dissolved, there are only individual women, being mothers.

Separation: The Reproduction of Broken Mothering

It turns out I was never there
where she was *where was she?*
All my weeks and months away;
no wonder no memory *where was she?*

where was she? that face whose smell
I never fathomed, whose day
I never grasped, whose life to me
was invisible *where was she?*

And where was I when my belly
swelled? Being sick and fighting
with myself. There was no mother in me
good enough or ready *where was she?*

Sarah Hopkins 'Not There'

From the evidence in Parts Two and Three, it is clear that there are
so many factors involved in mothers and children being separated it
would be misleading to claim one specific cause. Psychic and social,
personal and political play on one another in complex ways and are
threaded inextricably together.

But there is one common denominator that does tend to recur.
Despite their diverse circumstances, their highly different class,
educational and social backgrounds, nearly all the women whose
stories we have heard show just how strongly patterns of mothering
and parenting reproduce themselves from one generation to the next.
The first interview I did was with Meredith, the young woman who
successively 'gave away' three children over the years, and it was the
central structure of her psychological drama that came to influence
how I thought about the issue of separation.

Meredith was adopted, and the bonding with her adoptive mother

proved very weak, a damage reflecting and being reflected by continuous forms of emotional and sexual abuse. Meredith's adult life
since has acted out an apparently compulsive spiral of bearing and
leaving children, time after time. For other women, the break with the
biological mother may have been less literal or melodramatic, but none
the less a similar pattern emerges. Threaded through nearly all the
accounts is an experience of broken, damaged or deeply problematic
mothering.

As I began to identify this tendency, I saw more and more how
patterns of mothering were being mirrored from one generation to
another, that damaged mothering tended to reproduce itself. It was
uncanny to see just how much there was a mirroring from one
generation to the next, the parallels and reflections between mothering
received and mothering given becoming increasingly conspicuous.
Mothers had left children at precisely that age when they were left –
either literally, through adoption, mother's illness, or death – or
symbolically, through her emotional withdrawal. The reproduction of
broken mothering started to look like a form of compulsive repetition,
with incredible mirrorings, doublings and repetitions – as if there
were a set of unconscious impressions being passed from one
generation to another, repeatedly breaking through and being acted
out.

As a child, Ingrid Bergman lost both her natural and surrogate
mothers – a loss of two mother figures uncannily repeated in her own
experience of mothering, as she twice relinquished custody of the
children from her two marriages. In the narratives in Part Three,
Siobhan's early ministering to the needs of her withdrawn alcoholic
mother created an inner dynamic that was echoed in Siobhan's adult
relationships – trying to fulfil her own needs through meeting the
needs of others – as if through caring for mother substitutes she would
vicariously receive the mothering she lacked. Her mothering of her
own children (especially her daughter) was interrupted, as her own
experience of being mothered had been.

Many of us who become mothers are daughters of mothers who are
still children. We are expected to mother our mothers and parent our
children before we have properly separated out from either and with
very little sense of what being a mother means. As analyst Nini
Herman writes in her autobiography: "'Who is the mother? Who the

child?" my terror squealed continuously. "Look, you grown-ups everywhere, my mother simply cannot cope."'[1]

Amongst the personal accounts in Part Three, we have seen many further examples of problematic mothering. Daphne's mother withdrew from her into illness and depression, her parents' marriage disintegrated and her mother (who had herself been adopted) left the family home, as Daphne herself was to do a generation later. Charlotte read her experience of abuse and broken mothering as a repetition of what she had seen and felt as a child, the lack of emotional bonding with her mother transmitted from one generation to another. Leonie admitted to a very fraught relationship with her mother and found it difficult to let her approach her own baby daughter. Ruth commented on her mother's treatment of her as distant and lacking in physical affection, and believed the pattern of ruptured mothering was inherited. 'I find the repetition that runs through families, one generation to another, quite amazing . . . My mother was abandoned at birth. I was abandoned at 18 months. And I abandoned my children at 7 years.'

Other mothers apart from their children have reinforced this idea of broken mothering reproducing itself. Liz, the mother who left her fifth and autistic child, was adamant that she was utterly unprepared for motherhood and had no idea how to reverse her own heritage of effectively absent mothering. 'Even when she [mother] was there, she wasn't really with us. After living in a dysfunctional family like that, with no physical affection, no outward sign, it was difficult for me to hug my children.'

Sophie, in Westminster, came from a 'working-class dysfunctional family. My mother had a drink problem and various breakdowns. Her love was increasingly withdrawn – not actively but through drinking, illness, going in an out of mental hospitals.' Significantly, not only Sophie but also her one elder sister, after marrying young and having children, also moved out from her marriage and home some years later to live alone – both sisters left their children behind.

Paddy, whose lesbian history lost her children, had a mother she describes as dominating, critical, unsupportive and emotionally withdrawn: 'My brothers nicknamed her the Ayatollah!' She feels she was pressurised into an unsuitable early marriage both to please her mother and to escape from her.

Jan wrote from Liverpool: 'I have lived apart from my daughter for the past six years, and what's more, I also lived apart from *my* mother during some of my childhood.' Similarly Linda from Sussex: 'All I know is my natural mother was abandoned when she was seven years old and my mother had me adopted, so let go of me. Now, I have let go of my son (at a similar age).' Maureen in Wells: 'My mother was adopted. She had no idea how to mother me.'

In Charlotte Perkins Gilman's case, her mother had visibly recoiled from demonstrations of love and Gilman's resultant depression became an enormous obstacle in her own relationship with *her* daughter. As if, when she herself became a mother, her early sense of abandonment and despair were re-triggered. Such a post partum psychosis in women whose own mothering has been badly damaged is more than postnatal depression. Here, the mother can become profoundly self-destructive, turning against both herself and her child, and regressing to early unconscious states. [2]

Of all the women I encountered, only one boasted a positive relationship with her own mother and none had mothers who had been actively supportive after their separation from their children. Indeed, this broken mothering was such a repeated feature I began to see it as more than mere coincidence, and sought an explanation as to why it may be so: what the internal dynamics might be that affect this widespread reproduction of experiences of mothering.

Psychoanalysis and different schools of psychotherapy have long recognised the mirroring that takes place as we unconsciously repeat our early emotional experiences with parents or parent figures. And nowhere is this kind of repetition more evident than when we come to being parents ourselves, unconsciously acting out our own childhood formation. Emotional or physical abuse may be repeated, or we may try to over-compensate and force ourselves to give what we were denied.

The main thesis of John Bowlby's *Maternal Care and Mental Health* (1951) was that, as once deprived children in turn become parents, they will tend to reproduce the circumstances that led to their own deprivation. Michael Rutter's more recent survey of research in *Maternal Deprivation Reassessed* makes similar findings of 'intergenerational cycles of disadvantage', strong patterns of continuity, so that specific childhood experiences will influence the kind of parenting practised in later years. Early experience of physical or emotional violence or neglect is clearly linked with difficulties in parenting. Rejection in early life can deter attachment to others. So problems in mothering will rarely arise in a context of unproblematic social or family background: the greater the problems, as in Meredith's case, the more serious the history of adversity.

Extensive research shows that attachment behaviour in the mother does indeed follow that of her experience as a child, Rutter's conclusion being that 'a woman's experiences in childhood [are] associated with her behaviour as a mother.'[3] Thus she will tend to reproduce the same models of relationship with her children that she internalised during infancy: 'The way in which an individual's attachment behaviour becomes organised within her personality affects the pattern of affectional bonds she makes during her life. Because children tend unwittingly to identify with their parents, there is a tendency to behave in the same way towards their children when parents. A social cycle is therefore a distinct possibility.'[4]

The amazing mirroring and acting out that occurs in patterns of mothering, then, is a *social* rather than a genetic or biological repetition. A kind of maternal imprinting occurs and if the mother is emotionally broken, ill or depressed, her daughter will take this in during infancy and later reflect it back in her own mothering. It is as if there is an invisible legacy handed down through the process of mothering, and what happens to the parent is unwittingly done again to her own child.

Whether we will it or not, the kind of mothers we have had and the mothering we have received have deeply imprinted themselves on us and will show through our own forms of mothering. Relations of mothers and daughters will profoundly affect the patterns of the bonds we make in adult life.

Nini Herman, in her study of the mother-child dyad in *Too Long a Child*, argues that roots of troubled mother-daughter relations can be traced back several generations. And in Judith Arcana's words in *Our Mothers' Daughters*, 'As we are predominantly patterned after our mothers, most of us raise our children by reproducing the emotional dynamic we experienced as our mothers' daughters . . . our own mothering, in style and technique, remains based, quite firmly, in the models our mothers have presented . . .'[5]

Susie Orbach has identified our relation with our mothers as the most significant and formative one we have, the legacy that is indelibly etched into our emotional lives and unconsciously affects our sense of identity, choices and possibilities. The texture of it tends to be the blueprint of all our subsequent experience. The mother-daughter bond is a complex one, inevitably shot through with ambivalence, as mother and daughter identify together, making emotional separation deeply problematic. 'The mother's need for attachment, combined with her identification with her daughter, creates a fusion between the two of them (a merged attachment). The mother is not separate from her daughter . . . and the daughter . . . has an equivalent experience.' She retains her mother's presence inside her, and carries the emotional markers of her mother's needs into her adult relationships. [6]

Nor Hall has similarly defined 'Woman's original experience of herself in relationship to a mother [as] one of identity, a continuation of the blood bond of pregnancy.' [7] And to Adrienne Rich, it is this relationship that carries the greatest potential for both pain and pleasure for women. 'The cathexis between mother and daughter – essential, distorted, misused – is the great unwritten story. Probably there is nothing in human nature more resonant with charges than the flow of energy between two biologically alike bodies, one of which has lain in amniotic bliss inside the other, one of which has laboured to give birth to the other. The materials are here for the deepest mutuality and the most painful estrangement.' [8]

This links up too with the work of analyst Melanie Klein, who revealed time and again that the attitude and relationship of a mother to her child has much in common with her feelings as a child towards her own mother: any unresolved negative material or death wishes which, as a child, she bears towards her own mother, will be carried over to her own child when she herself becomes a mother. Thus any difficulties in relating, in her own childhood, to both parents – or to any brothers or sisters – will be likely to reproduce themselves in her adult life in difficult and unresolved feelings towards husband or children. [9]

A woman with a difficult relation to her own mother – whose mother, for example, has been unable to contain the child's naturally aggressive impulses and fantasies, and so help manage the guilt and anxiety to which they give rise – is unlikely to be able to move into a full maternal position with any ease. Because of the strength of these ties which link the relationship of a mother to her child with that of her own relation to her mother in babyhood, difficulties in mothering will tend to reproduce themselves from one generation to another.

The mothering a woman gives, then, is a mirroring, however unconscious or unwilled (hence Charlotte Perkins Gilman's sadness at not being able to give the mothering she longed *to be able* to give), of the mothering she felt she received, almost as if she were her own child. It should be emphasised that this is not a *conscious* copying or conditioning, but a mark of how deeply *unconscious* patterns and impressions reproduce themselves. 'The unconscious minds of the children very often correspond to the mother's unconscious mind . . .'[10]

So, in the case of a mother leaving or relinquishing her children, it is most likely to be a repetition and acting out of what happened to her with her own mother, or rather *what she experienced (internally) as having happened with her own mother.*

Nancy Chodorow's detailed and profound study *The Reproduction of Mothering: Psychoanalysis and the Sociology of Gender* shows how much this parenting is not a matter of imitation or learning a set of behaviour patterns but something that involves deeply complex *interpersonal* dynamics, impossible to learn by rote. Mothering, argues Chodorow, is not taught by mere conditioning, such as giving girls dolls to play with or *telling* them they should mother. Strong though behavioural imitation or coercion from a male ideology may be, it is much deeper than this. What enforces women's mothering is a deeply *internal* dynamic – a *taking in of oneself as maternal.* Thus the daughter will be able to take on a mothering position herself *only if this has been absorbed at an unconscious level* from the mother. And mothers who've left show Chodorow's thesis in action. No matter what the enormous social expectations and pressures to care for her child, even these are ineffective to make a woman provide 'good' mothering. This can only happen if the woman '*to some degree* and on *some unconscious or conscious level*, has the capacity and sense of self as maternal to do so.'[11]

Chodorow's point is central to my argument here. For though many of the women we have heard from have been in external circumstances that were dire and oppressive, nevertheless these are not so very different from what many other mothers also endure – *without* feeling they must leave. Thus the reaction to external forces (which are very real – marital, economic, social) interacts with this inner dynamic too. The woman may also, on some level, be demonstrating *a non-activating of the mother position* within herself – that *internal mothering figure* that is essential if women are to be able to sustain mothering over time in often hostile conditions. For many women who've left the traditional role – most clearly in the cases of Meredith, Sophie, Alice and Siobhan – this internal mothering position has simply been *unavailable* to them.

Symbolically, in these women's inner world, the 'good' mother is manifestly *not there*. So, with an inward feeling of being unmothered, a woman may leave as she was left. A woman who has experienced herself as cheated of mothering at the most primitive level will find it hard not to 'cheat' her own children, for the necessary figure of a good *inner* mother is simply unavailable to her. This reinforces the idea that it is less a question of women 'choosing' to leave, of *actively rejecting* their children, than of women who – for a number of complex reasons, inner as well as outer – have been *unwillingly ejected from* the mothering position.

It is impossible to separate out a woman's actions – as mother – from her complex relationship with her own mother. Thus women's actions in separating from children cannot be understood without placing them in the context of their mothers' histories. This too goes back generationally, as daughters of adopted mothers – like Ruth – demonstrate. Moreover, it may also be that by leaving the mothering position, a woman is unconsciously *repudiating* her own mother – *rejecting her* through rejecting the position and role she represents.

Such a reading is central to Jungian psychology. To Jung, a woman's 'mother complex' – that complex of feelings she holds towards the mother figure – exists somewhere between two poles. At one extreme is over-identification with the mother and at the other total resistance to her: either utter exaggeration of the feminine (maternal) side or its atrophy. In these latter cases of resistance to the maternal, which Jung calls 'the supreme example of the negative mother-complex', the woman's (largely unconscious) motto is 'Anything, so long as it is not like Mother!' According to Jung, this manifests as rejection of everything wherein the Mother's archetype is present:

> stubborn resistance to the power of the mother in every
> form has come to be life's dominating aim ... For
> example, the mother as representative of the family (or
> clan) causes either violent resistances or complete
> indifference to anything that comes under the head of
> family, community, society, convention and the like ...
> All instinctive processes meet with unexpected diffi-
> culties; either sexuality does not function properly, or
> the children are unwanted, or maternal duties seem
> unbearable, or the demands of marital life are
> responded to with impatience and irritation. [12]

Jung sees such resistance behind menstrual disturbances, troubles in
pregnancy, miscarriage, problems in mothering, or in the 'masculine'
development of the intellect 'for the purpose of creating a sphere of
interest in which the mother has no place'.

Whether driven by the non-activating of the mother position as
Chodorow describes it, or motivated by this unconscious resistance to
the mother archetype as Jung identifies it, mothers not occupying the
conventional mother role certainly do seem to be struggling with
separating from their own mothers and the negative impressions of
them that they carry.

Amongst the women I met, I found no examples of women whose
own mothers were conspicuously happy, fulfilled, or self-actuating. On
the contrary, they were graphic examples of dependance, often having
repressed their own needs and lived vicariously through their
children, so their relationships with their daughters were bound to be
double-edged and their daughters almost inevitably had ambivalent
attitudes to their mothers and to mothering. Most told of mothers who
were exceptionally needy, depressed, ill, manipulative or demanding.

Taking this a step further, one could say that these very daughters
were acting out their *mothers'* ambivalence. As if their mothers'
knotted feelings about mothering had finally come to the surface and
it was *their* repressed emotions that were returning and manifesting
in the next generation.

Once more, Donald Winnicott's work is helpful in understanding the
process of how mother and child interact so that an inner mothering
figure comes – or fails to come – into being. Winnicott believed that
an infant's healthy development depended on being able to fully

internalise the mother's (or Mother figure's) emotional presence. For this, the mother herself had to be able to go into what he calls a 'maternal reverie', where her own needs are (temporarily) completely subsumed into those of the child. She also needs to be able to come to terms with – both accept and contain – her own ambivalent and hostile feelings towards the child, which (as we saw in the previous chapter) may be considerable.

If – for whatever reason – this giving over to her child fails to happen, as is the case with a mother who is depressed, preoccupied or ill, there is none of this total absorption in the child – and hence no absorption by the child of that necessary inner figure. Instead of building up a strong sense of being and self-worth, there is a feeling of insubstantiality and self-destruction. And a continually depressed or withdrawn mother/parent exacerbates this inner state – Winnicott suggests that *emotional withdrawal* is just as devastating for the child as physical separation and can be a primary factor in causing psychic damage.

This may sound like traditional arguments for the mother taking primary infant care, but Winnicott (like Bowlby and Rutter) is using the term 'mother' to signify the child's first major attachment, and he is sensitive to the cost of all this to the mother – no blame devolves to the mother figure if she is unable to provide this nurturing environment, for that very inability has its roots in her own social and emotional life. He is aware that the balance between a mother being able or not able to meet the infant's needs is precarious, and reliant on many factors – her own happiness, her relationship with the father, her situation in the world, her health, her own experience of being mothered, etc. There are no value judgements involved. Not being able to enter the ideal 'reverie' or to supply on-going 'good enough' mothering is not necessarily a sign of wilful neglect, so much as a symptom of the woman's own inner state (and, in turn, the mothering she received).

The mother-infant relationship does not exist in a timeless vacuum but is played on by its economic, social and emotional context. Where this is hostile to the woman – through poverty, marital conflict, isolation, lack of support, unemployment, unhappiness – the likelihood of her relationship with her child suffering increases. Hence the difficulty of good mothering in a society where women are in disadvantaged positions.

What is more, if the experience of mothering does re-trigger and mirror the experience of having been mothered, then a mother leaving will go through a double trauma. For she is not only being separated from her real child in the world, but is once again experiencing the abandonment of her child within, and some of the trauma facing a woman apart from her children is that her *inner* world has been equally torn apart. Hence the deep disorientation that can follow separation, re-arousing the woman's original sense of loss. Thus, although maternal (or paternal) deprivation has its real effects, *child deprivation* can be equally traumatic. However much a mother *seems* to have colluded with, or even initiated, the separation from her child, loss of on-going daily contact can still be a major trauma for her. It can lead to intense feelings of shock, loss, grief and depression, sometimes paralysing and self-destructive in their effects.

Mothers apart from their children are often missing out on both sides. For it tends to be precisely those women who have themselves missed out (as children) on 'good' mothering who are most likely to find their experience of mothering their own children cut short, interrupted, blocked. As both daughters and mothers, they get a raw deal.

The evidence is that cycles of parenting *do* reproduce themselves from one generation to another, that damaged mothering *does* have a tendency to be repeated. But this does not mean there has to be an eternal stalemate. Studies of child deprivation have shown that even the most damaged psyche has surprising resilience and an urge towards reparation, whilst the more positive case stories in Part Three have shown that the spiral *can* be broken and not simply unwittingly reproduced *ad infinitum*.

The emotional damage which we – and our mothers before us – inherited *can* be healed, the patterns reversed. First, by becoming aware of the cycle of broken mothering, bringing it into conscious focus and then doing what we can to heal the relationships with ourselves, our children and our mothers. Secondly, by seeing how these negative patterns have arisen not from some peculiar isolated 'bad mothering' female psyche, but from the accumulated effect on women of living in a social context which makes their lives – and so their mothering – deeply problematic.

Reparation:
Mother and Child Reunion

> If we have been able, deep in our unconscious minds,
> to clear our feelings to some extent towards our parents
> of grievances, and have forgiven them for the frus-
> trations we had to bear, then we can be at peace with
> ourselves and are able to love others in the true sense
> of the word.
>
> Melanie Klein *Love, Guilt and Reparation*

One of the few sensitive film portraits of a mother who leaves, *Autumn Sonata* (which appeared, ironically enough, in 1978, the same year as the novel of *Kramer versus Kramer*), was made by Swedish director Ingmar Bergman. The originality of *Autumn Sonata* lies in its exploration of *both* sides of the story of a mother and child who have been emotionally severed. Charlotte Andergast, a highly successful concert pianist now in advanced years, visits her adult daughter, Eva, who is still harbouring resentment at having been left as a child. Eva remembers her mother as perpetually absent, whether on tour or preoccupied with her own work whilst at home, and she now hurls at her mother all the pent-up rage a rejected child can accumulate. 'People like you,' she accuses Charlotte, 'are a menace, you should be locked away and rendered harmless.'

But Bergman, with his characteristic attention to the details of complex human relationships, widens the focus away from a one-sided identification with the abandoned child. We learn that Charlotte has her inner pain too, her own difficult history, and we hear once more of someone whose own broken mothering reproduced itself when it came to mothering her own daughters. Charlotte reveals that her own parents, successful mathematicians, never touched her or played with her, so that artistic achievement became the only way she knew to try to gain their affection. All her childish needs and feelings were sublimated into her work, as she now realises:

> I was completely ignorant of everything to do with love – tenderness, contact, intimacy, warmth . . . [I feel as if] I'm not alive. I've never been born. I was squeezed out of my mother's body. It closed and turned at once to Father. I didn't exist . . . I've never grown up – my face and my body age, I acquire memories and experiences, but inside the shell I'm, as it were, unborn. [1]

It is as if she was asked to be a mother when internally, emotionally, she was effectively still a child – a recurrent dilemma for many of the mothers (and, in turn, their mothers) encountered in this book. And *Autumn Sonata* powerfully conveys just how hard it is to shift these inherited patterns of mothering that are handed down from generation to generation. Like Eva, we tend to go on blaming the individual mother for not being perfect, for helplessly reproducing broken or inadequate forms of parenting.

Only right at the end of the film, after much struggle, does Eva begin to see that throwing accusations at her mother is no solution: that the mother has suffered just as much as the daughter and is in equal need of compassion. In a letter which she writes to Charlotte, she finally tries to recognise and heal the wound that has remained open between them, admitting that she wronged her by meeting her with 'demands instead of affection. I tormented you with an old soured hatred which is no longer real. Everything I did was wrong and I want to ask your forgiveness . . . There is a kind of mercy after all. I mean the enormous chance of looking after each other, of helping each other, of showing affection . . . It must not be too late.'

After the emotional pain mother *and* child have endured, this is a marvellous gesture of reparation. It indicates the struggle there inevitably is before we can arrive at full forgiveness and under-standing, the challenge that faces all of us to accept completely our personal histories, no matter how hostile or deprived they may have been, rather than get stuck in a perpetual anger of railing against them. And Bergman knows this is no easy process. He wisely avoids a facile happy ending in *Autumn Sonata*: we know Eva has arrived at a point of good will, but we do not know whether mother and daughter will finally, or permanently, be reconciled. The future is open and uncertain and has to be repeatedly worked towards. In direct contrast to Hollywood's anodynes, here there are no guarantees.

For the first time on screen, *Autumn Sonata* represented a mother who has left children as someone with her own complex history, her own difficult emotional heritage and reality. And it managed this on a literal as well as symbolic level. For the actress chosen to play the part of Charlotte Andergast was none other than Ingrid Bergman – a woman who, as we have seen, knew only too well the cost and repercussions of not occupying the traditional motherly role. In fact, this was the last film Ingrid Bergman made before her death – returning also to the Swedish language once more, her own 'mother' tongue – and thus giving a fitting sense of completion to her career. Through her presence, fact (or association) could blur with fiction to give added resonance and, in more ways than one, move towards vindicating rather than incriminating a mother who leaves.

Yet Ingrid protested against Bergman's heavy tone – she insisted that the film should have been lighter, that with her own daughters, from whom she had obviously been separated, there were jokes and humour too. She objected to the harsh edge to Charlotte's character – 'She's so brutal in the way she expresses herself' – and argued strongly against the mother being represented as someone who had not seen her children for seven years – 'I went on arguing with him. "Seven years! Staying away from her children for seven years! Impossible!"' [2]

So, even within his sensitivity to the emotional depths between mother and child, it seems that Bergman could not avoid some of the (male) assumptions about such women – that they are hard, cold, and that the relationship with their children – where it survives – is bound to be heavy and shot through with doom and gloom.

* * *

Accounts of reparations between mothers and children outside these male fictions are much more heartening. One in particular, the story of the relationship between Elizabeth Fowles, the late wife of novelist John Fowles, and her daughter Anna, is a moving example of how – despite long periods of separation during Anna's childhood – a profound and intense bond between mother and child can nevertheless survive and be restored. [3]

Elizabeth Fowles (née Whitton) was born in 1925 to a working-class family in the Midlands. Her father was a theatre electrician, which fostered in Elizabeth a deep love of the theatre and a desire to act. She left school at 14, joined the WAAF during the war – a time which was, paradoxically, a positive one for her, taking her away from home and broadening her horizons – and after the war ended went, along with many others seeking a vocation, to teacher training college. But this proved unsuitable for her and, in the late 1940s, she moved to London to try to find more congenial and creative work. It was shortly after her arrival in London that she met Roy Christy, then teaching at a school of architecture in Kingston. Fairly quickly she fell pregnant by him, married and had her daughter, Anna, in November 1950.

When Christy, along with several other teachers, was dismissed from Kingston for his politics, he was invited by an old friend, Dennis Sharrocks, to the Greek island of Spetsai to take up a vacant position in the school there. Elizabeth, Roy and Anna arrived on Spetsai in 1952 and it was here that Elizabeth met John Fowles, also teaching English in the school. When the four of them returned to England the following year, Elizabeth left Roy almost immediately, and Anna remained with him.

The exact events surrounding the meeting and relationship of Elizabeth and John Fowles, and the story of Elizabeth's subsequent separation from both Roy and Anna, are obviously crucial to any discussion of John Fowles' life and work. Elizabeth, for example, was the model for the figure of Alison in *The Magus*, and we have to await a full biographical study to understand more exactly her own role and struggles. [4] Moreover, since Elizabeth Fowles died in March 1990, leaving behind her very little written material, there is unfortunately no direct record of the whole experience from her point of view.

Elizabeth's daughter, Anna Christy, though, still recollects the events of those years and her account of them and of her relationship with Elizabeth gives an encouraging sense of the ways in which relationships between mothers and children, though badly broken, can be healed. What emerges in the story of Elizabeth's life, reconstructed through Anna's memories and from surviving papers, is a woman deeply hurt by being separated from her child, but constantly struggling towards reunion.

Like Ingrid Bergman, Elizabeth Fowles had to face both the emotional heartache of not being with her child and the social stigma this entailed in the early 1950s, which was such a decade of motherhood and the feminine mystique. But in the relationship that evolved between Elizabeth and Anna, we also find a heartening example of reparation, with mother and child coming together again, perhaps drawn even closer by their early trauma of separation. Here, an incredibly strong, close relationship emerged between mother and daughter in later years, suggesting that no matter how hostile the circumstances, the intensity of their deep bonding and love can never be completely severed or erased.

The following pages record an interview I made with Anna Christy where she recounts the story from the point she herself remembers it.[5] This takes us first to the island of Spetsai in the early 1950s, then back to England, where her mother and father separated. Both Roy and Elizabeth had trouble finding jobs and accommodation, especially with a young child, as there were no benefits then for single parents. When John Fowles took a post teaching English at Ashridge College, near Berkhamsted, Elizabeth returned alone, for a while, to Birmingham to live with her parents.

From then on, for the next several years, Roy moved the young Anna around from one set of friends to another, making it very difficult for her mother to see her. It was not until Anna was finally settled with a family in London that Elizabeth was allowed to have regular contact again, but from then their relationship blossomed. Here are Anna's own words:

We must have spent a year on the island, and during that time, my mother met John [Fowles] who was teaching in the same school. We shared a house with a Greek family, a widow and her children and she became a kind of nanny for me, looking after me, mothering me. She's dead now, but I've been back to stay and I'm still in touch with the rest of the family. I'd stay with her whilst Liz, Roy and John would travel around Greece and Crete together. But I've discovered recently – from Liz's letters to my godmother – that Liz was torn at having to leave me behind on those trips, she hated not being able to take me. She'd get terribly anxious I'd have an accident, or fall down

*the well at the back of the house, she was always uneasy about
it.*

We came back to England, about 1953. My father and I
moved around to various families – he asked his sister, my
aunt, if she would adopt me and take me on, but she refused.
My father's an extremely difficult, egocentric man. For years
he's been a manic depressive and alcoholic, in fact he's now
been in an institution for some time. Prior to meeting my
mother, he'd had another marriage which had broken up and
since then, there's been another failed one, too.

He didn't really take over the parenting when he and my
mother separated. I was always settled with families who were
friends of my father's. We lived with two or three different
families and at one point, when I was quite little, I was put
into a convent for a while. So although my father did try to do
a certain amount, eventually he would always throw himself on
to one family or another who could take me on.

During that whole period, my mother had absolutely nothing
and I feel she suffered horrendously. She had to cope with the
ordeal of having left me, of trying to sort out her marriage
with John, which took some time, and of not being able to face
the prospect of returning to my father, despite his recriminating
letters. He was a converted Roman Catholic (he insisted I was
baptised a Catholic) and the religious side of things became
terribly heavy. There's one painful letter that's survived,
supposedly written by me to my mother, but actually my father's
hand doing childlike writing – I was only three then, I couldn't
write! – it says things like please forgive Daddy, I don't like it
when he's unhappy . . . It was a terrible kind of blackmail,
and my mother was having to receive letters like this. Or he'd
get me to pick bunches of primroses that he'd put in the post so
she'd find this crumpled bunch of dead flowers . . .

I never remember seeing my mother then, my father wouldn't
let her see me. It wasn't until I was older, about five or six,
when I was taken in with another family, that I began to see
my mother more. By that time, my father had another job
teaching architecture, and a colleague and his wife took me in,
in Forest Hill, southeast London. I must have lived there for

*four years, in what was effectively a fostering situation. My
father didn't live with us, he was leading a bachelor life by
then, so occasionally my mother was allowed to come and take
me out and visit. It was tough on her, he'd often cancel an
arrangement at the last minute. I know he denied her both
access and custody. It was terribly hard for her, it was such a
long haul for her to come over and take me out. But I
remember those visits quite well, we'd do lovely things like boat
trips up the river, picnics, but in those days I didn't actually
acknowledge or understand that she was my mother. She was
very beautiful – she had the opportunity of being a model
before she married – and so calm, such a lovely presence.*

*Liz and John married in April 1954, and they lived in
Hampstead for some years, so then my mother would come and
take me out, we'd go to the theatre, ballet and cinemas, she
introduced me to art and culture. We'd take buses, go on
outings, roam around London, then I'd be taken back to where
I was living. They were lovely trips, but unrooted, there was no
home base to them.*

*It wasn't until my father remarried, when I was 10 and I
went to live with him and his new wife that I began to see my
mother much more regularly. I remember that occasion of my
father's wedding, meeting my stepmother's family and searching
through the crowds for that other figure, that beautiful woman,
not being able to understand why she wasn't there.*

*Those first few years of my father's new marriage were the
most stable ones for me, that was quite a good time. It was my
first real experience of family life and I loved having a young
stepbrother and step-sister. But it deteriorated again when my
father became ill and self-preoccupied once more after the
second child. I still have difficult feelings to resolve towards
him, I find it hard to visit and he's only ever seen my children
once. When Liz died, he offered no sympathy to me, in fact he
was almost gleeful. He wrote a letter to John saying tough luck,
neither of us have got her now.*

*When I was old enough to transport myself, I'd go and visit
my mother, see more of her and John in Hampstead, stay
overnight. I adored those weekends, though it was awful going*

home again, having to suppress and hide that experience. And I really missed things like Liz never seeing me in any school performances – the rift was just too severe for her to attend any of those occasions, she was never included in them.

In the 1960s, after John had become successful, they moved down to Lyme Regis, Dorset, and then the bond between us developed and got even stronger. I was in my mid-teens so I could go and spend weekends and long holidays with her, we had much more time together and the relationship got much stronger. It was such a wonderful contrast to the way we'd had to meet before, all that travelling round London, sitting in coffee bars and eating ice creams. Now we could do things we'd never been able to do together before and our activities became much more domestic, much more home-based. We both loved house-making, we'd do shopping, cooking, jam-making, long walks, visiting churches and doing brass rubbings, simple mother-daughter things. And now that I was older it was easier with John, too.

That pattern of spending a lot of time together continued when I went to college to study graphic design, first at Exeter, then at Bristol. Liz would come up and stay, or I would go down there. She really enjoyed that, helping me find flats, sorting things out, we were great home-makers together. We were always doing this, making homes for each other. It was as if we were making up for our time apart, it happened again at the end of her life when Liz came out of hospital and I rearranged her room at home, she commented that it was like our setting up house again.

[When Anna was 23, she married a fellow art student. Two years later she had her first child, Tess, followed by a son. This marriage broke down, but Anna subsequently remarried and now she and her two children live with her second husband, Charles.]

By the time I started having children, the relationship with my mother was very close. I desperately wanted a girl, I think more for Liz's sake than mine. I can't stress enough how important having a daughter was for the relationship between us. It was as if I was giving her myself, giving back to her the years she'd missed. I remember being so proud to be able to hand this baby girl to her, it was just a few days before Christmas, the excitement was incredible. I know it was the best thing I could ever have done for her, and Tess was always so special for Liz.

When the children were little, we'd spend long holidays in Lyme, Liz loved it when we went down. She was so good with children, playing games with them, relating to them on their own level, entering their fantasy world. The other great tragedy in my mother's life is that she was unable to have any more children. She and John would have liked to have had children together, but because of gynaecological complications, it wasn't possible. So that was really a double blow to her.

[Through the 1980s, Anna and her mother made several trips back to Greece and Crete, some with the children, others with John and, later, Charles too. These cheap package holidays together, once and sometimes twice a year, proved immensely healing for them both – as if going back together to the scene of their original separation 30 years before provided deep emotional reparation on both sides. In this case, happily, the reparation between mother and daughter was profound, perhaps in ways that are less possible for mothers and sons, where the mutual identification may be rather less intense and intricate.]

I'd always had a hankering to go back to Greece, because I knew it was where this trauma had started and it was a place I had to really feel in my heart. I'd been back before with my father once, but Liz and I going back there with each other for the first time was what really brought us together. A lot of healing has gone on over the last few years, and I think it really started then when we went back to Greece. We found a place where it could be put right.

We didn't actually talk about it much, as Liz didn't like putting her feelings on show, they were very much held within, nothing much was said. Only occasionally, like the time I admitted I married young because I was insecure, did she try to tell me I didn't really know what it was like, and we almost faced something openly then. But I've always felt sympathetic to

*her. My father was such a difficult man, I could never blame
her for leaving.*

[In early 1990, Anna learnt that her mother was suffering from
cancer and she went to Lyme Regis to help John nurse her at
home. Two weeks later, in March 1990, Elizabeth Fowles died,
but Anna recollects their final time together with great affection.]

*I always had a premonition my mother would die young. I
knew it would be the most devastating event imaginable for
me, having to live without this woman who was my dearest
friend, so I'd been preparing myself for it for years. I knew she
was ill. She'd had bouts of depression over the years and
recently she'd been feeling less energetic, less enthusiastic about
life. When she was depressed, I would take her out, take the
children to visit, cook for her, it was as if I took on the mother
role to her.*

*She wouldn't openly pour out her feelings, as if she refused to
acknowledge her deeper emotions, and it was the same with
her physical being, she wouldn't go for medical checks. But she
smoked heavily and she developed cancer. By the time the
doctors realised what it was, she only had two weeks to live.
She was allowed to be at home, and I spent that last fortnight
with her at Lyme. It was such short notice, it was an immense
shock to John and he found it hard to accept. He couldn't give
up his optimism: he thought they might be able to give her a
few more months to live. Liz knew she was dying, but we didn't
say a lot. I think she just needed me there at that point, she
trusted me, it was what she wanted. She was in danger of
excluding John then and I had to make sure he was brought
into everything.*

*I know that, over the years, she'd had recurrent nightmares,
dreams of me as a baby, and she still felt some guilt. But she
never talked about it in great detail. Those last weeks, when
she did try to say how awful she felt for what had happened in
my life, all I wanted to do was to reassure her that it was past,
that she only had to look at me to see I was fine. I wanted her
to know that even though it had been a painful experience, it
wasn't something I really regretted having happened. It had
taught me so much.*

And in a similar way, though her dying was so painful, I was immensely grateful to have that last fortnight with her, it was so important being together then. I felt so fortunate to be with her at that time, preparing for her death and being so close physically, lifting her, walking her. I had a premonition the day before she was going to die, it was extraordinary, there was such an intuitive closeness between us. I remember cooking John some supper and saying we should go upstairs and have it at the table at the end of her bed, as if I knew she wasn't going to be there the next day. It was like a last supper.

Liz didn't have any religious beliefs, both she and John were atheists. But I believe she's not really gone, the presence of her is still so strong. She had such humour and wit, there was such great tenderness and warmth and affection from her.

I was so touched, when John put the announcement of Liz's death in The Times, *that he described her as 'mother of Anna' before anything else. It was as if he knew that was how she'd have wanted to be seen.*

John Fowles corroborates this reading of the closeness between Elizabeth and Anna, suggesting that 'Their last relationship was much more of two good friends, than the normal mother-and-daughter one.' And he emphasizes that their initial severance caused Elizabeth great pain, the memory of which could never be completely wiped away: 'leaving Anna seriously mutilated Elizabeth, and continued to recur all through her life and our life together, though one small compensation was their coming together again after the first painful years of separation . . .'[6]

One letter of Elizabeth's which has survived points to this long-term emotional cost – to her – of not being with her daughter. Describing a visit to Anna in Putney at the time of Roy Christy's third marriage, she expresses how moved she is to see her daughter having a home again, and tells of Anna 'waving furiously' as her mother departs on a bus. Then she goes on – uncharacteristically – to spell out the awful pain, for herself, of that (repeatedly re-enacted) separation.

> And I sit on the top of the bus in a kind of breathless
> choking despair, for a time I feel I shall never reach
> reality. I stay suspended and disconnected.[7]

Ultimately, Elizabeth and Anna were reunited, and there was obviously some profound healing of the wound that both had suffered. But for a long time, Elizabeth Fowles, like Frieda Lawrence (whose story is similar in so many respects) and like so many mothers who've left young children, constantly carried within her the wound of separation from her daughter. In John Fowles' words, 'Eternally, she missed her in those early years.'

* * *

Whether it is the child or the mother trying to come to terms with their separation 't is no easy process. As Ingmar Bergman shows in *Autumn Sonata*, reparation does not come for free. Being realistic, there are many instances where the obstacles to repairing the relationship are simply insurmountable. The children's father may – openly or insidiously – turn them against the mother, especially in cases where he is jealous of her new-found freedom or new partnership. It would be a rare man who could refrain totally from some manifestation of anger or revenge, and it is often children who are unwitting pawns in his strategy. In cases where this is most extreme, the mother may be so demoralised that she comes to feel she has to abandon attempts at fighting him.

Paddy, whose story was mentioned in Chapter 7, is one example of this. All her cards and letters to her children strangely disappeared, presents were destroyed, and her ex-husband refused to give her any news of them. Trying to arrange meetings in the face of her children's resistance and their father's manipulative behaviour ultimately became too distressing for her. Rather than waste energy fighting a losing battle indefinitely, Paddy finally decided to give up and pursue her own life. She now does not see her children at all.

Similar hostility has happened in many other cases. Ernest Weekley did not inform Frieda Lawrence of her children's address when he took them to London in 1913 and for years blocked access. Presents and cards that Diana Dors sent to her two sons in Hollywood for birthdays and Christmas mysteriously went astray every time, probably through the intervention of a jealous nanny, so the children thought she didn't care about them.[8] Meredith's child's father has refused to tell her where he and the child are living. Other women have reported parallel stories, of presents disappearing, letters getting lost, arrangements being cancelled at the last minute, an accumulation of evasive behaviour around access so that they have come to feel unwanted and that their relationship with their child or children is just too distressing or difficult to pursue. In these circumstances, it is hard not to be defeated. Yet if one does give up, one is then vulnerable to the additional accusation of not caring, of never getting in touch, of being selfishly engrossed with one's own life and pursuits. It can seem a no-win situation.

When parents separate, feelings of the children involved are bound to be complex, whether it is father or mother leaving, and the split inevitably has some emotional impact. Both child and mother survive best if some contact – or attempt at it – is sustained and if the child is told clearly both what is happening and that it is not his or her fault. Especially if the child is young, the contact needs to be regular, reliable and predictable, for the sake of both mother and child. But this can be very difficult in the face of hostility, whether from father, children's stepmother, relatives, or from the children themselves. And there may be practical obstacles to overcome, too. Poverty makes it difficult, especially in cases of geographical distances, where the mother may not be able to afford to travel to see the children. She may lack suitable accommodation in which to have them to stay, as in Caroline's case.

Yet these factors have to be fought. For her own sake as much as the child's, the mother needs to know she is doing her best to communicate and keep the relationship going. Even when there are vast distances involved, as for Charlotte, whose four daughters were abducted to the other side of the globe, or when there are immense time gaps, as for Frieda Lawrence and Elizabeth Fowles, determined attempts to mend the relationship have been rewarded. Especially, it seems, between mothers and daughters. Sons are often more intractable, perhaps because of their unconscious identification with the father who has been left – as in *Sorrell and Son* or *Daddy* – and here the reparation may be more problematic.

Mothers come to terms best with living apart from their children when there has been some *outer* reconciliation – when contact is on-going, when the children understand the reasons for her departure – and when the father does not poison them unduly against her. But equally important as this outer level is an inner one, where the mother may move towards acceptance of the situation for herself. For once the split is made, no matter what her best efforts, the kind of reparation of the relationship she would like *may not happen*. To deal with this, and for her own development, the process of coming to terms with the event *on an inner level* is just as vital as external attempts at healing, for the results of these are not entirely in her hands.

Helen Franks rightly suggests that the challenge facing mothers who leave is primarily one of self-forgiveness. One could even go a step further and say that more useful than self-forgiveness (which implies a sin needing to be forgiven) is the notion of *acceptance* – accepting that, at the time of separation, with her particular personal history, her particular set of social and economic circumstances, the particular context of mothering as an institution, there was no other way forwards, nothing else the mother could have done. It is not enough for this to be an abstract idea. It has to be an *emotional reality*, where the mother fully acknowledges that, at the time, with the resources she had (and did not have), leaving her children *was felt to be the only possibility available*.

Only those mothers who *have* started to accept this reading of their situation of being apart have been able to move on with their own lives, and to transform them into something positive. Moreover, women like Charlotte, Maggie, Leonie and Ruth, who have been able to use their experiences of psychotherapy (and their various spiritual philosophies) to explain this part of their personal history as the reproduction of a pattern inherited from their mothers, have thereby been able to sort out the exact nature of their responsibilities to themselves and their own children. This makes it more possible to ease out of guilt so that their freedom can be valued and used more creatively. Paradoxically, since leaving, all these women have developed *better, richer, lighter* relationships with their children, more fluid and pleasurable forms of interacting with them.

Without such perspective and support, there is a sad tendency for mothers apart to stay stuck in very negative places. Many of the women

I met were still locked in an emotional wasteland, lost in terrible feelings of frustration, grief, hopelessness and despair. States of depression and confusion often alternate with more angry feelings – blaming, resentful and bitter – especially towards men, the children's fathers, and (of course) their own mother, who is held to be the cause of much of the difficulty in the first place.

Some element of these feelings will be known to all mothers apart from their children, but it seems important not to let them fester and become self-destructive. We need to go on working through these feelings and trying to resolve them, in whatever way we can. Righteous anger against this negative definition – and against our own history – needs to be focused in creative ways, or it may backfire and turn into lingering resentment or incapacitating despair. It is not only guilt that sticks to us like tar, but anger and rage that, unacknowledged, can colour the whole emotional landscape with a bleak depression. But it is not hopeless. From the accounts in this book, it is obvious that it *is* possible to resolve some of these difficulties and even if the *external* reparation is blocked, *inner* healing can still take place.

One has also to attempt to understand the complex *political* as well as *personal* context in which such difficult situations arise, and to see that hostility towards us as 'bad mothers' is culturally induced. We have to recognise that many of the forces that drove us into destructive relationships or living situations – situations from which we then had to flee, with or without our children – came from our familial histories. Damage and deprivation, on whatever level, tend to reproduce themselves. But through making this negative heritage *conscious* – becoming aware of it, drawing attention to it, seeing how much it has conditioned our expectations and responses, compelled many of our actions – its destructive spell and effects can be undone. Whether we take the path of psychotherapy or other forms of healing, whether we try to become aware of these patterns alone or with others, the inheritance we have unconsciously taken on – from both our fathers and, more especially for women, our mothers – *can* be consciously dissolved. There is no magic wand to make this happen. It is a long process of coming to terms with our history, our backgrounds, our selves. It involves trying to understand, accept and forgive. It is part of a path of self-knowledge.

But if we are to accept that, as mothers who left, there was nothing else at the time that we were able, or felt able, to do, then we also have to accept that any inadequate mothering we received was the result of a chain of causes rather an act of malice. If we want not to be blamed we have to stop blaming. We can only move forwards by going backwards sufficiently to repair damage and stop perpetuating it.

This work on ourselves is helped enormously by remembering that though our life stories are unique, they mirror and are mirrored by so many others. We can be heartened in our own struggles towards acceptance and reparation by keeping in front of us those examples of women who have come through, mothers who – despite all the projections and obstacles against them – have fought to stay in touch with their children and have, finally, had profoundly creative and loving relationships with them.

Yet, paradoxically, it may be that far from working against them, the break from an ordinary pattern of mothering has served in many cases to make their eventual bonding even stronger. As if the separation opens a door on to a different dimension, however strange, painful or unsettling, and this serves to draw attention even more sharply to the bonding, forcing awareness to focus on the (broken) dynamic between mother and child, so that when the reparation and reunion does arrive it is deeper, more conscious, than it would be where the mother-child continuum is taken for granted.

Certainly, in the stories of Frieda Lawrence, Ingrid Bergman, Elizabeth Fowles and a host of lesser-known women whose mothering has been dramatically interrupted, the mother-child relation has become, in the end, extraordinarily rich and strong.

Epilogue:
Back to the Future

. . . it is a question of the meaning of motherhood in a
world where women are unequal. Women do not have
economic and hence personal and social independence;
they are judged by a patriarchal law. Natural instinct –
an oyster can be a mother, as Charlotte Perkins Gilman
put it – is not enough. If you infantilise women by
making them both statutorily dependant and psycho-
logically passive, should you simultaneously ask them to
be responsible mothers?

Juliet Mitchell *Women: The Longest Revolution*

I have argued that leaving children is *not* a feminist act, and that a
mother who leaves is no feminist heroine, for any such assertion would
feed dangerously into a misogyny that caricatures feminists as
irresponsible and unloving. But of course any woman who repudiates
conventional roles, particularly the role of mothering, *is* treading new
ground.

We have become so accustomed to double standards in viewing male
and female behaviour, we take them as read. Just as men have
traditionally been given more licence than women in their sexual
freedom, so fathers who leave are nothing unusual and have invited
relatively little censure. It is still seen as 'natural' for a man to pursue
fulfilment (whether professional or erotic) outside the family, yet a
woman who makes the same claims is seen – at best – as eccentric, at
worst as selfish. A 'normal' woman is still held to be someone who lives
primarily *through her relationship* to others: her very identity is
defined through her connectiveness rather than her independence. A
woman is not meant to nourish her own life as much as or more than
a man's or child's.

If women in general are meant to support others, to play the mother, this is even more so with their biological children. Attached, receptive, surrendering her claims to self-determination, mother by definition is a sacrificial and flexible figure whose own needs melt in the face of others'. Mothers floating free from this 'natural' function as nurturer and provider, mothers leaving, become contradictions in terms. People do not know how to place them.

I have stressed, too, that a mother separated from her own children is a phenomenon deeply rooted in the social and political: that it is not a sign of individual aberration so much as a symptom of something deeply flawed in our concept, construction and practice of mothering. Seen in this way, as *symptomatic* of cultural difficulties, the increased numbers of such mothers today indicates something profoundly wrong with our social fabric and its organisation of parenting. The rising number of mothers leaving is *not* an index of female morals on the wane, but is indicative of a system that is seriously at fault.

In this sense, the very theme of mothers leaving their children demands to be read on a collective rather than personal level. For as we have seen in the analysis of images in mainstream literature and popular culture, mothers who leave first appear in any major way at the beginning of the modern age. From Defoe's *Roxana* and novels from the early Industrial Revolution onwards, representations of such mothers start to proliferate – some sympathetic, some deeply hostile – but if we search for their appearance in culture prior to that time, they are remarkably absent.

In classical, medieval and Renaissance culture, we find types of the 'Bad' mother in the archetypal form Jung identified – women like Medea who devour their young, or scheming stepmothers – but the motif of the mother who leaves, as such, is conspicuously absent.

This in itself is very telling. The motif – and the social reality it represents, with cultural forms reflecting and refracting that reality for their own purposes – comes into being at *precisely that moment* when modern forms of motherhood are born. Prior to that, with family life being less separative and not enclosed in bourgeois units, there was no need for the mother to leave to escape the nuclear family's intolerable pressures, and more surrogate forms of mothering were part of everyday life. Only with the progressive impact of the Industrial Revolution and the resultant displacement of collective and shared responsibilities for child care by an exclusive focus on a woman mothering alone does the issue of mothers leaving start to emerge in the West as a social phenomenon.

Mothers who leave manifest historically, then, at exactly that time when extended families were superseded by the nuclear family, and the role of woman as mother took on such specific definitions and functions. According to these definitions, the actions of 'unmothering' mothers are flawed, signs of some kind of ill-health. They are not as 'whole' as other women, something has 'gone wrong' in their make-up and psychological development. (Indeed, Chapter 21 partly feeds into such a reading).

Yet the phenomenon can be read in a light entirely different from this, one that makes these women's actions less a mark of ill-health than the exact opposite. Far from being simply the destructive shadow side, the inverse of good mothers, women moving away from the pattern of the nuclear family actually serve as a reminder of all that was left behind when the specific and relatively recent institution of mothering as we know it was inaugurated.

For just as unusual physical symptoms may be constructed as illness or as attempts by the organism to restore itself to wholeness and balance, so these symptoms of unusual mothering may be seen as negative faults to be cured, or as much more hopeful signs of life. Indeed, on the level of the collective, the whole phenomenon of mothers leaving can be seen as a welcome indication that something refuses to be suppressed, as an attempt on the part of the social organism to right itself.

Whatever is rotten in the state of motherhood will no longer be ignored, but is rising to the surface with greater intensity day by day and our numbers are increasing. This does not mean things have got worse, nor that feminism has finally got us to burn our maternal apron strings. It means that we are no longer able to lie or repress. Whereas generations of mothers before us tended not to leave, our own finds itself more able to do so – or more unable to go on resisting the reality and pressure of unconscious forces that are insisting on being felt.

Symptoms of illness in the physical body will go on perpetuating themselves until true health is restored (even if it means physical death), and these symptoms of breakdown in the social body will go on similarly accumulating and repeating themselves until a more profound transformation occurs. They may appear negative or destructive in the short term (and of course being separated *is* painful to some degree, for mother *and* child), but behind them is a much more positive drive – towards real reparation, social as well as personal, as if the collective unconscious is attempting to repair our cultural damage.

It would be wrong, then, to concentrate too exclusively on the individual woman or her 'failure' to adapt. She is trying to exit not from her children, but from the travesty of the institutionalised form of being with her children that this culture presents as natural. If she seems damaged, it is because she shows the heavy toll that nuclear mothering has taken on women, especially in less privileged economic groups, over the last two centuries – a toll passed on from generation to generation and so affecting her children (particularly daughters) in their turn. Damaged mothering does not come out of nowhere.

From this perspective, when I turn to look at my own personal history, I see my relationships with both my mother and my child as having been severely damaged by the forms of mothering socially available (especially to particular economic groupings) in modern times. In my mother's unfulfilled life, poverty and powerlessness, with her own early (economic and emotional) deprivation repeating itself in fraught relations with her children, I see a woman who has deeply repressed her own feelings and needs, martyring herself to the myth of the Good Mother in a way that has, tragically and ironically, militated against the very mothering she has tried to provide.

For different but related reasons, my relation with my own son has been deeply compromised. Prejudice and inflexibility around mothering positions (as well as simple external factors such as lack of money for nannies, nurseries or travel) have inevitably coloured the relationship between us. Only through determination and persistence has it survived into its present, relatively healthy state, which is one I would describe as neither better nor worse than that of most women I know with sons of a similar age, social background and estranged parents. There is a general move forwards and the future always holds hopeful possibilities, yet it would be hypocritical to deny that, somewhere, for both of us, there remains the scar of years missed.

Maggie Mountford, whose sensitive poems frame this book and who has gone through parallel experiences of struggling against the odds with her two sons, hints at some of these tensions and difficulties in 'The Unearthing', the poem whose opening introduces Chapter 7. Having celebrated some of the reparation and healing that has eventually taken place, she goes on to admit that the recovery is always fragile and forever vulnerable:

> better now. Yes, better!
> Grown over year by year
>
> except for a sort of
> winter
> in the heart, with blizzards
> any time of day, at any hour.

A mother who has left is never completely immune.

Yet if, as I have come to believe, the phenomenon *is* some kind of attempt on the part of the collective, however blind or unwitting, to expose the limits of motherhood as a cultural institution and to move towards different social forms and practices, we have to respect it. It then becomes neither a syndrome to lament nor a symptom to reverse, but something with meaning for the future. If women – and men – in greater and greater numbers are continuing to leave their isolated family units, this is not simply because they cannot 'take the responsibility' any more, but because they want a more fulfilling and meaningful way of life.

On a wider, collective level the reactions of mothers leaving are not necessarily either unhealthy or irresponsible. Symptomatically, they represent an unconscious drive, *within the social fabric itself*, to move back to something much less enclosing and individualistic than the nuclear family structure – a desperate gesture to get back to some other form of living and of parenting.

The age that was born with industrial capitalism is an age of consumption and possessiveness, of private property, individualism and narcissism. Here, not only objects but children (and women) are seen as extensions of the self, things to be owned and branded as 'mine'. Mothers who leave offer a dramatic image of something other.

They remind us that relationships with children need not be narcissistic, simply reproducing ourselves in our own image, nor need they be so possessive that only our biological children have ultimate claims on our resources. They remind us (and so deeply offend the individualistic assumptions on which a nuclear family structure depends) that children do not 'belong' to parents alone, that there are other forms of responsibility and that relationships – between parents and children, as between adults – can be more fluid, open and free.

Not that this more optimistic reading is always obvious. The ways in which the actions of such mothers manifest themselves may be muddled, shot through with guilt and confusion, involving pain rather than liberation. But still, informing their actions and at a level deeper than conscious social judgements, there does seem to be a much more profound message trying to break through. A message, as it were, from the *collective* unconscious, and one which is being spelt out constantly on a day-to-day level – in the form of mothers leaving, families disintegrating, nuclear units falling apart. Look, it says, at the suffering this social structure has caused. Look how untenable and damaging it is. Look at how it divides men and women, distorts parenting, cripples women, constrains mother and child.

It is as if, no matter what the personal cost to us as individual women – and there *is* a price to be paid for venturing outside the nuclear shelter – we are being compelled towards the point where we *have* to take a wider and longer-term view of our actions. We have to see that our moving away from traditional positions is not some neurotic reaction, but the reflection of an increasingly desperate social need, the need to find an alternative to the nuclear family unit, with all the possessiveness, individualism and patriarchal assumptions it implies. One of the messages seems to be that unless we move (back) to less individualised and exclusive forms of living (of which mothering is the most concentrated example), we will never be able to move forwards to a fuller or freer future; indeed, there may be no future at all.

One of the obstacles to a more fluid view is the rush to moral judgements about good and bad mothers, fed in part by that unconscious polarising discussed in Chapter 20. Either you are a good mother, or a bad: definitions of mothering have been very black and white. One of Franks' conclusions in *Mummy Doesn't Live Here Any More* is that there are 'women who can't or won't mother'. But women can and do move in and out of different mothering positions: 'unmothering' is not a fixed identity any more than mothering is. Many mothers who leave go on to have more children whom they do not leave. It is not a question of either/or. One *can* leave *and* still love, one can be responsible *and* leave, one can be a loving mother *and* not be permanently present, or one can be present *and* still fight to be that part of oneself that is *not* a mother. Our lives are fluid: the plots and stories we inhabit can change.

Motherhood is only *one aspect* of a woman's possible range of experiences, not an all-defining and delimiting identity. It is a mobile part of her being, a position to move in and out from, not to occupy permanently.

Yet the mythology surrounding the perfect Mother dies hard. In our contemporary Western world, she is undergoing a strong revival (and the current preoccupation with the Goddess figure could be seen as a displaced version of the same longing for the ideal eternal Mother). This is not surprising. In times of rapid social flux like our own, there is always a tendency to want to hang on to the comfort of traditional mores and habits. Hence the desperate right-wing backlash and the attempt to reinstate familiar forms of living.

Once more, the 'normal' family is being defined as 'husband and wife living with their own children, the husband the major earner, the spouses intending and trying to stay together.'[1] Opposition to female independence or to living units other than the heterosexual couple is as intense as ever. A woman's greatest fulfilment is supposed to lie in her experience of mothering, her greatest misery in a failure to conceive. Symptomatic of this trend, even Franks' *Mummy Doesn't Live Here Any More* concludes with a peroration to maternal love.[2]

In the face of fears of change, such a reactionary trend is understandable, for the idealised 'Mother' is one of the most comforting fantasies of all. As psychoanalysis has explained, it is the image of the longed-for mother held in our unconscious minds that comes to represent all we have lost in our entry into the human. Mother is the whole from which, in order to mature into human beings, we have to endure separation. Thus in our fantasy life, Mother is deeply lodged as an image of the pre-human and pre-social, the place of unity and oneness that precedes language, separation and individuation.

If the movement into the human realm of language and cultural order is thought of as a kind of fall from Paradise, it is the realm of the Mother that then becomes the one and only space in which fantasies of a pre-social, pre-linguistic and non-alienated being can be placed (at least in a secular culture). Working primarily on this unconscious imaginary level, the Maternal space serves as an imagined lost wholeness – as everything that the fragmented, alienated and separated human realm is not. The mother's (imagined) body is the lost domain, the lost Eden. Mother is the perfection, the Paradise from which, as humans, we are permanently exiled.

Separating out *real women as mothers* from this fantasy of Mother is not easy. As Julia Kristeva's work has shown, many cultures have reabsorbed otherwise subversive female energies into exactly such a Maternal space and, in the West especially, the whole history of our civilisation has been predicated on the value of the Maternal. It is precisely *through* the icon and image of the mother that femininity has been made respectable. As Kristeva writes: 'The *consecrated* (religious or secular) representation of femininity is absorbed by motherhood.' And Western Christianity, with its cult of the Virgin Mary, has brought that process of absorption to a peak. [3]

But why do we, as women, allow this process to happen? Kristeva suggests that the reason women – quite as much as men – collude with this Maternal enterprise is because it is precisely these fantasies of the Maternal that give to the women who carry them an otherwise non-existent power. Women are consoled for their real loss of power in the (male) cultural order by being told that, as mothers, they are entering a higher, more privileged realm.

> This feminine (maternal) power must have been experienced as denied power, more pleasant to seize because it was both archaic and secondary, a kind of substitute for effective power in the family and city . . . the underhand double of explicit phallic power. [4]

Hence the conspiracy between women and patriarchy that still exists. Consoled by fantasies of sharing that 'privileged' Maternal space, believing that the Maternal is some kind of special place to be, female masochism has managed to perpetuate itself largely intact and unabated. Despite the onslaughts of feminism, and fearful of its full implications, women as well as men now advocate and practise a renewed movement back to this 'special' position, once again seizing substitute gratification for their actual lack of power.

In *The Rocking of the Cradle and the Ruling of the World*, Dorothy Dinnerstein argues strongly against this kind of conspiracy that forces women into unconscious collusion with the Maternal. Making full use of psychoanalytic understanding, Dinnerstein too recognises that women's experience – and particularly our experience of mothering – is clouded by projections and unconscious images of the Mother. Indeed, Dinnerstein holds this fantasising process and construction to be largely responsible for women's subordinate position in general.

It is because Mother is apprehended as a fantasy realm, confused with that area of experience prior to differentiation and individuation – our 'fall' into the human – that our social definitions and expectations of the female, or feminine, have been formed as they are. In Dinnerstein's view, *the problem is that woman has been constantly apprehended as a fantasy Mother and not a separated being in her own right.* 'She (a woman) is this global, inchoate, all-embracing presence before she is a person, a discrete finite human individual with a subjectivity of her own.'[5]

If men 'rule the world' and women 'rock the cradle', this is because of that widely sustained desire for a kind of infantile dependency upon the mother – a regression to an infantile state of union. Dinnerstein sees this as the key to women being kept in subordinate positions. She points out our repeated reluctance to separate fantasy from reality, our resistance to seeing mother *as an individuated being* rather than (the imaginary) Mother who is an extension of the self.

For Dinnerstein, this tendency comes not from some innate and unchangeable unconscious formation, but from the specific social practices that operate around the care of infants and children. She argues that it is the pattern of making the first primary care-taker a woman that has led to this fantasising process itself. 'One result of female-dominated child care . . . is that the trouble every child has in coming to see that the magic parental presence of infancy was human, a person, can be permanently side-stepped: Women can be defined as quasi persons, quasi humans . . .' The nuclear family too Dinnerstein regards as a regressive model, based on a similar nostalgia for infantile unity, 'a wish to return to an illusion of oneness'.[6]

In an attempt to reverse this deeply entrenched pattern, that has come to seem so natural, Dinnerstein urges women to make a conscious decision *not* to collude with the fantasy. We have to try to *undo the very mental processes* that make us fall only too readily into maternal and care-taking positions. We (women as much as men) have to stop keeping woman in the position of the Mother (to adults as well as children) and to resist the fantasy of the Maternal which, as women, we are made to carry.

A start towards this massive reversal lies in the development of a much more fluid theory and practice around parenting. Only an equal sharing of the *emotional* as well as *physical* responsibility of infant and child rearing can help start to redress the imbalance and to stop that unconscious equation of woman as the sole maternal function.

Whether or not Dinnerstein's ideas are possible to realise on the global level she desires – and whether a shift in child care practice would actually effect a dissolution of that deeply unconscious fantasy of the Mother we all seem to carry – certainly there does need to be a radical and widespread re-orientation if the relation between the sexes – and between parents and children – are ever to improve.

After all, the usual lack of participation by the adult male in current child rearing is *not* a biological given but another cultural construction. Not only are mothers no more real than other women, but women need not be better mothers than men. The 'mother' role can equally well be taken by a man – and without investing him with the super-heroics found in *Sorrell and Son, Kramer versus Kramer,* or *Daddy.*

Women are not merely there for the child's holding. They have their own equally vital needs. And mothers need not be biological, nor must the continuous adult figure needed for the child's emotional stability and maturity be female. Men can mother as well. But to make this happen, women, too, have to let go of the power of the Maternal fantasy.

As Ann Kaplan writes: 'The mother . . . is not a fixed, monolithic construct; "mother" does not signify in fact any particular attributes.'[7] We have to resist regressive fantasies of the romanticised biological Mother, to undo constructions of the Maternal on imaginary (unconscious) as well as real (social) levels – in our own minds as well as in the world.

Yet an idealised discourse of motherhood still floats around us in our patriarchal culture, constantly undermining our resistance. It insists on our failures, on the imperative of bridging the gap between that impossible fantasised perfection of Mother and our own reality. We are berated for falling short of the ideal, we berate ourselves and we berate our own mothers in their turn. We find it hard not to attack them too for not being 'good' mothers. Such is the grip of our unconscious desire for that great omnipresent Mother.

There are further ways, too, of reading this longing. In Leonie's story in Part Three, it was clear that she viewed the yearning for wholeness with the Mother in much more spiritual terms. Traditional psychology (locked into materialist ways of thinking) would read Leonie's longing for a non-worldly Mother as a displacement of the desire for an earthly one – the result of disappointment at not being met by her own mother. But it is also possible to stand this psychological reading on its head and offer a completely different interpretation. What if the desire for Mother, the nostalgia for a floating, non-human Maternal space, is instead a reflection of a deeper, spiritual longing – that desire for ultimate union beyond the individuated, ego-identified self?

In a secular culture, such transpersonal notions are scoffed at, not least by ego-based psychology and psychoanalysis. But that may be part of the problem. In our exclusive focus on a *human* realm of fulfilment, there is nowhere else to put our longings for union, totality and wholeness; thus desire *will* fall back into the human, particularly into nostalgia for the imagined body of the Mother. We will look backwards to that time of pre-human merging and ultimate containment in a way that is inevitably infantile and regressive.

Perhaps the time has come to look beyond this fixation with the Mother to what it represents, to start searching beyond our secular culture towards a different kind of wholeness. For the fantasy of the Maternal may be read as nothing but a reflection, on a psychological level, of that yearning for wholeness which is the ultimate goal of all forms of mysticism and spirituality. This desire to merge with something beyond the personalised separated self, to move into a non-linguistic, oceanic state, need be neither unconscious nor regressive. It is the bliss of union consciously sought as the height of mature mystical experience. [8]

Fantasies of the Mother take on such power and numinosity precisely because we are locked in a materialistic and secular society, where desire for another realm has nowhere else to locate itself. [9] When yearnings to get beyond the human have nowhere else to go, inordinate attention *will* be given to the imagined, imaginary body of the Mother: she will become the vision of Paradise and bliss. Thus, issues around mothering and the maternal cannot be separated from the deepest crises facing our society. It is not merely a sexist culture that is the problem, but a secular one.

In relation to this, it is no accident that many of the mothers discussed in this book left their children not out of personal ambition nor selfishness, but as part of a move (however unconscious) to try to find more satisfactory ways of life than the small, individualistic outlook of the nuclear family unit made possible. Like Doris Lessing's fictional Martha Quest, who relinquished a child she loved because the forms of mothering available to her were so stifling, they too have felt driven to move towards a fuller, deeper, non-secular vision as did Martha in *The Four-Gated City*. Many have become involved with different forms of spirituality, healing, and creativity.

The women whose stories we have heard frequently felt themselves unable to stop the process that pushed them out of the conventional mothering position. Many have described a sense of a deeply unconscious force compelling them out of their nuclear families and driving them to give their lives a different focus and alignment. And although some have chosen to find their identity once again as mothers, this time proving themselves excellent Good Mothers by having more children or by taking on jobs and relationships in which their roles are notably nurturing ones, many have resisted this option and have tried to come to terms more fully with the phenomenon of leaving their children, examining it for what it might mean in both personal and transpersonal terms.

I have certainly found this true for myself over the years, the weight of my double disappointment in mothering made lighter by reading my personal situation in a context of spiritual (for want of a better term) evolution. And whether it proves to be a dubious consolation or an authentic alternative view, I have found it helpful to keep in mind the notion that our complex human relationships – especially with mothers and children – may be formed not only by our connections with one another in this lifetime, but also by our previous lives.

As Blake said, 'Anything possible to be believed is an image of truth' and it might indeed be true, as so much Eastern philosophy maintains, that *all* our human involvements and actions (even the writing of this book) are deeply karmic ones.

Karma is a Sanskrit term and refers to the law of action and reaction, cause and effect that is conditioned, or shaped (not, though, crudely predetermined) by one's past lives. According to this belief, during each incarnation the many experiences taken in by the individual – physical, emotional and mental – are stored in the psyche as impressions, or *sanskaras*, and are reactivated, or spent, in subsequent lives. [10]

Thus, our experiences, relationships and human interactions are influenced and formed by these impressions and patterns brought with us from past incarnations – the load of our karmic heritage. According to this theory, not only may we have known one another before, but all our very close encounters, especially of the family kind, are inevitably affected by this residue carried over from past lives. Our various knots of human intimacy are deeply tied and entangled in what are, to our limited conscious perspectives, inscrutable ways.

Such a reading, taking into account as it does the *possibility* of reincarnation (and thereby offending any exclusively materialist philosophy or ego-based psychology), gives an added dimension to the usual psychoanalytic concentration on the mother-child bond. For it introduces the possibility that, as we move through successive incarnations, our roles with one another – especially our most intimate familial ones – may be repeatedly polarised and reversed as the sanskaric impressions and debts work themselves out. Thus the child of a mother in a previous life may be the mother (of a child who was previously that same mother) in this lifetime, and so on.

Isabel Allende's novel, *The House of Spirits* (1985) beautifully dramatises such complex incarnating through the saga of a family history. And Shirley MacLaine – a mother who left her child – reflects interestingly on this possible reversal of roles in close relationships through successive lives and reads our human knots from a more transpersonal perspective, in her best-selling memoir *Dancing in the Light* (1985).

This notion of reincarnation has particular bearing on the issue of mothers who leave, for it is in the relation between mother and child that any unresolved material from past lives is held to be most likely to manifest. Indeed Roger Woolger, a Jungian psychotherapist who has worked for some years in this (controversial) area of possible past life material and its residual impact on the psychology of the present, has gone so far as to identify the mother-child dyad as being not only the most tightly bound pair of psychic opposites, but as also being *the very place where past life tensions and conflicts will most assert themselves.* [11] It is with our mothers and children that karmic entanglement will be at its most intense – hence the deep roots of the emotional tensions we feel around them, roots that may go beyond our perceived or visible history.

Such a sense of conflicts and problems around mothering (given and received) having origins deeper than the most immediately apparent ones of social or personal history shifts the slant on outer events in an interesting way – though it does not negate any of the desperate need for profound political and cultural change around the institution of mothering which, I hope, has become so apparent in this study.

Rather, once light has been thrown on, or from, this other dimension, we can see that our usual, more secular perspective is somewhat limited in its approach. We are so used to judging events in their external manifestation, we tend to forget there may be these other less visible (yet no less real) dimensions within and behind them and that our relationships with parents and children (amongst others) may be permeated by a heritage that carries as much invisible material beneath the surface as it shows above it. From these transpersonal perspectives, my main focus in *Mothers Who Leave* can be seen as having touched on only *part* of the full range of possibilities and complexities affecting human relationships – of which the mother-child interaction remains the most fraught. And although there are many feminists and material thinkers who will resist strongly any idea of reincarnation or karma, holding such doctrines to be both regressive and deterministic – as if they do away with the need for social action or responsibility – yet, understood properly, a conviction of the importance of past and future as well as present lives can work differently and to radical effect.

For what else but a knowledge that we have been here before and will be back, time and time again, until we have faced fully our responsibilities as human beings, will wake us up to the imperative of confronting them this time round? What else but a realisation that we exist in a much larger, longer time-scale than these tiny finite lives, can make us fully sensitive and compassionate to every aspect of the earth, others and ourselves, or stop us grabbing instantly at whatever gratification we can get?

What else but an understanding that *we are not fixed absolutely* in our present identity – as *this* person, *this* ego, *this* sex – can really undermine our over-identification with one gender and what are taken to be its 'natural', essential qualities?

This time round, for whatever inscrutable reasons, I find that part of the experience of being here has involved being female, being a mother, being separated from a child, feeling the pain of that, the guilt, the anxiety, the regrets, the determination and struggle to repair and heal and hold, and the need to name and wrest meaning from it all by writing – writing in a way that stays open to possibilities and comes, hopefully, back to the present and future.

When I speak about it now
I see November mist.
That damp afternoon of my life.

It goes with excitement
and fear: my body's truth.
Opening my freedom

like a letter bomb,
seeing everything
explode.

Surviving, I hear:
You alright?
Where does it hurt?

How do you measure
mind-ache?
How do you tell of

amputations this invisible?
See, I smile, I talk,
I walk . . .

I even speak about it now
without a tremor in my voice
when I need to say their names.

And the reasons have faded too.
Like an old print in the sun.
Leaving residues of something

which isn't exactly guilt
but wears the same drab colour
and which jolts me awake at two

to choose and choose
and choose again
what always seems

impossible
and will remain
forever so.

Maggie Mountford 'When I Speak'

Notes

Introduction

1 Lesser, 'One of the last great crimes: Women who leave children.' Paper presented at 44th annual AAMFT family therapy conference, Orlando, Florida, October 1986.

2 For American figures, see *New York Times* 9 May 1987; 16 June 1988; *Newsweek* 4 June 1990.

3 Figures in report on Government's new Child Support Agency, *Guardian* 5 April 1993.

4 Brandt, *Five hundred and seventy-four deserters and their families*.

5 Kaplan, *Motherhood and Representation: The Mother in Popular Culture and Melodrama*, gives a full theoretical account of the different discourses that construct mothering. Her study is highly recommended for readers not intimidated by cultural theory.

6 Edwards, *How Could You?: Mothers Without Custody of Their Children*, p. 12. I am indebted to Edwards for many of the examples found in this chapter.

7 Brabazor, *Dorothy L. Sayers: A Biography*, pp. 103–4. Sayers did not, however, completely disappear from her son's life. She visited and wrote regularly, paid for his maintenance and education, and on her death in 1957 he became sole heir to her literary estate.

8 Greer, *The Female Eunuch*, p. 322.

9 Weldon, *The Sunday Times* 5 August 1990.

Chapter 1

1 Morton, *Diana: Her True Story*, p. 9.

2 Morton, pp. 9–22, 38, 53–4, 120, 151.

3 Morton, pp. 17–18. On p. 137 he implies this negative view of

Frances Shand Kydd has been influenced and sustained by the
Queen Mother, who remains 'unfavourably disposed' to Diana
and her mother.

4 Greif and Pabst, *Mothers Without Custody*, p. 2.
5 Franks, *Mummy Doesn't Live Here Any More: Why Women Leave
   Their Children*, p. 28.
6 Ingrid Bergman (and Alan Burgess), *My Story*, p. 299.
7 Dors, *Dors by Diana*, pp. 288–309.
8 Trudeau, *Beyond Reason*, pp. 228, 249.
9 Raske, *The Killing of Karen Silkwood*. Edwards, *How Could
   You?*, p. 10, adds the postscript to the story: 'Five years later a
   federal court jury found Kerr-McGee negligent, and awarded the
   Silkwood estate over $10 million in damages. Far from being weak
   and irresponsible, Karen Gay Silkwood's tenacious pursuit of
   what she perceived as justice and fairness showed remarkable
   courage. So, perhaps, did the course she took in re-ordering her
   life.'
10 Fildes, 'Maternal feelings reassessed: child abandonment and
    neglect in London and Westminster 1550–1800', in Fildes (ed.),
    Women as Mothers in Pre-Industrial England, p. 157.
11 Lawyer Leonard Kerpelman, *Time* 2 April 1980.
12 Greif and Pabst, *Mothers Without Custody*, p. 5.
13 Interview by David Sheff, 'John Lennon and Yoko Ono', *Playboy*
    January 1981, pp. 99–101.
14 Franks, *Mummy Doesn't Live Here Any More*, pp. 28–29.
15 On issues of representation and the male gaze, see Mitchell,
    Psychoanalysis and Feminism; Mulvey, 'Visual pleasure and
    narrative cinema', *Screen* 16, 3 (1975), pp. 6–18; Kuhn, *Women's
    Pictures: Feminism and Cinema*; Kaplan, *Women and Film: Both
    Sides of the Camera* and 'Is the Gaze Male?' in Snitow (ed.),
    Desire: The Politics of Sexuality, pp. 321–338; Suleiman (ed.), *The
    Female Body in Western Culture: Contemporary Perspectives*.
16 Orbach and Eichenbaum, 'Merged Attachments', in *Bittersweet*,
    pp. 43–61.
17 Wynd, *The Ginger Tree*, p. 182.
18 Faludi, *Backlash: The Undeclared War Against Women*, p. 190.
19 Kaplan, *Motherhood and Representation*, p. 182.

Chapter 2

1 Housman, *Pains and Penalties*. I am grateful to Katharine Cockin for this reference.
2 Showalter, *A Literature of Their Own: British Women Novelists from Brontë to Lessing*, p. 171.
3 Mrs Henry Wood, *East Lynne*, p. 491.
4 Mitchell, 'Introduction', *East Lynne*, p. xii.
5 Wood, *East Lynne*, p. 237.
6 As the first wife who comes back to haunt the second marriage, Isabel recalls other stories of female doubles: the mad and sexual first wife in Charlotte Brontë's *Jane Eyre*, violently killed by fire; the unnameable shadow in Gilman's *The Yellow Wallpaper*; the ghostly sexual first wife in Daphne du Maurier's *Rebecca*; the subversive wife haunting the husband's new relationship in Fay Weldon's *Life and Loves of a She Devil*. Like these, Isabel represents part of the female psyche that doesn't fit, that eludes identity as 'wife' or 'mother', a slippage of female desire and power that can never be fully exorcised.

Chapter 3

1 The primary fear evident on almost every page of *Sorrell and Son* is of a mother who is also sexual. In psychoanalytic terms, this can obviously be read as an Oedipal struggle and the obsessive father-son bond as a narcissistic defence against adult sexuality.

   Significantly, Deeping has a diatribe against Freud within the novel itself, rejecting any psychoanalytic reading or theory. Repeatedly misspelling Freud's name, he writes: 'It was sex that was troubling Christopher, and all that sex implied – his mother, other fellows' mothers. Sorrell had dipped into Frued [sic], and his inclination was to laugh at Frued . . . As for the so-called 'Oedipus complex', it did not appear to exist in Kit. Nor had it existed in Sorrell . . . He rather thought that the abnormality could be looked for on the Continent, and in the mental make-up of a certain sort of Continental youth who grew up to be a professor.' This is a fascinating piece of denial, all the more so in a novel where every critical scene betrays Oedipal patternings – the horror of mature female flesh, the depiction of women's sexual desire as vampirism, the recurrent terror of mother seducing – and the father and son's retreat into an exclusively male enclosure is purely defensive.

2 Dors, *Dors by Diana*, p. 289.

3 Brecht, 'The Augsburg Chalk Circle', in *Collected Short Stories*, p. 198.

4 Faludi, *Backlash*, p. 72.

Chapter 4

1 Kaplan, *Motherhood and Representation*, pp. 100–106: 'unlike the nineteenth-century British novel, which was written by a woman primarily addressing a female audience, the twentieth-century American films, directed and adapted within the Hollywood system, construct a cleanly sealed phallocentric discourse . . . the Hollywood versions of *East Lynne* recuperate even the mildly subversive aspects of Ellen Wood's novel.'

2 Amongst these are the Hollywood versions of *Anna Karenina* starring Greta Garbo in 1935, one with Vivien Leigh in 1947 and a Soviet one by Alexander Zarkhi in 1967.

3 Some films in the 1970s gave positive portraits of women leaving home, on temporary or permanent moves, including *Diary of a Mad Housewife* (1970), *A Woman Under the Influence* (1974), *An Unmarried Woman* (1978), *Alice Doesn't Live Here Any More* (1974) and *The Turning Point* (1977). It was in reaction against their potential feminism that films like *Kramer* and *Fatal Attraction* emerged. See Faludi, 'Fatal and Foetal Visions: The Backlash in the Movies', in *Backlash*, pp. 140–170.

4 Kaplan, *Motherhood and Representation*, p. 184. '*Kramer versus Kramer* was the archetype for this imaginary paradigm, especially in the negativity accorded the departing mother, who later appears to regret her decisions, and its obvious invitation to the spectator to identify with the father. The fantasy was repeated in many other films.'

5 The one exception was Sherry Lansing, then Senior Vice-President of Columbia, but she was effectively on the men's side. She collaborated on the editing, reordering sequences to increase sympathy for Ted Kramer. Mass, 'The Mirror Cracked: The Career Woman in a Trio of Lansing Films' (*Film Criticism* xii, 2, Winter 1987–8, pp. 28–36), argues that despite Lansing's claims

to be 'a very strong feminist', those films in which her influence has been most marked, *Kramer versus Kramer*, *The Verdict* (1982) and *Fatal Attraction* (1987) have shown the opposite and presented any movement away from the nuclear family – through leaving children, career success or adultery – as inviting severe punishment.

6 Silverman, 'Life Without Mother', *American Film* 9, 4, pp. 50–53 gives details of Jaffe, Benton and the film's production. Columbia bought the film rights for $200,000 – a large sum for a book that only sold a total of 12,000 copies in hardback – and $6.5 million were invested in production costs. Taking only 64 days to shoot on location in New York, *Kramer* was a relatively low-budget film which generated vast box office returns. Amongst Jaffe's previous titles were *Love Story* and *The Godfather*.

7 It was unfortunate that French director François Truffaut, who expressed interest in adapting *Kramer* for screen, was too busy to take it on: we might have had a rather different result.

8 Malloy, 'Kramer vs Kramer: A Fraudulent View', *Jump Cut* 26, December 1981, pp. 5–7: 'The structure bears a resemblance to stories of superheroes whose powers are concealed until dire need triggers a metamorphosis. Dustin Hoffman as Mighty Mouse. That makes Streep Sue Storm The Invisible Girl.'

9 Silverman's term.

10 Corman, *Kramer versus Kramer*, pp. 230 – 231.

11 George Sand, pen-name of Amandine Dupin, married Baron Dudevant in 1822 and they had two children. She left them in 1831 to lead an independent life in Paris, writing and having love affairs – amongst her lovers were Alfred de Musset and Frédéric Chopin.

12 Cited in Paskowicz, *Absentee Mothers*, p. 23. It may be no coincidence MacLaine has often been cast in eccentric roles, such as the alcoholic 'bad' mother in the film *Postcards from the Edge*.

13 Bailin, 'Kramer vs Kramer vs Mother-Right', *Jump Cut* 23, October 1980, pp. 4–5.

14 Silverman, 'Life Without Mother' quotes Jaffe's sense of widespread family break-up being caused by women's personal irresponsibility: 'Would that this story were science fiction. But it is not science fiction. The seventies are quite a neurotic time, and families are under a great deal of pressure. To me, what happens to Ted and Joanna Kramer in this film is what happens ten years

later to the couple in *The Graduate*. That generation ran off and got married, maybe had a child or two, then split up rather than face the situation. It is sad. This has become the accepted way, the norm.'

15 Malloy, 'Kramer vs Kramer: A Fraudulent View', p. 6: 'Phallocentric compositions segregate Streep from the spaces within the film where most of the action takes place, as well as from audience identification. An upper, male-dominated domain is created . . . the action takes place on the very top floors of these phallic monsters (the Kramers' apartment building and both of Hoffman's office buildings) . . . (Thus) Hoffman's grossly over-determined male right to privilege of ownership and position comes across as fitting and neat.'

16 Malloy, p. 5: 'They cannot only do without a woman but they can now do things together that are particularly male and that might be interrupted by a woman's presence . . . The domestic scenes that are shown take on a men's club atmosphere. The two "men" carry on a silent morning ritual. They pee in the same way and read at the breakfast table together. A breakfast scene is shown at the end of the film that rhymes humorously with that first breakfast scene; everything is the same, except that the boy and Hoffman work together like a well-oiled machine. Billy has facilitated Hoffman's control of domestic space; the men are now as smooth and natural together in the kitchen as if the mother had never been there.'

17 In *Love and Death in the American Novel*, Leslie Fiedler identifies this tradition as rooted into the genre from *Huckleberry Finn* and *Moby Dick* to *One Flew Over the Cuckoo's Nest*. Whether read as Oedipal or not, it is a decidedly misogynistic bonding of sons with fathers or surrogate father figures, part of the same male coupling found in *Easy Rider, Butch Cassidy, Rain Man* and *Midnight Cowboy* and proliferating in later backlash films: *18 Again, Like Father, Like Son* and *Daddy*. All celebrate male bonding or father and son relationships with mother definitively excluded.

18 O'Brien's 'Love and Death in the American Movie', (*Journal of Popular Film and Television* ix, 2, Summer 1981, pp. 91–93) draws analogies between the misogyny of *Kramer* and *Ordinary People*, whilst Keeler's 'The Shining: Ted Kramer has a Nightmare' (*Journal of Popular Film and Television* viii, 4, Winter 1981, pp. 2–8) detects beneath *Kramer*'s surface

liberalism the same sadism and horror found in *The Shining*.

19 Faludi, *Backlash*, p. 297.

20 Quoted Faludi, p. 299. *New York* magazine called the film of *Kramer* 'a tragic and ironic summing-up of the decade of self-realisation and women's lib.'

21 Malloy, 'Kramer vs Kramer: A Fraudulent View', p. 6.

22 Some independent cinema, however, has depicted mothering from the mother's point of view, both thematically and formally – notably *Riddles of the Sphinx* (1976) by Laura Mulvey and Peter Wollen. See Kaplan, *Women and Film*, pp. 171–188.

23 Faludi, *Backlash*, p. 165.

24 Kaplan, *Motherhood and Representation*, p. 198.

25 *Observer* 23 March 1980. Vincent also quotes a Fleet Street male remarking of *Kramer*: 'It makes you appreciate people who stay together for the sake of the children.'

Chapter 5

1 Atkinson, 'Female Sanctity in the Late Middle Ages', in *Mystic and Pilgrim: The Book and the World of Margery Kempe*, identifies many medieval mothers who left families behind to go on their own quests. Margery Kempe, for example, left 13 children, Birgitta of Sweden 8, Dorothea of Montau 9. Shorter, *The Making of the Modern Family*, p. 168, argues that in traditional societies children under age two were treated with relative indifference.

2 Franks, *Mummy Doesn't Live Here Any More*, p. 31. Kaplan, *Motherhood and Representation*, pp. 17–24.

3 Greer, *The Female Eunuch*, p. 234.

4 John C. Abbott, 1830s, quoted Rich, *Of Woman Born: Motherhood as Experience and Institution*, p. 44.

5 McIntosh, *Woman in America: Her Work and Her Reward*, quoted Rich, p. 45.

6 Crawford, 'The construction and experience of maternity in seventeenth-century England' in Fildes (ed.), *Women as Mothers*, p. 6.

7 Rich, *Of Woman Born*, p. 52.

8 Mitchell, *Women: The Longest Revolution*, p. 122. Her whole chapter, 'Feminism and the Question of Femininity', pp. 115–124 is devoted to discussing rewrites of and responses to *A Doll's House*.

9   Kaplan, *Motherhood and Representation*, p. 192. She also cites
    Caplan's study *Don't Blame Mother: Mending Mother-Daughter
    Relations*, which identifies mothers as being blamed for more
    than 70 kinds of their children's problems and fathers for almost
    none.
10 Levine, *Who Will Raise the Children?*, p. 25.
11 Schaffer, *Mothering*, p. 110.
12 On child care under apartheid, see Cook, *Maids and Madams*;
    on female slaves separated from children, see Chesler, *Mothers on
    Trial*.
13 Kaplan, *Motherhood and Representation*, p. 200: 'It seems that
    the end of the 1980s marks, in relation to women, a return to
    rigid polarization of sex, work and motherhood in the social
    imaginary . . . Fathers begin to steal the show in regard to
    parenting (they are the new heroes in this role), and the baby
    steals the show from both fathers and mothers.'
14 Faludi, *Backlash*, pp. 69, 298.
15 Faludi, p. 63. 'A National Academy of Sciences panel in 1982
    concluded that children suffer no ill effects in academic, social or
    emotional development when mothers work.'
16 David, 'Putting on an Act for children?' in Maclean and Groves
    (eds.), *Women's Issues in Social Policy*, pp. 95–116.
17 Rich, *Of Woman Born*, pp. 53, 14.
18 Rutter, *Maternal Deprivation Reassessed*, pp. 207–8. 'Cross-
    cultural data appear to suggest that mothers who are home alone
    all day with their children, without other adults who can share
    the tasks of child care, are more likely to become rejecting in
    their attitudes and behaviour.'
19 Oakley, *Telling the Truth About Jerusalem*; Rich, *Of Woman
    Born*, p. 13.
20 Kaplan, *Motherhood and Representation*, p. 42.

Chapter 6

1   Stone's claim, in *The Family, Sex, and Marriage in England
    1500–1800*, that mothers 'chose' to treat their children brutally
    and even killed them has been challenged by feminist historians.
    See Crawford, 'Maternity in seventeenth-century England,' in
    Fildes (ed.), *Women as Mothers*, pp. 3–38.
2   Fildes, 'Maternal feelings reassessed', in Fildes (ed.), p. 139.

3 Fildes, p. 155.

4 Fildes, p. 153.

5 Franks, *Mummy Doesn't Live Here Any More*, p. 100. 'Unmarried mothers in rural areas would have their newborn infants taken to the foundling hospitals in the cities to save themselves from shame and ostracism. Domestic servants were in danger of losing their jobs if they had children.'

6 Franks, pp. 206–12.

7 Faludi, *Backlash*, p. 8.

8 See Hanmer and Maynard (eds.), *Women, Violence and Social Control*.

9 Paskowicz, *Absentee Mothers*, p. 70.

10 Rutter, *Maternal Deprivation Reassessed*, p. 139.

11 Rutter, p. 206, argues for maternal behaviour being affected by the sex of the child: 'differential treatment of male and female offspring has also been reported in sub-human primates. Thus, socially isolated monkeys tend to become generally rejecting and indifferent mothers but they are much more likely to physically abuse male infants.'

12 Fischer and Cardea, 'Mother-child relationships of mothers living apart from their children', (*Alternative Lifestyles*, Fall 1982), pp. 45, 49: 'All male children in the non-custody group (a sample of non-custodial mothers) lived with the father or were in father's custody.'

13 Franks, *Mummy Doesn't Live Here Any More*, p. 37.

14 Paskowicz, *Absentee Mothers*, p. 84.

15 Golombok, 'Children in Lesbian and Single Parent Households: Psychosexual and Psychiatric Appraisal', *Journal of Child Psychology and Psychiatry* 24 (4), 1983.

16 Richardson, 'Lesbian Mothers,' quoted by M. Steel, *Lesbian Mothers: Custody Disputes and Court Welfare Reports*), p. 3.

17 Steel, p. 7.

18 Franks, *Mummy Doesn't Live Here Any More*, pp. 221, 7.

19 Paskowicz, *Absentee Mothers*, p. 93. Individual histories in MATCH newsletters confirm these findings: stories of 'dysfunctional backgrounds', violent early years that witnessed destructive battles between parents, equally unsatisfactory marriages for themselves, struggles with poverty and material survival, women's inner worlds already at risk in some way before their own experience of mothering.

20   Franks, *Mummy Doesn't Live Here Any More*, p. 6. 'Research by
      Dr Eva Frommer in 1973 suggested that women separated from
      either parent before the age of eleven found it difficult to cope
      with their own babies. More recent work from Tirril Harris,
      George Brown and Antonia Bifulco showed that loss of a mother
      before the age of seventeen, whether through adoption, death or
      separation lasting at least a year, was linked with depression in
      adult women.'
21   For the effects of postnatal depression and other problems on
      bonding, see Franks, pp. 151–158.
22   Cookson's short autobiographical pamphlet 'For the Sake of the
      Children' (1989), cataloguing these and other dire events, can be
      ordered directly from her through MATCH (see page 323 for
      address).
23   Herrerias, 'Noncustodial mothers: Loving is leaving' (1984), paper
      presented at Annual Meeting of Society for Study of Social
      Problems, San Antonio; cit. Greif and Pabst, *Mothers Without
      Custody*, pp. 71–72.
24   Greif and Pabst, p. 255.

Chapter 7

1   David, 'Putting on an Act for Children?' in Maclean and Groves
     (eds.), pp. 95–116: 'The reforms . . . reinvigorate notions of the
     privacy of the family, through reinforcing the key concept of
     parental responsibility. They reduce state responsibility for child
     care, except to assess the extent of risk of dangerousness or need
     for support . . . No additional resources are to be devoted to our
     children who are our future. It seems that it is resources for
     child care to support parental responsibility that should also be
     the key concept of the Children Act – or the children themselves
     will pay the price.'
2   *Guardian* 5 April 1993.
3   Ibsen, *A Doll's House*, in *Plays*, p. 334.
4   Hardwick, *Seduction and Betrayal: Women and Literature*, p. 46
     makes a similar criticism of Nora's departure: '. . . the severance
     is rather casual and it drops a stain on our admiration of Nora.
     Ibsen has put the leaving of her children on the same moral and
     emotional level as the leaving of her husband and we cannot, in
     our hearts, assent to that. It is not only the leaving but the way

the play does not have time for suffering, for changes of heart. Ibsen has been too much of a man in the end. He has taken the man's practice, if not his stated belief, that where self-realisation is concerned, children shall not be an impediment.'

5 Mitchell, *Women: The Longest Revolution* p. 124 disputes this notion of Ibsen's insensitivity to the aftermath. 'I do not want to suggest that self-realisation should come before children, nor that women or, for that matter, men, should leave their children; though I would not agree to a dogmatic opposite. That is not the point . . . I would argue that it is not a question of Ibsen's masculine sensibility predominating at the end, it is a question of the meaning of motherhood in a world where women are unequal . . .'

6 Ian Lyness, *Daily Express* 5 April 1990, reviewing the BBC TV documentary *How Could She?*

7 Dors, *Dors by Diana*, pp. 214–17, 275–6, 288–317.

8 Franks, *Mummy Doesn't Live Here Any More*, p. 7.

9 Greif and Pabst, *Mothers Without Custody*, p. 16.

10 Rutter, *Maternal Deprivation Reassessed*, pp. 124–5.

11 Schaffer, *Mothering*, p. 112.

12 Rutter, *Maternal Deprivation Reassessed*, p. 126.

13 Rutter, p. 27.

14 Paskowicz, *Absentee Mothers*, pp. 118–9: 'suicidal behaviour during childhood is a condition that appears in suspicious degree among non-custodial mothers. A person who has had difficulty sustaining her own existence is more likely to have difficulty sustaining that of another as well.'

15 Fischer and Cardea, 'Mother-child relationships of mothers living apart from their children', p. 52.

Chapter 8

1 Gilman, *The Living of Charlotte Perkins Gilman: An Autobiography*, pp. 91–2.

2 Gilman, p. 163.

3 Kaplan, *Motherhood and Representation*, p. 130: 'Gilman was one of the first to theorize that a different social organization was essential for more humane interpersonal relations, and to base the new ethic specifically around motherly qualities. *Herland* projects an all-female society based on a caring ethic, itself

premissed on mothering. The loving mother-daughter relationship provides the model for all bonding in the community . . . the women are all gentle, nurturing and yet not boring.'

4 Letter from Bergman to her first husband, Dr Petter Lindstrom, 6 October 1950. Bergman, *My Story*, p. 315.

5 Bergman, p. 422.

6 Thorpe's British Council pamphlet *Doris Lessing*, p. 6.

7 See, for example, Nini Herman's discussion of Lessing in *Too Long a Child: The Mother-Daughter Dyad*, pp. 276–289.

8 There are signs such writing may soon materialise. When I invited Doris Lessing to make a contribution to this book, she declined on the grounds that she was writing about the subject herself. Personal correspondence 20 June 1992.

9 Lessing, *A Proper Marriage*, pp. 224, 226.

10 Rich, *Of Woman Born*, p. 52.

11 I am indebted to Jan Relf for this discussion of *Gaining Ground*. In her unpublished Ph.D. thesis on feminist Utopias, Jan writes: 'notwithstanding its low-key narrative and realist discourse, [*Gaining Ground* is] a radical, subversive and uncompromising text . . .[It] proposes a radical rupture with conventional options for female protagonists and an alternative, viable model of female autonomy.' (University of Exeter 1992).

12 Rogers, *The Ice is Singing*, pp. 152–3.

Chapter 9

1 All letters quoted are from *Frieda Lawrence: The Memoirs and Correspondence* (ed. D. W. Tedlock). Here, p. 342, letter from Frieda Lawrence to John Middleton Murry, 1954; pp. 339–40, letter from Frieda to her son Monty, 1954.; p. 294, in a letter from 1950 she admits 'I couldn't get on with their father (he didn't know how I felt).'

2 Frieda's unfinished fictionalised autobiography 'And the Fullness Thereof . . .', reprinted in Tedlock, pp. 88–89.

3 Letter from Lawrence 14 May 1912, quoted by Frieda Lawrence in *Not I, But the Wind*, p. 23.

4 Lawrence, *Not I, But the Wind*, pp. 5–6. Moore, *The Intelligent Heart: The Story of D.H. Lawrence*, p. 162 says the travelling with Lawrence began in 'hope and agony'.

5 Frieda's letter to Edward Garnett, January 1913 in Tedlock, pp.

189–90. Later, in 1950, she recalls: 'Then when I left and they were not allowed to see me, Monty couldn't eat for six months and was sick. I am glad I didn't know that then. What hells L. and I went through anyhow! Their father was awful to them. If he was cruel to me, all right, but to them, no. I couldn't go to England, I couldn't. Even for *their* sakes, I would only be a queer creature to them. But I felt pleased that they want me . . .' p. 294.; her missing them is obvious in a note to Henry Savage, December 1913: 'Your boy, *do* enjoy him, when I think of the joy mine gave me and now I haven't got them.' p. 201.

6 Letters to Edward Garnett, April, May and June 1913. Tedlock, pp. 194–5, 197.

7 Lucas, *Frieda Lawrence: The Story of Frieda van Richthofen and D. H. Lawrence*, p. 100.

8 Tedlock, *Frieda Lawrence*, p. 432. Barbara Barr's (née Weekley) memoir of her mother, 'I Look Back', was first published in *The Twentieth Century*, March 1959.

9 Lawrence, *Not I, But the Wind*, p. 61.

10 Tedlock, *Frieda Lawrence*, pp. 359–60. A similar message had gone to her son Monty in 1953, pp. 318–9: 'I wish sometimes I felt kindlier towards your father. I wish him well, but I cannot forget that he had made an image of me and did not know anything about the real me.'

11 Lawrence, *Not I, But the Wind*, p. 56.

12 Lawrence, *Not I, But the Wind*, p. 38. She also quotes (p. 57) a letter from Lawrence of 14 Dec 1912 which justifies his resistance to Frieda returning to Weekley because of the pressure this would put on the children to make up to her for the sacrifice: 'if Frieda gave up all to go and live with them, that would sap their strength because they would have to support her life when they grew up. They would not be free to live of themselves – they would first have to live for her, to pay back . . . So we must go on, and never let go the children, but will, will and will to have them and have what we think good.'

13 Tedlock, *Frieda Lawrence*, p. 360. Evidence of Lawrence's detachment is found in a letter Frieda sent to Lady Cynthia Asquith in Dec 1913, p. 201: 'You wrote me such a frightfully nice letter, don't be too sympathetic, I warn you, or I shall come and weep to you when we are in England. Don't be too sorry either, after all we are very happy too, and I believe in the miracle too; only it's hard, I miss them so, like one would miss a

leg.' Lawrence made his own scribbled addition to the letter at this point, noting only half-jokingly, 'one wouldn't, after a fortnight.'

14 Letter to Edward Garnett, Tedlock, p. 202.
15 Lawrence, *Not I, But the Wind*, p. 133.
16 Feinstein, *Lawrence's Women: The Intimate Life of D. H. Lawrence*, pp. 131, 194.
17 John Bayley, 'Lawrence's comedy, and the war of superiorities', in *Rethinking Lawrence*, ed. Keith Brown, pp. 1–11, introduces this reading of *The Woman Who Rode Away* as a piece of revenge against Frieda's maternal feelings.
18 Tedlock, pp. 220; 221; 223; 233; 236, 238; 243; 342; 360. Lawrence, *Not I but the Wind*, pp. 167–69.
19 Feinstein, *Lawrence's Women*, pp. 97, 10.
20 Feinstein, *Lawrence's Women*, pp. 81, 205, 215.
21 Feinstein, *Lawrence's Women*, pp. 88, 12.
22 Tedlock, p. 269.

Chapter 10

1 I have taken the liberty of changing the gender of pronouns here.

Chapter 11

1 Fischer and Cardea, 'Mother-Child Relationships of Mothers Living Apart from their Children,' pp. 47–48 and p. 50 notes that: 'noncustody mothers cited fathers' bribing, coercing, and taking the children . . . the children were vulnerable to bribery by the material benefits the fathers offered.'

Chapter 12

1 Fay Weldon's novel was published in the U.S. under the title . . . *And the Wife Ran Away*, in Britain as *The Fat Woman's Joke*; both in 1967.

Chapter 14

1 The institution of motherhood is, by my [Shirley Glubka's] definition, a system of customs, laws, ideals, and images that (1) determines how the *work* of mothering is generally defined, organized, and performed in a society; (2) powerfully influences the form and quality of the mother-child *relationship* in that society. For an excellent description of the working of this institution, see Adrienne Rich's *Of Woman Born: Motherhood as Experience and Institution* (New York: W. W. Norton & Co., 1976) [London: Virago, 1976].

2 For more writing by women who have given up their children, see the following: Louise Billotte, "Mothers Don't Have to Lie," *Mother Jones*, May 1976: 22–25; *The Living of Charlotte Perkins Gilman: An Autobiography* (n.p., Katharine Beecher Stetson Chamberlain, 1935; reprint, New York: Harper & Row, 1963); Martha Jane Cannary Hickok, *Calamity Jane's Letters to Her Daughter* (n.p., Dr. Nolie Mumie, n.d., limited ed.; n.p., Don C. Foote and Stella A. Foote, n.d., limited ed.; reprint, San Lorenzo, Calif: Shameless Hussy Press, 1976); Patricia Preston, "Parenting in Absentia," *Branching Out*, May/June 1977: 8–10; Judy Sullivan, *Mama Doesn't Live Here Anymore* (New York: Pyramid Books, 1974); Lucia Valeska, "If All Else Fails, I'm Still a Mother," *Quest* 1 (Winter 1975): 52–63.

Chapter 18

1 Marion Woodman is a Jungian analyst, author of four books on the psychology of women: *The Owl was a Baker's Daughter: Obesity, Anorexia Nervosa and the Repressed Feminine*; *Addiction to Perfection*; *The Pregnant Virgin: A Process of Psychological Transformation*; *Leaving My Father's House: A Journey to Conscious Femininity*.

Chapter 20

1 De Beauvoir, *The Second Sex*, pp. 528–9.

2 Paskowicz, *Absentee Mothers*, p. 168, quotes some of the cases of violence caused by 'society's insistence that a mother remain with

her children no matter what'. She instances mothers threatening to kill children, burn them or beat them to death. She quotes the terrible case that Rich (*Of Woman Born*) also cites, of Joanne Michulski, aged 38, mother of 8 children from 18 years to 2 months, who on 11 July 1974 'took a butcher knife, decapitated and chopped up the bodies of her two youngest on the neatly kept lawn of the suburban house where the family lived outside Chicago' (Rich, pp. 256–8). Rich goes on to analyse the history of the Michulski case: a tale of years of withdrawal, depression and lack of contraception: 'The minister who lived next door said that she seemed "quietly desperate from the moment the family moved into the home" in 1959.' There had been no offers of help in the intervening 15 years.

3 Rich, *Of Woman Born*, p. 277.
4 Cited Mullan, *Are Mothers Really Necessary?*, p. 141.
5 Winnicott, 'Hate in the Counter-Transference', in *Through Paediatrics to Psycho-Analysis*, p. 201.
6 Winnicott, 'Hate in the Counter-Transference', p. 202: 'Sentimentality is useless for parents, as it contains a denial of hate, and sentimentality in a mother is no good at all from the infant's point of view.'
7 Winnicott, 'Primary Maternal Preoccupation', in *Through Paediatrics to Psycho-Analysis*, pp. 300–305.
8 Jung, 'Psychological Aspects of The Mother Archetype', in *Aspects of the Feminine*, pp. 101–140.
9 Kristeva's essay, 'Stabat Mater,' in *Tales of Love*, p. 234 explores some of the unconscious complexities informing this idealisation of the maternal. She suggests that it is not only an idealised archaic mother that is being invoked, but an idealisation of the relationship that binds us (men and women) to the mother – an idealisation of primary narcissism.

Chapter 21

1 Herman, *My Kleinian Home*, p. 19.
2 Karnosh and Hope, 'Puerperal Psychoses', *American Journal of Psychiatry* 94 (1937), p. 208. Melges, 'Postpartum Psychiatric Reactions', *International Encyclopaedia of Psychiatry, Psychology, Psychoanalysis and Neurology*, 1977 ed., vol 8 discusses the phenomenon of postnatal depression in women whose own mothering has been problematic.

3 Rutter, *Maternal Deprivation Reassessed*, pp. 198–208.
4 Mullan, *Are Mothers Really Necessary?*, p. 43.
5 Arcana, *Our Mothers' Daughters*, pp. 192–3.
6 Orbach and Eichenbaum, *Bittersweet*, p. 53.
7 Hall, *The Moon and the Virgin*, p. 134.
8 Rich, *Of Woman Born*, pp. 225–6.
9 Klein, 'Love, Guilt and Reparation,' in her book *Love, Guilt and Reparation*, pp. 306 – 343.
10 Klein, p. 320.
11 Chodorow, *The Reproduction of Mothering*, p. 33. 'Role training, identification, and enforcement certainly have to do with the acquisition of an appropriate gender role. But the conventional feminist view . . . which understands feminine development as explicit ideological instruction or formal coercion, cannot in the case of mothering be sufficient.'
12 Jung, 'The Mother Archetype', in *Aspects of the Feminine*, p. 119.

Chapter 22

1 Ingmar Bergman, *Autumn Sonata*, quoted by Paskowicz, *Absentee Mothers*, p. 31.
2 Ingrid Bergman, *My Story*, pp. 514, 516. On page 519, she expands on this difference with Ingmar Bergman over the film's mother not seeing her children for a seven-year gap: 'I went on arguing with him . . . So to keep me quiet, he cut it to five – even though I noticed seven came back in the finished picture – and he still insisted: "There are women who stay away from their children like that; they don't want to be bothered with them; they don't want to hear their problems. They have their own careers, their own lives; they just block everything else out." '
3 I am deeply indebted to Jan Relf for making possible the material in this section. She generously shared facts and ideas from work in progress on her biographical study of John Fowles, and kindly put me in touch with both John and his stepdaughter Anna Christy. All this material has been seen by Jan, Anna and John and is reproduced with their consent.
4 In *The Magus*, for example, the imaginary location was inspired by the island of Spetsai, and the relationship of Alison to the protagonist drew heavily on that between Elizabeth and John.

John Fowles informs me, however, that the real drama on which
The Magus draws occurred following their return to England in
1953 and during his teaching post at Ashridge College. In a letter
to me, 14 June 1993, he writes: 'I fell in love there with a South
African girl; and remained in love with Eliz. I put the dilemma
in which my typical male selfishness put me in into *The Magus*.
Everyone thinks that took place in Greece; it really happened in
England.'

5 What follows is the transcription of part of a personal interview
with Anna Christy, 24 May 1993.

6 Letter to the author from John Fowles, 1 June 1993.

7 Letter from Elizabeth Fowles to Monica Sharrocks, 1 September
1959.

8 Dors, *Dors by Diana*, pp. 301–2.

Chapter 23

1 Digby Anderson from The Institute of Social Affairs, 'Ripe for a
British majority', *The Times* 15 October 1985.

2 Franks, *Mummy Doesn't Live Here Any More*, p. 224: 'Our
children offer us the greatest gift in the world. They allow us to
experience altruistic love. We are enriched by them; we enrich
those who do not have children themselves . . . it would be tragic
if . . . women chose to flee from motherhood while men,
sometimes reluctantly, picked up the pieces.'

3 Kristeva, 'Stabat Mater', in *Tales of Love*, p. 234.

4 Kristeva, p. 245.

5 Dinnerstein, *The Rocking of the Cradle and the Ruling of the
World*, p. 93.

6 Vivien Bar's 'Introduction' to Dinnerstein, p. xiii.

7 Kaplan, *Motherhood and Representation*, p. 50. Similarly p. 39:
'I see the female body (and in particular mother/child bodies) as
constructed by/through the patriarchal Imaginary to fulfil specific
or capitalist needs.' For a fuller discussion of the idea of the
mother in the Imaginary, see Kaplan's chapter 'The
Psychoanalytic Sphere and Motherhood Discourse.'

8 For a distinction between the infantile longing for union (with the
mother) and mystical longings, see Wilber, *The Atman Project: A
Transpersonal View of Human Development*.

9 This does not negate Kristeva's arguments about the use of the

fantasy of the (pure, virginal) maternal within religious cultures too.

10 For fuller elaboration of ideas of karmic evolution and the formation and function of *sanskaras* in human development, see Meher Baba's *Discourses*.

11 Woolger's *Other Lives, Other Selves: A Jungian Psychotherapist Discovers Past Lives* discusses the possible effects of reincarnation on psychology.

Bibliography

Non-fiction

Arcana, Judith, *Our Mothers' Daughters* (1979; reprint London: Women's Press, 1981)

Aries, Philippe, *Centuries of Childhood* (London: Cape, 1962)

Arney, W. R., 'Maternal Infant Bonding: The Politics of Falling in Love with Your Child,' *Feminist Studies* 6 (3), 1980, pp. 547–82

Atkinson, Clarissa, 'Female Sanctity in the Late Middle Ages', in *Mystic and Pilgrim: The Book and the World of Margery Kempe* (Ithaca, NY and London: Cornell University Press, 1983)

Baba, Meher, *Discourses* (Myrtle Beach, SC: Sheriar Press, 1989)

Badinter, Elizabeth, *The Myth of Motherhood in Modern History* (New York: Macmillan, 1980)

Bailin, Rebecca A., 'Kramer vs Kramer vs Mother-Right', *Jump Cut* 23, October 1980, pp. 4–5

Balint, Michael, 'Love for the Mother and Mother-Love' 1939, in M. Balint (ed.), *Primary Love and Psycho-Analytic Technique* (New York: Liveright Press, 1965)

Berke, P.; Black, M.; Byrne, M.; Fields, F.; Gallagher, B. and Paley, N., 'A study of natural mothers who terminated the primary parental role', unpublished master's thesis, University of Southern California School of Social Work, Los Angeles, 1979

Bernard, Jessie, *The Future of Motherhood* (New York: Dial Press, 1974)

—, *Women, Wives, Mothers* (Chicago: Aldine Press, 1975)

Billotte, Louise, 'Mothers Don't Have to Lie,' *Mother Jones* May 1976, pp. 22–5

Birns, B., 'The Mother-Infant Tie: Fifty Years of Theory, Science and Science Fiction,' in B. Birns and D. F. Hay (eds), *The Different Faces of Motherhood* (New York: Plenum, 1988)

Bowlby, John, *Maternal Care and Mental Health* (Geneva: World Health Organization, 1951)

——, *Child Care and the Growth of Love* (Harmondsworth: Penguin, 1953)

——, *Attachment and Loss* (vol. I: *Attachment*, vol. II: *Separation*, vol. III: *Loss*; Harmondsworth: Penguin, 1975, 1976, 1981)

Brandt, Lilian, *Five hundred and seventy-four deserters and their families* (1904; reprint New York: Arno Press, 1972)

Brown, Keith (ed.) *Rethinking Lawrence* (Buckingham Open University Press, 1990)

Campbell, Bebe Moore, 'Mothering long-distance', *Essence* October 1981, p. 92

Caplan, P., *Don't Blame Mother: Mending Mother-Daughter Relations* (New York: Harper & Row, 1989)

Cassady, Margie, 'Runaway Wives', *Psychology Today* 8, May 1978, p. 42

Ceplair, Larry (ed.), *Charlotte Perkins Gilman: A Nonfiction Reader* (New York: Columbia University Press, 1992)

Chesler, Phyllis, *Mothers on Trial* (New York: McGraw-Hill, 1986)

——, *Sacred Bond: Motherhood Under Siege* (1988; reprint London: Virago, 1990)

Chodorow, Nancy, *The Reproduction of Mothering* (Berkeley, CA: University of California Press, 1978)

Cook, Jacklyn, *Maids and Madams* (Johannesburg: Raven Press, 1984)

Crawford, Patricia, 'The construction and experience of maternity in seventeenth-century England', in Fildes (ed.), *Women as Mothers in Pre-Industrial England* (London: Routledge, 1990), pp. 3–38

Dally, Ann, *Inventing Motherhood: The Consequences of an Ideal* (London: Burnett, 1982)

David, Miriam, 'Putting on an Act for children?', in M. Maclean and D. Groves (eds), *Women's Issues in Social Policy* (London: Routledge, 1991), pp. 95–116

De Beauvoir, Simone *The Second Sex*, trans. H. M. Parshley (1953; Harmondsworth: Penguin, 1972)

Deckert, Robert A., 'Mothers minus their children', *Working Woman* October 1983, pp. 180–184

Dinnerstein, Dorothy, *The Rocking of the Cradle and the Ruling of the World* (London: Women's Press, 1987)

Doudna, C., 'The weekend mother', *New York Times Magazine* 3 October 1982, pp. 72–75, 84–88

Eckersley, Jill, 'Could you walk out on *your* children?' *Living* October 1989

Edwards, Harriet, *How Could You?: Mothers Without Custody of*

Their Children (Freedom, CA: Crossing Press, 1989)
(this has an excellent bibliography which includes children's books
on the subject)

Faludi, Susan, *Backlash: The Undeclared War Against Women*
(London: Chatto and Windus, 1992)

Fiedler, Leslie, *Love and Death in the American Novel* (New York:
Stein and Day, 1966)

Fildes, Valerie (ed.), *Women as Mothers in Pre-Industrial England*
(London: Routledge, 1990)

Firestone, Shulamith, *The Dialectic of Sex* (New York: William
Morrow, 1970; London: Women's Press, 1979)

Fischer, Judith, 'Mothers living apart from their children', *Family
Relations* 32, 1983, pp. 351–357

Fischer, Judith and Cardea, Jane, 'Mothers living apart from their
children: a study in stress and coping', *Alternative Lifestyles* Spring
1981, pp. 218–227

——, 'Mother-child relationships of mothers living apart from their
children,' *Alternative Lifestyles* Fall 1982, pp. 42–53

Franks, Helen, *Mummy Doesn't Live Here Any More: Why Women
Leave Their Children* (London: Doubleday, 1990)

Friday, Nancy, *My Mother, My Self: The Daughter's Search for
Identity* (1977; reprint London: Fontana, 1979)

Friedan, Betty, *The Feminine Mystique* (New York: Norton, 1963)

Genevie, Louis and Margolies, Eva, *The Motherhood Report: How
Women Feel about Being Mothers* (New York: Macmillan, 1987)

George, V. and Wilding, P., *Motherless Families* (London: Routledge,
1972)

Gillis, J. R., *For Better, For Worse: British Marriages 1600 to the
Present* (Oxford: Oxford University Press, 1985)

Gladstone, Valerie, 'The Bad Mother', *New York Woman* February
1989, pp. 87–89

Glubka, Shirley, 'Out of the stream: An essay on unconventional
motherhood', *Feminist Studies* Summer 1983, pp. 223–234

Goldstein, Sol, *Divorced Parenting: How to Make it Work* (London:
Methuen, 1987)

Golombok, Susan, 'Children in Lesbian and Single Parent
Households: Psychosexual and Psychiatric Appraisal', *Journal of
Child Psychology and Psychiatry* 24 (4), 1983.

Greif, Geoffrey, 'Mothers without custody', *Social Work* 1, 32, 1987,
pp. 11–16

Greif, Geoffrey and Pabst, Mary S., 'Weekend Mothers', *Single Parent* 24, 4, 1986, pp. 14–17

—, *Mothers Without Custody* (Lexington, MA: Lexington Books, 1988)

Greenwood, Lynne, 'Mothers who pay the price for another man', *Sunday Express* 21 October 1990

Greer, Germaine, *The Female Eunuch* (1970; reprint London: Paladin, 1971)

Hall, Nor, *The Moon and the Virgin* (London: Women's Press, 1980)

Hanmer, Jalna and Maynard, Mary (eds), *Women, Violence and Social Control* (London: Macmillan, 1987)

Hardwick, Elizabeth, *Seduction and Betrayal: Women and Literature* (London: Weidenfeld and Nicholson, 1974)

Heffner, E., *Mothering: The Emotional Experience of Motherhood after Freud and Feminism* (New York: Doubleday, 1978)

Herman, Nini, *My Kleinian Home* (London: Free Association, 1988)

—, *Too Long a Child: The Mother-Daughter Dyad* (London: Free Association, 1989)

Herrerias, C., 'Noncustodial mothers: A study of self-concept and social interaction,' unpublished doctoral dissertation, University of Texas, Austin, 1984

HMSO, *An Introduction to the Children's Act 1989* (London: HMSO, 1989)

Holdsworth, Angela, *Out of the Doll's House: The Story of Women in the Twentieth Century* (London: BBC Books, 1988)

Hutter, Bridget and Williams, Gillian (eds), *Controlling Women* (London: Croom Helm, 1981)

James, Adrienne, 'What happens to mother when father takes custody of the child?', *Vogue* September 1978, p. 122

Jung, C. G., *Aspects of the Feminine* (London: Ark, 1986)

Kaplan, E. Ann, *Women and Film: Both Sides of the Camera* (London: Methuen, 1983)

—, 'Is the Gaze Male?', in A. Snitow (ed.), *Desire: The Politics of Sexuality* (London: Virago, 1984), pp. 321–338

—, *Motherhood and Representation: The Mother in Popular Culture and Melodrama* (London: Routledge, 1992)

Kaplan, M., *Images of the Mother* (New York: Routledge, 1991)

Karpf, Anne, 'How Could She?', *Guardian* 3 April 1990, p. 17

Keane, Noel and Breo, Dennis, *The Surrogate Mother* (New York: Everest House, 1981)

Keeler, Greg, 'The Shining: Ted Kramer has a Nightmare', *Journal of Popular Film and Television* viii, 4, Winter 1981, pp. 2–8

Klaus, Marshall and Kennell, John H., *Maternal-Infant Bonding* (St Louis: C. V. Mosby, 1976)

Klein, Melanie, *Love, Guilt and Reparation* (London: Hogarth Press, 1981)

Koehler, J. M., 'Mothers without Custody', *Children Today* 2, xi, 1982, pp. 12–15

Kristeva, Julia, 'Stabat Mater', in *Tales of Love* (1976; reprint New York: Columbia University Press, 1987), pp. 234–263

Kuhn, Annette, *Women's Pictures: Feminism and Cinema* (London: Routledge, 1982)

Lazarre, Jane, *The Mother Knot* (New York: McGraw-Hill, 1976; London: Virago, 1987)

Levine, James, *Who Will Raise the Children?* (Philadelphia: Lippincott, 1976)

Malloy, Eileen, 'Kramer vs Kramer: A Fraudulent View', *Jump Cut* 26, December 1981, pp. 5–7

Margolis, M., *Mothers and Such* (Berkeley, CA: University of California Press, 1984)

Markey, Judy, 'When *he* gets custody', *Cosmopolitan* April 1984, p. 164.

Mass, Roslyn, 'The Mirror Cracked: The Career Woman in a Trio of Lansing Films', *Film Criticism* xii, 2, Winter 1987–8, pp. 28–36

Miller, Alice, *The Drama of Being a Child* (London: Virago, 1987)

——, *For Your Own Good* (London: Virago, 1987)

——, *Banished Knowledge: Facing Childhood Injuries* (London: Virago, 1990)

Millett, Kate, *Sexual Politics* (London, Rupert Hart-Davis, 1971)

Mitchell, Ann, *Coping with Separation and Divorce* (London: Chambers, 1986)

Mitchell, Juliet, *Psychoanalysis and Feminism* (Harmondsworth: Penguin, 1974)

——, *Women: The Longest Revolution*, (London: Virago, 1984)

Mullan, Bob, *Are Mothers Really Necessary?* (London: Boxtree, 1987)

Mulvey, Laura, 'Visual pleasure and narrative cinema', *Screen* 16, 3 (1975), pp. 6–18

Mungen, Donna, 'Forgotten women: Non-custodial mothers', *Ms* February 1986, p. 70

Murray, Linda, 'The runaway wife phenomenon', *Practical Psychology for Physicians* June 1975, pp. 40–45

New, Caroline and David, Miriam, *For the Children's Sake: Making Child Care More than Women's Business* (Harmondsworth: Penguin, 1985)

Oakley, Ann, *Subject Women* (Oxford: Martin Robertson, 1981)
—, *From Here to Maternity* (Harmondsworth: Penguin, 1986)
—, *Telling the Truth About Jerusalem* (Oxford: Basil Blackwell, 1986)
O'Brien, Thomas W., 'Perspectives: Love and Death in the American Movie', *Journal of Popular Film and Television* ix, 2, Summer 1981, pp. 91–93
Orbach, Susie and Eichenbaum, Luise, *What Do Women Want?* (London: Michael Joseph, 1983)
Orbach, Susie and Eichenbaum, Luise, *Bittersweet* (London: Arrow, 1988)
Paskin, Sylvia, 'She's leaving home', *New Statesman and Society* 6 April 1990, pp. 12–14
Paskowicz, Patricia, *Absentee Mothers* (New York: Allenheld/Universe, 1982)
Petley, Sylvia, 'Women who close the door on their children', *She* February 1988
Preston, Patricia, 'Parenting in Absentia', *Branching Out* May/June 1977, pp. 8–10
Reichers, M., 'Mothers Without Custody: Reversing Society's Old Stereotypes', *Single Parent* October 1981, pp. 13–15
Rich, Adrienne, *Of Woman Born: Motherhood as Experience and Institution* (London: Virago, 1976)
Rogak, Lisa, 'When Mommy moves out', *New York* 5 January 1987, pp. 36–41
Rosenblum, Karen, 'The route to voluntary non-custody: How mothers decide to relinquish custody', *Journal of Alternative Lifestyles* Spring 1984, pp. 175–185
—, 'Leaving as a wife, leaving as a mother', *Journal of Family Issues* 2, vii, June 1986, pp. 197–213
Rowbotham, Sheila, 'To be or not to be: the dilemmas of mothering', *Feminist Review* 31 (1989), pp. 82–93
Rutter, Michael, *Maternal Deprivation Reassessed* (Harmondsworth: Penguin, 1972)
Schaffer, Rudolph, *Mothering* (London: Fontana, 1977)
Scott, Gail, 'Singles: the mother's case for non-custody', *Washington Post* 6 May 1981, p. 5
Segal, Hannah, *Klein* (London: Fontana, 1979)
Shahar, Shulamith, *The Fourth Estate: A History of Women in the Middle Ages* (London: Routledge, 1983)
—, *Childhood in the Middle Ages* (London: Routledge, 1992)
Shorter, Edward, *The Making of the Modern Family* (London: Collins, 1976)

Showalter, Elaine, *A Literature of Their Own: British Women Novelists from Brontë to Lessing* (Princeton, NJ: Princeton University Press, 1977)

——, *The Female Malady: Women, Madness, and English Culture, 1830–1980* (New York: Pantheon, 1985)

Silverman, Stephen, 'Life Without Mother', *American Film* 9, 4, pp. 50–53

Silverzweig, Mary Zenorini, *The Other Mother* (New York: Harper & Row, 1982)

Steel, Moira, *Lesbian Mothers: Custody Disputes and Court Welfare Reports* (Norwich: Social Work Monographs, University of East Anglia, 1990)

Stern, D., *The First Relationship: Infant and Mother* (Cambridge, MA: Harvard University Press, 1976)

Stone, Lawrence, *The Family, Sex and Marriage in England 1500–1800* (New York: Harper, 1977)

Suleiman, S. R. (ed.), *The Female Body in Western Culture: Contemporary Perspectives* (Cambridge, MA: Harvard University Press, 1985)

Sullivan, Judy, *Mama Doesn't Live Here Anymore* (New York: Pyramid Books, 1974)

Tudor, Andrew, Review of 'Kramer vs Kramer', *New Society* 24 April 1980

Valeska, Lucia, 'If all else fails, I'm still a mother', *Quest* 1 (Winter 1975), pp. 52–63

Warner, Marina, *Alone of All Her Sex: The Myth and Cult of the Virgin Mary* (New York: Knopf, 1976)

Westhoefer, Janet, 'Mothers under stress: the psychological correlates of relinquishing custody', *Dissertation Abstracts International* 8b, 45, February 1985, p. 2675

Wilber, Ken, *The Atman Project: A Transpersonal View of Human Development* (London: Quest, 1980)

Winkler, Elisabeth, 'Abandoned', *Options* (September, 1993), pp. 64–65.

Winnicott, Donald, *The Child, the Family and the Outside World* (Harmondsworth: Penguin, 1964)

——, *The Maturational Processes and the Facilitating Environment* (London: Hogarth Press, 1987)

——, *Through Paediatrics to Psycho-Analysis* (London: Hogarth Press, 1987)

Woodman, Marion, *The Owl was a Baker's Daughter: Obesity, Anorexia Nervosa and the Repressed Feminine* (Toronto: Inner City Books, 1980)

—, *Addiction to Perfection* (Toronto: Inner City Books, 1981)

—, *The Pregnant Virgin: A Process of Psychological Transformation* (Toronto: Inner City Books, 1985)

—, *Leaving My Father's House: A Journey to Conscious Femininity* (Boston: Shambhala, 1993)

Woolger, Roger, *Other Lives, Other Selves: A Jungian Psychotherapist Discovers Past Lives* (New York: Bantam, 1988)

Worth, Jill, 'Where's Mummy Gone?', *Under Fives* September/October 1990, pp. 25–6

Autobiography, Biography and Fiction

Adams, Jane, *Good Intentions* (New York: New American Library, 1985)

Alpert, Harriet, *We Are Everywhere: Writings By and About Lesbian Parents* (Freedom, CA: Crossing Press, 1987)

Arms, Suzanne, *To Love and Let Go* (New York: Knopf, 1983)

Barfoot, Joan, *Gaining Ground* (1978; reprint London: Women's Press, 1980)

Bergman, Ingrid (and Alan Burgess), *My Story* (London: Sphere, 1980)

Bergman, Ingmar, *Autumn Sonata* (film, trans. Alan Blair; New York: Pantheon, 1978)

Billotte, Louise, 'Mothers Don't Have to Lie', *Mother Jones* May 1976, pp. 22–5

Brabazor, James, *Dorothy L. Sayers: A Biography* (New York: Scribners, 1981)

Brecht, Bertolt, 'The Augsburg Chalk Circle,' in *Collected Short Stories* (London: Methuen, 1983)

Cate, Curtis, *George Sand: A Biography* (New York: Avon, 1975)

Chopin, Kate, *The Awakening* (1899; reprint New York: Avon, 1972)

Corman, Avery, *Kramer versus Kramer* (New York: Collins, 1978)

Deeping, Warwick, *Sorrell and Son* (London: Cassell, 1930)

Defoe, Daniel, *Roxana* (London: 1724)

Dors, Diana, *Dors by Diana* (London: Macdonald Futura, 1981)

Feinstein, Elaine, *Lawrence's Women: The Intimate Life of D. H. Lawrence* (London: HarperCollins, 1993)

Gilman, Charlotte Perkins, *The Living of Charlotte Perkins Gilman: An Autobiography* (1935; reprint New York: Harper & Row, 1963)

—, *The Yellow Wallpaper* (1892; reprint London: Virago, 1981)

Hickok, Martha Jane Cannary, *Calamity Jane's Letters to Her Daughter* (San Lorenzo, CA: Shameless Hussy Press, 1976)

Holligon, Sheila, *House of Gingerbread* (London: Dunscaith, 1990)

Housman, Laurence, *Pains and Penalties* (1911; reprint London: Jonathan Cape, 1937)

Ibsen, Henrik, *A Doll's House* (in *Plays*, trans. Peter Watts; Harmondsworth: Penguin, 1965)

Lawrence, D. H., *The Woman Who Rode Away and Other Stories* (Harmondsworth, Penguin, 1990)

Lawrence, Frieda, *Not I, But the Wind* (London: Heinemann, 1935)

Lessing, Doris, *A Proper Marriage* (1965; reprint St Albans: Panther, 1966)

Lucas, Robert, *Frieda Lawrence: The Story of Frieda van Richthofen and D. H. Lawrence* (London: Secker & Warburg, 1973)

MacLaine, Shirley, *Dancing in the Light* (London: Bantam, 1985)

Miller, Sue, *The Good Mother* (New York: Harper Collins, 1981)

Moore, Harry T., *The Intelligent Heart: The Story of D. H. Lawrence* (Harmondsworth: Penguin, 1960)

Morton, Andrew, *Diana: Her True Story* (London: Michael O'Mara, 1993)

Prouty, Oliver Higgins, *Stella Dallas* (Boston: Houghton Mifflin, 1923)

Raske, Richard, *The Killing of Karen Silkwood* (Boston: Houghton Mifflin, 1981)

Rogers, Jane, *The Ice is Singing* (London: Faber, 1987)

Sklar, Anna, *Runaway Wives* (New York: Coward McCann and Geoghegan, 1976)

Steel, Danielle, *Daddy* (London: Bantam, 1989)

Sullivan, Judy, *Mama Doesn't Live Here Anymore* (New York: Pyramid, 1974)

Tedlock, E. W. (ed.), *Frieda Lawrence: The Memoirs and Correspondence* (London: Heinemann, 1961)

Thorpe, Michael, *Doris Lessing* (London: Longman, 1973)

Tolstoy, Leo, *Anna Karenin* (trans. Rosemary Edmonds; Harmondsworth: Penguin, 1963)

Trudeau, Margaret, *Beyond Reason* (New York and London: Paddington Press, 1979)

——, *Consequences* (Toronto: Seal, 1982)

Weldon, Fay, *. . .And the Wife Ran Away* (first published 1967; retitled *The Fat Woman's Joke*; London: Coronet, 1982).

Wood, Mrs Henry (Ellen Price), *East Lynne* (1861; reprint New Brunswick, NJ: Rutgers University Press, 1984)

Wynd, Oswald, *The Ginger Tree* (1977; reprint London: Eland, 1988)

Permissions

The author and publisher gratefully acknowledge the following for permission to include material:

extracts from *Diana: Her True Story* by Andrew Morton, Copyright © 1992 Andrew Morton, reprinted by permission of Michael O'Mara Books Ltd.

extracts from *Ingrid Bergman: My Story* Copyright © 1980 by Ingrid Bergman and Alan Burgess, reprinted by permission of estate of Ingrid Bergman.

extracts from *Backlash* by Susan Faludi, Copyright © 1992 Susan Faludi, reprinted by permission of Chatto & Windus.

extract from *The Fat Woman's Joke* by Fay Weldon, Copyright © 1967 Fay Weldon, reproduced by permission of Hodder and Stoughton Ltd and Sheil Land Associates.

extract from the 'Playboy Interview: John Lennon and Yoko Ono', *Playboy Magazine* January 1981, Copyright © 1980 Playboy, reprinted by permission of Playboy Enterprises Inc.

extract from *The Shameless Hussy* by Alta, Copyright © 1980 Alta Gerrey, and extracts from *How Could You?* by Harriet Edwards, Copyright © 1989 Harriet Edwards, both reprinted by permission of The Crossing Press.

extract from 'The Network of the Imaginary Mother. 4 The Child,' from *Upstairs in the Garden: Poems Selected and New 1968–1988* by Robin Morgan, Copyright © 1990 by Robin Morgan, reprinted by permission of Edite Kroll Literary Agency.

extracts from 'A Doll's House' from *Plays* by Henrik Ibsen, translated by Peter Watts (Penguin Classics, 1965), Copyright © 1965 Peter Watts, reproduced by permission of Penguin Books Ltd.

extracts from *Frieda Lawrence: The Memoirs and Correspondence* by Frieda Lawrence, edited by E. W. Tedlock, Jr. Copyright © 1961, 1964 by the Estate of Frieda Lawrence. Reprinted by permission of

Key Addresses

(Please note that all queries to these organisations *must* be accompanied by a sae.)

UK

MATCH (Mothers Apart from Their Children)
c/o BM Problems
London WC1N 3XX

USA

Mothers Without Custody
PO Box 27418
Houston Texas TX 77227-7418
Tel: 713 840-1622

'Mothers Without Custody (MWOC) is a non-profit, self-directed organisation. Our primary purpose is to enhance the quality of life for our children by strengthening the role of non-custodial parents in regard to custody, child support, visitation and parenting.'

AUSTRALIA

MATCH (Mothers Apart from Their Children)
PO Box 918
Rockingham 6168
Western Australia

Index